BEHIND THE HORROR

TRUE STORIES THAT INSPIRED HORROR MOVIES

BEHIND THE HORROR

TRUE STORIES THAT INSPIRED HORROR MOVIES

Written by
Dr Lee Mellor

Senior Editor David Fentiman
Designer David McDonald
Jacket Design Lisa Lanzarini
Picture Research Sumedha Chopra
Senior Production Controller Louise Daly
Senior Production Editor Jennifer Murray
Managing Editor Sarah Harland
Managing Art Editor Vicky Short
Art Director Lisa Lanzarini
Publisher Julie Ferris
Publishing Director Mark Searle

With thanks to Victoria Armstrong and Nicole Reynolds
for editorial assistance; John Friend for proofreading.

First Published in Great Britain in 2020 by
Dorling Kindersley Limited
One Embassy Gardens, 8 Viaduct Gardens, London SW11 7BW

10 9 8 7 6 5 4 3 2 1
001–316402–Jul/2020

A CIP catalogue record for this book
is available from the British Library.

ISBN: 978-0-24140-943-5

Set in 10.5/13.5pt Bembo MT Pro
Typeset by Jouve (UK), Milton Keynes
Printed and bound in Great Britain by Clays Ltd, Elcograf S.p.A.

For the curious

www.dk.com

This book is made from
Forest Stewardship Council™
certified paper–one small
step in DK's commitment
to a sustainable future.

Contents

M: A City Searches for a Murderer 1931

The Serial Killers of Weimar Germany

In 1931, the German director Fritz Lang wowed audiences around the world with *M: A City Searches for a Murderer.* Lang drew from the unprecedented number of serial killers who had emerged in Weimar-era Germany to formulate his sinister antagonist, Hans Beckert; those who worked tirelessly to catch them inspired Lang's protagonist, Inspector Karl Lohmann.

Serial killers have walked among us since time immemorial. Still, there have been eras and locations that have spawned an over-abundance. The United States saw an alarming spike in the number of serial killers between the mid-1960s and final decade of the 20th century: a period beginning with the so-called Boston Strangler and ending with Jeffrey Dahmer. Victorian Britain experienced a similar outbreak. Weimar Germany (1918–33) – that ill-fated Republic sandwiched between the First and Second World Wars – was so ridden with serial murderers that collectively they inspired the fictional child killer, Hans Beckert, in Fritz Lang's timeless 1931 thriller *M*.

Less than a year before *M* was released, Berlin police inspector Ernst Gennat coined the term "Serienmörder" to refer to this strange "new" violent phenomenon. Gennat himself served as the main inspiration for *M*'s Inspector Lohmann.

M begins with a murderer already on the prowl – children play games about who will be next, and their anxious parents escort them home from school. A young girl is approached by a mysterious man, who offers to buy her a balloon. Shortly thereafter the girl is shown to be missing. In the wake of her disappearance, public panic is compounded when the murderer writes to the papers, promising to kill again. Led by Inspector Lohmann, the city police try to catch the killer, conducting psychiatric analysis of released prisoners, and new forensic tests, such as handwriting analysis and fingerprinting. The city's crimelords are so disrupted by the increased police pressure that they start their own manhunt for the killer, using the city's numerous beggars as lookouts. The police find the killer's rooms, which contain incriminating evidence, and lie in wait for him. Meanwhile, the killer is on the hunt for more victims. A blind beggar identifies the killer's distinctive whistling, and is aided by other beggars, who mark "M" for *Mörder* (murderer) in chalk on the back of his coat. Shortly thereafter, the killer is cornered and abducted by the crimelords. Put "on trial" in an abandoned distillery, the killer delivers an impassioned defence, claiming that he cannot help himself – that his urge to kill is uncontrollable – and questioning why other criminals feel they have a right to judge him. Before the mob can kill the "defendant", the police arrive, break up the proceedings, and arrest him and the other criminals. The film ends with the killer, Hans Beckert, facing the judges at his real trial, while the mothers of his victims weep in the gallery.

Like Alfred Hitchcock's *The Lodger*, released four years earlier, *M* broke new ground by exploring the subtle psychological and social factors around sexual homicide, instead of simply portraying murderers as mindlessly "evil". Peter Lorre's depiction of a torn, baby-faced, seemingly non-threatening killer made him an international star and cemented *M* as one of the greatest films of all time.

Six Weimar-era serial killers served, to varying degrees, as inspiration for Hans Beckert: Johann Mayer, Friedrich Schumann, Carl Großmann, Fritz Haarmann, Karl Denke, and perhaps most of all, Peter Kürten, the so-called "Vampire of Düsseldorf".

—

In March 1918, while his countrymen were mired in the trenches of Belgium and northern France, Johann Mayer committed his first murder. Born in 1886 to an impoverished single mother, he had spent much of his childhood roaming western Germany begging for alms. After losing his left forearm in an accident involving explosives while working at a quarry, he was nicknamed "Stump Arm", and deemed unfit for military service. Due to his disability, Mayer was unable to find steady work and ended up poaching, stealing, and sleeping in hollow tree trunks to survive.

Despite his wretched situation, Mayer was able to establish friendships and relationships – connections that he would abuse to repeatedly and successfully commit murder. In March 1918, he shot Maria Dahm, a 23-year-old ex-girlfriend, with his carbine rifle in the woods near Mayen in the Rhineland. Eleven months later, he fatally shot 28-year-old Maria Falk. As with many Germans at the time, Falk made her living travelling from industrial Bonn to the countryside to trade city products for natural goods. Mayer, the poacher, dealt in wild game. When Maria learnt about his unsavoury past, she attempted to end their relationship. Sadly, she was found with a bullet in her head, lying in a forest between Masburg and Hauroth.

Later in that spring of 1919, Mayer shot his friends Nikolaus Schüller and Lorenz Reuter with a rifle in the pine forest outside Reimerath-Boos. Reportedly, Mayer decapitated both men, swapping their heads in a gruesome attempt to mislead the police. Schüller's body and Reuter's head were soon discovered under juniper brushes by a group of youngsters. Reuter's decapitated corpse was found quite some time later, half a mile north of Franzen Mill in the Arbachtal.

Mayer's final victim was his lover, Katharina Forst, a 34-year-old mother-of-three who had lost her husband in World War I. The two were occasionally seen dancing together in Kelberg, and Katharina provided shelter for the known criminal at her home in the hamlet of Mannebach-Sickerath. In return, he brought her venison and other wild meats. When she discovered his reputation for violence, Mayer concluded she could no longer be trusted and would have to be eliminated. In May 1919, he lured Katharina out of town under the pretext of going to buy a goat, shot her in the back, and concealed her body under brushwood in a forest near Illerich.

Though Mayer – a known criminal with convictions for violence, poaching, and theft – was investigated by the police on July 9, he remained at large until August 10, 1922, when he was recognized by travellers in Eulgem, where he worked as a farmhand. By this time, the very mention of his name struck terror into the hearts of the inhabitants of the south Rhineland, and there was a reward for his capture. Naively, he approached a group of travellers and asked them for a cigarette, only to be apprehended. Turned over to the authorities, he was transferred to a prison at Koblenz. Mayer was convicted on four counts of murder and one of manslaughter, and sentenced to die on February 7, 1923. Though he stubbornly refused to admit to his crimes, in the days before his execution, Johann "Stump Arm" Mayer finally cracked and confessed to his priest. The penitent 37-year-old was executed by guillotine on December 29, 1923, at Cologne prison.

—

The second killer in Lang's "rogues' gallery" was Friedrich Schumann. Born in Spandau – the westernmost borough of Berlin – in 1893, Schumann came from a long line of miscreants. His grandfather was a convicted child molester and his father, Hermann, a habitual criminal and alcoholic. Unlike the disabled Mayer, Schumann served in World War I, and was awarded an Iron Cross for his marksmanship – a grim irony, since in 1909, at the age of 16, he had "accidentally" shot a female cousin dead while playing with his gun in Spandau Forest. Years later, he would admit that he had killed her simply because she was being too loud. Less than two years after shooting his cousin, he shot and robbed a woman on the Spandauer roadway, earning a paltry nine-month prison sentence.

Having absconded while on leave from the army, in May and July of 1917 Schumann gunned down a security guard and two policemen in Falkenhagen. In fact, this tiny east German community became Schumann's favourite hunting ground – especially the local forest. His preferred modus operandi was to wait for couples seeking privacy among the trees and then unexpectedly attack them. Like many "lovers' lane" slayers, he killed the males outright, before raping and murdering their female partners. "The Terror of Falkenhagen Lake" was in many ways an opportunistic offender, preying on hunting parties, foresters, hikers, and motorists.

The beginning of the end for Schumann came at 8 p.m. on August 18, 1919, when he was approached in Falkenhagen forest by Wilhelm Nielbock, a woodland supervisor. Schumann shot Nielbock in the stomach, but the hardy 52-year-old fired back with his shotgun, hitting Schumann in the shoulder and causing him to flee. Before dying in his hospital bed, Nielbock described his attacker as being of average height, blond with a slim build, and dressed in field-grey clothing. Two days later, Schumann was arrested while seeking treatment for his wounds at a doctor's office in Spandau. Between July 5–13, 1920, he stood trial in Berlin for a slew of crimes. On July 13, he was convicted on a half-dozen counts of murder, 11 attempted murders, and multiple thefts, earning him seven death sentences. While awaiting execution, Schumann confessed to his attorney that he had killed 25 people in total. Early in the morning of August 27, 1921, "The Terror of Falkenhagen Lake" walked calmly into the courtyard of Plötzensee Prison and placed his neck on the executioner's block.

—

Another Weimar-era killer, Carl Großmann, would become infamous not just for his crimes, but for the horrifying way he disposed of his victims. A butcher by trade, Großmann owned and operated a food stand at Berlin's Silesian railway terminus. The stand opened for business at dawn and served hot meat well into the night. As his name suggests, Großmann was an imposing figure – beneath his dark moustache, his wrinkled, toothless mouth rarely spoke or smiled, though most of his customers were in such a hurry they didn't pay him much mind anyway. By the summer of 1922, however, the taciturn butcher with the twitchy eye would haunt them for the rest of their lives.

A relatively successful local businessman, Großmann lent money to his neighbours, employed an array of female housekeepers, and was a regular client of sex workers. One particularly street-smart sex worker, Erika, would later go on record stating that she had found Großmann creepy, and refused to enter his third-floor apartment at a Lange Straße tenement. Though unattractive and dislikeable, Großmann benefited from being relatively wealthy in a city scarred by crushing poverty.

During the Weimar era, the impoverished, crime-ridden area around the Silesian station was flooded with transients from the eastern provinces. Most had migrated to the capital seeking employment, although, ironically, Berlin had one of the highest unemployment rates in the country. While mandated to record their places of residence with the local police, the majority of these migrants failed to do so.

Similarly, though prostitution was legal in Germany, all sex workers were required to register with the government and undergo routine medical examinations. Those who complied comprised a professional class of sex workers known as the *Kontrollmädchen*. Yet, the dire economic situation compelled a great number of women, both married and unmarried, to occasionally turn to sex work simply to get by. Never intending to make a career of it and well aware that the stigma of having been a *Kontrollmädchen* would follow them for the rest of their lives, these "casual sex workers" – *Gelegenheitsdirnen* – failed to register, too. This meant that a significant portion of people inhabiting the Silesian station area naturally avoided any interaction with the police. Incredibly, it is estimated that there were five to ten times more *Gelegenheitsdirnen* than *Kontrollmädchen*.[1]

Observing the situation in his Berlin neighbourhood first-hand, the journalist and cultural historian Hans Ostwald wrote: "In the sooty Koppenstraße at the Silesian train station, poor, weathered, and wrecked creatures walk around nightly, especially on Saturdays, without head-covering and with blue kitchen aprons. They count on the drunken workers returning home, to whom they can offer themselves for one to two marks."[2] Nearby Andreasplatz was also a popular meeting place for sex workers and their clients. The economic situation meant that some women were willing to sleep with men such as Großmann simply in exchange for food or clothing.

Even a city hardened to the macabre was shocked, however, when the dismembered remains of numerous unidentified women began surfacing in the Luisenstadt Canal and Engelbecken Reservoir. In August 1921 the police began posting notifications of these murders throughout the city, along with their supposition that the killer lived near the Silesian train station. At this point, Großmann's neighbours, Helene and Mannheim Itzig, started to suspect the toothless old butcher might be the culprit. Having heard women's screams, spotted red liquid oozing from the drains, and gagged all summer long on the rancid stench coming from his apartment – Großmann said it was spoiled chicken meat – the couple decided to bore a small hole in his door to spy on him. Observing his brutal treatment of women further convinced them that he was responsible for the recent spate of *Lustmörds* (sex murders).

On August 21, 1921, police were summoned to Großmann's apartment after neighbours reported seeing a naked woman screaming and frantically signalling to them from the window. Upon entering, they discovered the nude, blood-soaked butcher standing over the corpse of a naked woman on a cot. Großmann was arrested on the spot. The victim had either been repeatedly stabbed or bludgeoned to death (sources are conflicting), and may have been partially dissected. Worse, the manner in which she was bound resembled a hog prepared for butchery. Investigators found several trays of what appeared to be human sausage meat in the kitchen, along with a suspicious stash of women's clothing in the cupboard. Inspecting the tags on the garments, the investigators immediately realized that the items belonged to girls who had been reported missing, many of whom were last seen at the Silesian station. As Carl Großmann was hauled to police headquarters, law enforcement officers raced to confiscate his food stand at the terminus before word of his arrest reached the press.

Accounts differ as to what happened next. According to one source, Großmann was subjected to weeks of interrogation before he finally confessed to murdering three women. Initially, he insisted he had killed them in a fit of rage upon discovering they were attempting to steal money from him. And while he had dismembered their corpses, he had done so purely as a means of body disposal. A second account has him admitting to four murders.

Unfortunately for Großmann, the human sausage meat and overwhelming evidence of sadistic rape told a different story. By now it had been determined that the latest victim had been rendered unconscious with cyanide and sexually assaulted. She was quickly identified as 34-year-old Maria Theresa Nitsche, a recently released prisoner. Her precarious situation made her a typical target for "The Butcher of Berlin".

Besides preying on desperate *Gelegenheitsdirnen*, it turned out that Großmann was also in the habit of waiting at the Silesian railway terminus for migrant women to alight from the fourth-class carriage, seeking those with confused expressions on their faces. He would immediately approach them and ask if they required assistance. If they said they were looking for work, he would feign surprised delight, remarking that he was currently on his way to an employment agency to find a housekeeper.

Exactly how many innocent women and girls fell victim to this trick is unknown.

On July 2, 1922, the trial of 58-year-old Carl Großmann began in Berlin. Over the next three days, multiple surviving victims testified against him. As in the case of Maria Nitsche, Großmann had spiked one witness's coffee with a sedative. When she regained consciousness, she found herself tied to his bed and in immense pain. Another female visitor to his apartment had simply been overpowered. It is alleged that Großmann burst out laughing during the court proceedings. On the morning of July 5, he assumed control of the situation by hanging himself in his prison cell.

In retrospect, Carl Friedrich Wilhelm Großmann was a sexual psychopath hiding in plain sight. Born on December 13, 1863, Großmann grew up 30 miles (48 km) northwest of Berlin in the garrison town of Neuruppin. His parents ran a butcher's shop, and he would often work in the back, preparing meat. By some accounts, his father was an abusive alcoholic. Young Carl was an overweight child with a notoriously unpleasant personality – rumour has it he lured younger girls into his clutches with the promise of meat, then sexually molested them. It is also alleged that he sexually abused animals, including goats.

Attending school until the age of 14, Großmann then worked at a textile mill for two years before leaving Neuruppin for Berlin. There, in the German capital, he bounced from job to job, before being conscripted into the military at the age of 19. Released on medical grounds – a hernia – he went on to work as a farmhand in Pomerania, Mecklenburg, and northern Bavaria. Predictably, his unnatural activities with animals continued during this sojourn in the country, and in 1896 he was convicted of committing bestiality with a sheep in Mannheim.[3] Two years later, Großmann garnered another criminal conviction for sexually assaulting a 10-year-old girl in Nuremberg. He must not have lingered long in prison, for, while in Bayreuth in 1899, he sexually assaulted two more young children. Arrested and taken before a local court in 1899, he was sentenced to 15 years' hard labour.[4] Soon after the verdict, the younger child died as a result of her injuries.[5]

Carl Großmann was released from prison on the eve of World War I. Ironically, his heinous criminal history prevented him from serving in that bloody conflict in any capacity. He moved to a cabin on an allotment garden in eastern Berlin, but left in 1919, setting up in the apartment on Lange Straße. His neighbours were all too aware of his use and abuse of sex workers and housekeepers – their pained cries could be heard through the walls – but domestic violence was sadly tolerated in Weimar Germany. Occasionally, when it was disturbing their own peace, other residents would attempt to intervene, only to be told to "shut your face"[6] by the disagreeable butcher.

In 1921, an inebriated Großmann had even told a drinking buddy: "I don't work, just kill people and take their money. I am a butcher by profession, but I don't slaughter cattle, I only slaughter women. I cut them into pieces and burn the pieces. I prick the horses' eyes, I cut out the dogs' eyes with a knife, and I kill little children with a stone."[7]

While Carl Friedrich Wilhelm Großmann was undoubtedly responsible for the murders of at least three women, police estimated that between 20–50 victims had died by his hand, with many apparently making their way into the sausages he peddled to hungry travellers at the Silesian train station. But he was not the last of his kind – far from it.

—

Almost two years after Großmann's demise, in May 1924, children playing by the River Leine happened upon the skull of an adolescent male and brought it to the police. What initially seemed a freak occurrence foreshadowed a sinister pattern. Additional skulls – all male and between the ages of 11 and 20 – soon washed up on the banks of the Leine. The knife marks on the bone, indicating decapitation, confirmed what the police already knew: these were murder victims. When a second group of children uncovered a sack brimming with human bones, the citizens of Hanover took matters into their own hands and began searching the riverbed. They retrieved approximately 500 human body parts.

Assembling this macabre jigsaw, police determined that the pieces comprised at least 22 different male individuals – the vast majority teenagers. This appeared to account for the large number of young men reported missing in the city over the past five years. No sooner had this puzzle presented itself, than a woman entered the police station with an extraordinary claim: a local butcher named Fritz Haarmann had sold her a steak that did not derive from any animal. Rather, she suspected the meat was human. Under normal circumstances the police might have thought this accusation outlandish, but given the news from the capital regarding "The Butcher of Berlin" and the grim discoveries in the Leine, they decided to take it seriously. Mirroring the Großmann case, a brief search of Haarmann's apartment revealed clothing belonging to some of the missing boys. Protesting his innocence, Haarmann was immediately arrested. The police then conducted a more thorough search of his home, along with the residences of some of Haarmann's associates. Eventually, they uncovered multiple caches of personal effects linked to the murdered boys. Haarmann's young lover, Hans Grans, was also arrested on suspicion of murder.

When confronted with the evidence, Haarmann's dapper facade melted away. He confessed to having murdered countless young men between 1918–24, engaging in sexual intercourse – consensually or non-consensually – then overpowering them and biting through their windpipes. After they lay dead, he claimed to have been overcome by a profound sadness when gazing upon their dead bodies. This did not stop him from carving up their corpses and peddling their meat, often minced and intermingled with horse, beef, and pork to cunningly disguise it. The case took an even more bizarre turn when Haarmann claimed he had crushed all but one of his victims' craniums, and that the skulls recovered from the Leine were therefore from young men who had committed suicide or fallen prey to other murderers (more likely, he was lying). Although they were completely ignorant of each other's existence, let alone homicidal activities, Haarmann's case bore another astonishing resemblance to Großmann's. He would procure victims from the local train station, offering desperate boys meals and accommodation, or sometimes just cigarettes.

Haarmann's past had been anything but normal. He was born into an affluent family in Hanover on October 25, 1879, the sixth and last child of a violent, philandering father and an overindulgent mother. After a male teacher molested him at the age of 8, young Fritz began to act out sadistically, tying up his sisters and prowling the streets at night. His family was generally dysfunctional – his older brother was jailed for raping a 12-year-old girl and all of his sisters' marriages rapidly crumbled in a time when this was far from the norm.

Haarmann left school at the age of 16, and almost immediately began molesting young boys. He left Hanover to attend a military academy at Neuf-Brisach, but suffered a severe head injury while doing gymnastics during training and was subsequently plagued by hallucinations; medical doctors determined that Haarmann was epileptic.

He returned home, but was soon arrested for child molestation and admitted to a psychiatric hospital. Terrified by the conditions there, he escaped on several occasions and finally found sanctuary in Switzerland. Eventually, he returned to his parents in Hanover, who demanded he settle down with a German woman and have a child. He duly impregnated a girlfriend, but, given his homosexuality, predictably became uninterested in her, and she aborted the child. However, the pair remained on good terms.

Haarmann was conscripted by the military in the autumn of 1900, only to be hospitalized the following year for a nervous disorder.

In 1902, it was determined that he was medically unfit for military service, and he was released with a pension. Returning to civilian life, he tried and failed to run a fishmongers with his ex-girlfriend. He also started his first sexual relationship with another adult male – an older man – in 1905, but did not enjoy the experience, and they soon parted ways.

It was at this point that Haarmann began raping young men whom he had lured back to his apartment. Somehow, he also managed to become a police informant, and often used this status to lower his victims' guards. Often before the attacks occurred, he would take them to the station where he made a show of questioning people and asking them for their papers. His soon-to-be victims may have even heard locals call him "Detective Haarmann".

As a consequence of his repeated sexual offences, Haarmann spent most of 1905–18 incarcerated. When he was finally released back into Hanover, he rented a one-room apartment and immediately resumed his criminal activities, engaging in theft to top up his meagre military pension. Now, whenever Haarmann raped a young man, he didn't leave any witnesses. He co-habited with a young bisexual lover, Hans Grans, who may have participated in the murders. At the very least, it is difficult to believe he couldn't have known about them. Grans was arrested shortly after Haarmann, and charged with murder when "The Werewolf of Hanover" spitefully implicated him.

Fritz Haarmann's trial commenced on December 4, 1924, and lasted two weeks. He was convicted on 24 counts of murder and sentenced to death by beheading. Addressing the court, he proclaimed, "Condemn me to death. I ask only for justice. I am not mad. Make it short; make it soon. Deliver me from this life, which is a torment. I will not petition for mercy, nor will I appeal. I want to pass just one more merry night in my cell, with coffee, cheese, and cigars, after which I will curse my father and go to my execution as if it were a wedding."[8] At a separate trial, Hans Grans was sentenced to die for a single murder.

At first, Haarmann seemed inspired by his impending death, declaring, "I want to be executed on the marketplace. On the tombstone must be put this inscription: 'Here Lies Mass-Murderer Haarmann.' "[9] However, with his requests denied and the hour drawing ever nearer, his outlook soon changed, and he penned a furious letter condemning all of Germany and warning "you won't kill me; I'll be back – yes, I shall be amongst you for all eternity. And now you yourselves have also killed. You should know it: Hans Grans was innocent! Well? How's your conscience now?"[10]

After the guillotine fell at Hanover Prison on April 15, 1925, Fritz Haarmann's head was saved for further analysis. A subsequent medical examination revealed areas of his brain pressing against his skull – it was argued this was a result of a genetic defect, childhood meningitis, his gymnastics head injury, or some combination of the above.

Haarmann's letter would not only spare Grans the guillotine, but ultimately free him. Incredibly, though he was a notorious "sexual deviant", Grans somehow managed to live through the Third Reich without falling prey to Nazi persecution.

—

Among the disturbing number of cannibal killers in Weimar Germany, "The Cannibal of Ziębice", Karl Denke, holds the dishonour of beginning his homicidal career earlier than Großmann and Haarmann, evading capture for longer, and potentially claiming more victims than both combined. Yet comparatively little is known about his life and crimes, a reality acknowledged by his second nickname: "The Forgotten Cannibal".

Denke was born in 1860 in what was then the Kingdom of Prussia. His early life was apparently uneventful. By the early 1900s, the bearded bachelor (affectionately known as "Papa" by the residents of the Silesian town of Ziębice) was making his living renting out a boarding house and selling pickled meats at a local store. He even played the organ at the community church.

Things began to unravel for Denke on the night of December 21, 1924, when a coachman heard cries emanating from an apartment in the boarding house. By the time he had entered the structure, a young man was stumbling down the hallway, head in hands, blood streaming through his fingers. The coachman raced towards him, but the youth fell to the floor. Before he slipped into unconsciousness, he proclaimed that Papa Denke had hit him with an axe.

Racing out of the building, the coachman reached the local law enforcement, and recounted everything he had seen and heard. The police headed straight to the boarding house and arrested Denke. Further investigation revealed a stash of clothing consisting of various styles and sizes – few of which fit Denke – along with identification documents belonging to a dozen travelling salesmen. But these items were merely the most innocuous clues in a rapidly unfolding mystery. Opening a ledger, the policemen found a table listing the names, dates, and weights of Denke's visitors. They were at a loss as to why he needed their weights.

To their horror, they found their answer in the kitchen – two enormous tubs stuffed with pickled meat and a giant pot of fat and bone. The remains were obviously human. Immediately, the policemen began imagining all of the terrible possibilities. Was Papa Denke a cannibal? Was he serving up human-based recipes to his guests? Had the people of Ziębice inadvertently consumed human flesh, and if so, how often? By the time they approached Karl Denke with these questions, he had hanged himself from the prison bars using his trouser braces. He had taken his secrets to the grave.

In the end, the people of Silesia were able to determine that "Papa" Denke had murdered at least 31 people between 1921–24, although he may have been killing since the turn of the century. Besides targeting salesmen, he also preyed on vagabonds and other transients – those who, in the chilling words of the criminologist Dr Steven Egger 60 years later, comprised "the less-dead".

—

The final killer who served as inspiration for *M*'s Hans Beckert was perhaps the most depraved of them all. From May 1913 to 1930, a "vampire" stalked the industrial Rhineland. He wasn't ugly like the villain in *Nosferatu* – the contemporary masterpiece of German expressionist horror then wowing audiences – to the contrary, he was a dapper and unassuming gentleman named Peter Kürten. And he realized the importance of making a good first impression. After being released from prison in 1913, he stole a double-breasted pin-stripe suit and fedora from a tailor's and slipped back into the population.

On May 25 of that same year, while stealing from an inn in the town of Köln-Mülheim, he made his way upstairs to find nine-year-old Christine Klein asleep. Later he would recall "strangl[ing] her for about a minute and a half. The child woke up and struggled but lost consciousness . . . I had a small but sharp pocketknife with me and I held the child's head and cut her throat . . . the whole thing lasted about three minutes. Then I locked the door again and went back home to Düsseldorf."[11] After the child was buried, he returned to Köln-Mülheim on several occasions to visit her grave. Two months later, he fatally strangled 17-year-old Gertrud Franken in Düsseldorf – apparently finding the event sexually arousing – before finding himself back in prison on July 14, for countless arsons and burglaries.

In April 1921 Kürten was freed again, and moved to Altenburg. There he met and married Auguste Scharf, a former sex worker and convicted murderer, and began working at a factory as a trade union official. He and his bride relocated to Düsseldorf in 1925, where he landed himself back in prison for six months after seducing and threatening a servant girl.

Kürten's killing spree began in earnest on February 8, 1929, when he stabbed eight-year-old Rosa Ohliger a dozen times with a pair of scissors, then doused her clothing with kerosene and lit a match in an unsuccessful attempt to incinerate the corpse. He concealed her barely burned body behind a hedge. Four days later he attacked 45-year-old Rudolf Scheer in a nocturnal stabbing frenzy, while the mechanic stumbled home from a local beer hall. The next morning, as investigators cordoned off the crime scene, the killer returned to observe them. He managed to parry the suspicions of one detective by explaining that he'd heard about the murder over the telephone. Apparently, his voice was so soft and gentle the detective found it hard to believe he could have perpetrated such a heinous crime.

Kürten would make four unsuccessful attempts at strangling women over the next six months, but eventually succeeded in killing after returning to stabbing weapons. On August 11, he rendezvoused with Maria Hahn – a young single woman whom he'd met three days earlier – in Düsseldorf's Neandertal district. After spending several hours in her company, he lured her to a meadow where he stabbed and strangled her to death. He buried her body in a cornfield, but found himself returning to the makeshift grave. At one point, he unearthed the rotting corpse, and attempted (but failed) to nail it to a tree in a mock crucifixion.

The early morning hours of August 21 proved to be a particularly violent night. Kürten plunged a dagger into the back of a housewife returning home from a county fair, then went on to stab eight-year-old Anna Goldhausen and Gustav Kornblum, 38 – all within half an hour. Though none of these attacks proved fatal, the incidents caused a mass panic in the city, prompting the Düsseldorf police to increase their presence on the street.

Despite their best efforts, the killer struck again within three days, attacking foster-sisters Louise Lenzen, 14, and Gertrude Hamacher, 5, in an allotment bean patch as they made their way home from the market. After strangling them unconscious, he slit their throats, and stabbed Louise four times in the back.

On Monday, September 30, Kürten decided to try something new. Clad in his finery, he convinced a 31-year-old servant girl, Ida Reuter, to accompany him to a café for a beer, and afterwards the two strolled down to the Rhine. There, he repeatedly smashed her skull with a hammer and sexually assaulted her corpse. He similarly clobbered 22-year-old Elizabeth Dörrier unconscious and raped her on October 11. Horribly wounded, she died the next morning without ever regaining consciousness.

Though he would continue his hammer attacks well into 1930, Kürten claimed his final murder victim around sundown on November 7, 1929. He approached five-year-old Gertrude Albermann playing in the street outside her home. He told her he wanted to show her something and led her away by the hand. Once the two reached a remote factory, he sexually assaulted and strangled her, before stabbing her 36 times in the chest and skull.

Before Gertrude's body could be discovered, Kürten mailed an anonymous letter to a local newspaper, offering directions to the five-year-old's corpse along with a hand-drawn map of Maria Hahn's grave. The former victim was found lying face down in a patch of nettles by a factory wall on November 9, while the latter was disinterred on November 14.

The crimes of the "Düsseldorf Ripper" – the moniker bestowed on the killer by the media – now concerned all of Germany. An elite team of sleuths entered the investigation, led by the esteemed Detective Chief-Inspector Ernst Gennat from Berlin's Alexanderplatz (the German counterpart to Scotland Yard). But the letter-writing was the first sign that Kürten was losing control of his impulses and actively engaging with the authorities. Gennat would not be long on the case before the killer made it all too easy.

On Wednesday, May 21, 1930, 46-year-old Peter Kürten spotted Maria Büdlick, a woman he had tried to rape a week earlier, in the communal hallway of his apartment building at 71 Mettmanner Straße. She was in the company of DCI Ernst Gennat. Looking back, the killer knew his initial mistake had been taking Büdlick to the address in the first place; his second, attempting to sexually assault her in another part of the city; and his third, letting her live to tell the tale. Kürten quietly slipped away to speak with his wife, Auguste, at her place of work. He informed her of the situation, and told her that he had to leave the apartment immediately as "it was enough to get me fifteen years' penal servitude."[12]

After spending the night walking the streets, Kürten sneaked back into his apartment the following morning, placed some items in a bag, and departed to a room he had rented on Adlerstraße. He spent Thursday the 22nd sleeping.

On Friday, May 23, 1930, Auguste Kürten received a visit from two detectives at her workplace. They escorted her back to the apartment she shared with Peter and began searching the premises. Soon after they left, Peter returned home. When Auguste informed him about the investigators, he admitted to a second transgression: the attempted rape of a 26-year-old servant girl the preceding summer. If he was apprehended for the crime, he reminded her, he was looking at a minimum of 10 years' imprisonment. Auguste burst into tears. Not only would this mean the end of their marriage, but she would struggle to provide for herself, and possibly face starvation. Noting the hopelessness of their situation, she proposed they both commit suicide.[13]

Peter said he had a better solution. To her astonishment, he candidly admitted to being the "Düsseldorf Ripper" and reminded her that there was a substantial reward for the person who gave information leading to his capture. This would not be a betrayal on her part, he assured her; in fact, she would be serving humanity by turning him in. Auguste eventually agreed, promising her husband she would never commit suicide. The couple decided to meet at 3 p.m. the following day outside St. Rochus church, and Peter bid his wife a final farewell. Once he had left the apartment, Auguste contacted the police.

Everything went according to plan. Peter Kürten was arrested on the afternoon of May 24, 1930, and taken into custody. To the detectives' surprise, he not only confessed to the "Düsseldorf Ripper" attacks of 1929–30, but also to the previously unconnected slayings of Christine Klein and Gertrud Franken in 1913, along with nearly two-dozen arsons, and bizarrely, the slaughter of a majestic swan: "I used to stroll through the Hoftgarten very often, and in the spring of 1930 I noticed a swan sleeping at the edge of the lake. I cut its throat. The blood spurted up from the stump and I drank it."[14]

Kürten revealed to the detectives that he had been sexually aroused by the sight of blood since childhood. Furthermore, he told them that he had drunk the blood of a number of his victims.[15] Once this news reached the outside world, Kürten's "Düsseldorf Ripper" moniker was forever replaced by another: he was now the "Vampire of Düsseldorf".

On April 22, 1931, Peter Kürten was convicted of nine counts of murder and sentenced to die by guillotine. Upon hearing this he became visibly excited, asking the prison doctor, "after my head has been chopped off, will I still be able to hear, at least for a moment, the sound of my own blood gushing from the stump of my neck?"[16] To Kürten's apparent delight, he was executed at dawn on July 2, 1931.

Detective Chief-Inspector General Ernst Gennat would later write about the case in his seminal *Die Düsseldorfer Sexualverbrechen*. In the book he coined a new term for the types of homicides committed by Peter Kürten and his ilk: *Serienmörder* (serial murder).

Rope 1948

The Murder of Bobby Franks

The experience of viewing this psychological thriller from Alfred Hitchcock is akin to watching a play – everything transpires in real time. Indeed, it was adapted from a 1929 theatrical work by Patrick Hamilton, an English author and playwright. Hamilton was inspired by the so-called "crime of the century", a murder perpetrated just five years earlier by two students: Nathan Leopold and Richard Loeb.

Alfred Hitchcock's first Technicolor feature, *Rope*, is distinguished for unfolding in a single setting and creating the illusion that it was filmed in one 80-minute take. Unsurprisingly, *Rope* made a lasting impact on both editing and cinematography. Yet, the masterpiece merely broke even at the box office, an outrage that screenwriter Arthur Laurents proposed stemmed from widespread discomfort about the possible homosexual relationship between lead characters Brandon Shaw and Philip Morgan.

In the film, young intellectuals Shaw and Morgan contemplate the moral thought experiments of their mentor, Rupert Cadell, and decide to prove their superiority by committing murder. They lure a former classmate, David Kentley, to their Manhattan penthouse apartment, strangle him to death with a length of rope, and conceal his body in a wooden chest. Minutes later, they have Cadell, Kentley's father, Kentley's girlfriend, and several other guests over for dinner, using the chest as a table. With some prompting from Shaw, the conversation repeatedly turns to David's mysterious absence and how murder is an art form, which makes Cadell suspicious. Cadell relentlessly questions the visibly apprehensive Morgan, prompting him to seek refuge in drink and lose his wits. Meanwhile, the unflappable Shaw gleefully tries to acquaint David's girlfriend with another male guest. Tripping over their own smug cleverness, the duo's ghoulish game eventually comes to light, and they find themselves openly disavowed by Cadell as police cars race to the apartment.

Rope was the first and best of several films to be directly inspired by the so-called "crime of the century", in which the affluent young geniuses Nathan Leopold and Richard Loeb meticulously planned and carried out the 1924 murder of schoolboy Bobby Franks, in an attempt to prove they were "beyond good and evil".

—

It could be said that Richard Loeb was fire to Nathan Leopold's gasoline. The spoiled children of wealthy Chicago families, Leopold and Loeb had first met in childhood, but only truly bonded in 1920 while attending the University of Chicago. Besides their affluent backgrounds, Jewish heritages, and similar ages – Leopold was born on November 19, 1904 and Loeb on June 11, 1905 – they both had genius-level IQs, placing them in the top one per cent of the global population. However, in all other ways they were complete opposites. Where Leopold was intellectual, reclusive, and loathed sports, the gregarious and handsome Loeb devoted as little time to his studies as possible, choosing instead to drink, socialize, and engage in athletic endeavours. While Loeb constantly boasted of his sexual conquests, in reality, he was indifferent to sex – today he might be described as asexual – and instead, he was stimulated by perpetrating crimes. Leopold, on the other hand, was equally indifferent to criminality – breaking the law neither excited nor repelled him. He was, however, smitten with the handsome and charming Loeb. With Loeb in need of a criminal accomplice and Leopold obsessed with Loeb's companionship and carnal favours – Loeb consented to sex, albeit apathetically – they forged a close and deadly bond.

Ever-cerebral, Nathan Leopold sought intellectual justification for criminal activity, and quickly found it in the halls of academia. While earning his B.A., he had become acquainted with the works of the Prussian existentialist philosopher Friedrich Nietzsche, taking particular interest in his concept of the *Übermenschen* (supermen). One of the most misunderstood and misappropriated ideas in human history, the *Übermensch* was Nietzsche's solution to a complex problem of moral philosophy. With the rise of the scientific method, critical thinking, and scepticism, more and more academics were taking on agnostic and atheistic worldviews – a trend that was trickling down to the masses. Even for those who still claimed to be nominally Christian, the role of religion was vastly diminished in their day to day lives, and most now lived outside its strictures. Observing this trend, Nietzsche wrote:

"God is dead. God remains dead. And we have killed him. How shall we comfort ourselves, the murderers of all murderers? . . . Must we ourselves not become gods simply to appear worthy of it?"[1]

The paragraph, often shortened to "God is dead", is sometimes misinterpreted as an arrogant declaration of triumph. In actuality, Nietzsche was using emotionally-charged language to convey the sheer gravity of what this revelation meant for humanity – the implications of a world in which there was no God. If morality came from God and God did not exist, Nietzsche reasoned, then moral values were actually just a matter of opinion. Nietzsche realized that humanity would be forced to confront this reality ("nihilism") in the coming 20th century and would either be paralyzed by it, flee back to the comforting lie of faith, or adopt "secular religions" – a prediction that was borne out by the rise of the Nazi and Communist ideologies. Nihilism typically left people jaded and paralyzed by a lack of purpose. Nietzsche believed that only a small number of great individuals would be able to truly confront nihilism – fully accepting that there were no objective moral values. These people would go on to create their own morality and goals, which would give structure and meaning to their lives. They would have overcome the challenge of nihilism, making them *Übermenschen* ("overmen" or "supermen").

Despite his reported IQ of 210, Nathan Leopold seems to have either fundamentally misunderstood Nietzsche's concept, or simply used it to justify his own cognitive biases. He reasoned that since he and Loeb were not only atheists from highly successful families, but also possessed superior intellects, this automatically meant they were Nietzsche's prophesied *Übermenschen*.

Viewing crime as a means to prove their elite status, Leopold joined Loeb in committing petty transgressions – stealing items they could easily afford or engaging in acts of vandalism. Eventually, the two graduated to arson, but were crestfallen when their crimes received little or no media coverage. While transcending the need for others' validation seems implicit in Nietzsche's writings, this was lost on the two "geniuses". Indeed, Loeb apparently found Leopold's constant philosophizing tedious. He was, however, an avid reader of detective novels, and argued that becoming a master criminal was a valid aspiration in itself. Why did they need any further justification?

Over a period of six months, the two men conspired to commit a crime that not only would prove they were criminal geniuses and beyond common morality, but which was guaranteed to make media headlines. They would kidnap a boy from a wealthy family, demand a ransom, then kill the child to prevent him from identifying them. There were not motivated by the money – given their backgrounds, they already had plenty – it would simply be for the thrill.

On the morning of Wednesday, May 21, 1924, Nathan Leopold attended classes at the University of Chicago. At 11 a.m., he met Richard Loeb outside the law school, and the two men headed to their respective vehicles. Leopold led the way to his family's mansion at 4754 Greenwood Avenue in his maroon Willys-Knight sports car, with Loeb following closely behind in his mother's dark-green Cadillac – the paint schemes of the cars would later prove crucial. Reaching the Leopold residence by 11:30 a.m., Leopold went inside to gather the necessary tools: two bottles, one containing ether and the other hydrochloric acid; cloth gags; hip boots; duct tape; a chisel; and a revolver. Bundling these implements of murder inside a blanket, he placed them in the back of his car. Next, Leopold and Loeb drove to the Rent-a-Car lot on Michigan Avenue, where they hired another Willys-Knight, this one dark green. They returned to the Leopold mansion at around 12:30 p.m., where they transferred the blanket bundle from Leopold's Willys-Knight to the rental car. Before leaving, Leopold asked the family chauffeur if he would mind fixing the brakes on his car: they had been annoying him for quite some time, and he would not be needing the vehicle today anyway.

With that, Leopold and Loeb set out to look for a young boy from a wealthy family to abduct. They drove around for hours, even lingering around the old Harvard School on Ellis Avenue, which Leopold had attended in his own childhood. After a while they began to get frustrated – there were plenty of potential targets, but the opportunity never seemed to present itself. Around 5 p.m., the pair were almost ready to give up when they noticed a brown-haired boy walking down Ellis Avenue by himself. He looked around 14 years old, and as they drew nearer, Loeb realized it was his cousin Bobby Franks. Bobby lived practically across the street from Loeb's home, and he and Bobby had even played tennis together the day before. Loeb secretly despised his cousin and had no qualms about selecting him. They caught up with Bobby on 48th Street.

Leopold was driving, while Loeb called out to the boy from the backseat of the vehicle, offering him a ride. Bobby replied that he could walk, since he was almost home. Loeb countered that he wanted to chat about Bobby's tennis racket, saying he wanted to purchase one himself. This seemed to do the trick, and Bobby climbed into the front of the car, next to Leopold. After the car made a few turns, Loeb suddenly reached into the front seat, clamping his left hand over Bobby's mouth. Before the boy had a chance to realize what was happening, Loeb repeatedly stabbed him in the head with the chisel. To Loeb's astonishment, though, Bobby didn't die immediately. Loeb pulled him into the backseat, where he put a rag into the boy's mouth, sealing it in place with tape. Moments later, Bobby Franks finally passed away.

Leopold drove the car out of the city in the direction of Gary, Indiana. The plan was to dump the body in the vicinity of Wolf Lake – a wetland area, which, as an ornithologist and bird hunter, he knew well. They reached the area at sundown and decided to wait until the cover of night to hide the body. In the meantime, they picked up some hotdogs and root beer from a nearby eatery. As the sun disappeared on the horizon, the two would-be *Übermenschen* parked the rental car on an embankment overlooking Wolf Lake, and rolled Bobby's bloodied corpse onto a blanket. Together they carried it down to a culvert, placing the body on the ground and stripping it naked. To prevent easy identification, Leopold poured the hydrochloric acid over the body. Then, with some difficulty, they managed to wedge Bobby's body into the culvert. Believing that they had just committed the "perfect murder", the pair made their way back up the embankment to the road, and returned to Chicago.

Back in the city, Leopold pulled out a ransom note he had typed up days earlier on his portable typewriter. After locating the Franks' phone number in a drugstore phone book and buying stamps, at around 10 p.m., Leopold enclosed the ransom letter in an envelope, which he quickly made out to Jacob Franks. He deposited it in a mailbox on 55th Street.

Next, they headed to the empty Loeb residence where they bundled Bobby's clothes into the furnace and burned them. As the blanket was absolutely soaked in blood, they opted to conceal it in the greenhouse for the time being – any attempt to incinerate it would surely fill the house with a foul stench. It was at this stage they realized they had misplaced one of Bobby's black and white chequered socks. They told themselves that this minor error would not matter.

To complete the night's vile work, at 10:30 p.m., Leopold and Loeb drove to the Walgreens drugstore on 47th and Woodlawn, and headed for the payphone in the back. Both students managed to squeeze into the phone booth, albeit with some difficulty, and Leopold dialled the Franks residence. A maid answered the phone and replied that Mr Franks was currently out, so Leopold asked to speak with his wife, Flora. When Flora Franks came to the phone, Leopold began reciting his carefully chosen lines, "This is Mr Johnson . . . Your boy has been kidnapped. We have him and you need not worry: he is safe. But don't try to trace this call . . . We must have money. We will let you know tomorrow what we want. We are kidnappers and we mean business. If you refuse us what we want or try to report us to the police, we will kill the boy."[2]

Then, hanging up the receiver, the two men headed home to get some sleep. Everything seemed to have gone according to plan. They would vigorously clean the rental car at the Leopold residence in the morning, then make a second telephone call to the Franks family.

At 8 a.m. on Thursday, May 22, 1924, Jacob Franks anxiously opened an envelope addressed to him, and read the enclosed typewritten letter.

"*DEAR SIR:*

As you no doubt know by this time your son has been kidnapped. Allow us to assure you that he is at present well and safe. You need not fear any physical harm for him providing you live up carefully to the following instructions and such others as you will receive by future communications. Should you, however, disobey any of our instructions, even slightly, his death will be the penalty."[3]

The letter then stated that the kidnappers had three requests. Firstly, that the Franks family should make no attempt to communicate with the police. Secondly, that they must secure, before noon that day, $10,000. The money had to be composed entirely of old bills, and placed in a large cigar box, securely sealed with paper and wax. Thirdly, that they should remain home from 1 p.m., with the telephone not in use, and await further instructions. The letter was signed "GEORGE JOHNSON".[4]

That same morning, Tony Minke, a worker for the American Maize-Products Company, was walking home on a path that ran alongside the Pennsylvania Railroad tracks near the Indiana state line. Glancing down at a ditch on his left, he spotted a human foot protruding from a culvert. Minke approached the drainage pipe to get a better look, and was confronted by the nude body of a teenage male lying face down in the sludge. He immediately called over to some nearby railway workers for assistance. As the men carried the body to a railway handcar, signal-repairman Paul Korff searched the vicinity for any discarded clothing that might help the investigation. On the embankment beside the culvert, he happened upon a pair of tortoiseshell-frame glasses. Korff placed them in his pocket and hurried over to the handcar.

When news of the discovery reached the Franks family in Chicago, they told themselves it could not be Bobby. After all, he was being held captive by the kidnappers, and he never wore glasses. Nevertheless, their lawyer, Samuel Ettleson, asked Bobby's uncle, Edwin Greshan, to go down to the morgue at 13300 South Houston Avenue, just to make sure. In the unlikely event that it was Bobby, Ettleson instructed Greshan to telephone the extension line in the living room and simply say "yes". The dreaded call came soon after. There would be no opportunity to pay the ransom. Fourteen-year-old Bobby Franks was dead.

The police realized that the tortoiseshell glasses were their strongest lead. Their owner would have needed a prescription to purchase the lenses, meaning they would have been custom-made by an optician who presumably kept records of his clients. Consulting with a Chicago optician, they learnt that the lenses were a common convex cylindrical pattern meant to treat an exceedingly common problem: astigmatism. Though thousands of Chicago residents owned these types of glasses, the tortoiseshell frames – technically, Newport zylonite – with square corners and distinguishing hinges were manufactured in Brooklyn, and sold in Chicago solely by Almer Coe and Company opticians.

By Thursday, May 29, the clerks at Almer Coe were rifling through thousands of prescription files, and jotting down the names of anyone who had purchased that specific lens-frame combination. By the afternoon, the police had a name: Nathan Freudenthal Leopold Jr.

Leopold had in fact already been questioned – four days earlier he had been interviewed by Captain Thomas Wolfe of the Eighth Police District. Wolfe had learnt that Leopold reportedly gave ornithology classes by the Pennsylvania Railroad tracks, and asked the young man to provide him with further information. Leopold had confirmed that he often travelled to the area; as a matter of fact, on Saturday, May 17, he had been out at Wolf Lake bird hunting with his pal George Lewis.

Three Chicago police officers arrived at the Leopolds' three-storey stone manor in Kenwood, to take the 19-year-old to Hotel LaSalle for further questioning. The Leopolds were a rich and prominent family, and as there was no direct evidence tying their youngest son to the killing, State Attorney Robert Crowe had opted to be discreet. At the hotel, Nathan Leopold assured Crowe that his glasses were in a suit pocket, and if the police would be so kind as to drive him back home, he could retrieve them. Back in his bedroom at 4754 Greenwood, Leopold found that his glasses case was empty. He pocketed the case, headed back downstairs with the officers, and returned to the hotel.

Leopold provided an alibi for May 21 – one he had carefully formulated and rehearsed with Loeb. After attending his morning classes, Leopold had picked up Loeb in his maroon Willys-Knight sports car, and they had gone to have lunch at a grill, before heading to Chicago's Lincoln Park. Leopold was on the lookout for a heron that had been spotted in the area, while Loeb had been happy just to sit in the car swigging a pint of gin. They had realized they could not drive back to Loeb's house as his father was a fervent teetotaler. Instead, the two had headed for the Coconut Grove Restaurant to dine, and then driven up 63rd Street a few times looking for bored girls. They had eventually met two – named May and Edna – and drove out to Jackson Park, where they had stopped and shared some drinks with their female companions. However, when the girls refused to have sex with them, Leopold and Loeb had kicked them out of the car and instructed them to walk home.[5]

While Leopold was amusing himself playing cat-and-mouse with State Attorney Crowe, investigators from the Chicago police were scouring his bedroom and study for clues. During the process, they confiscated a Hammond typewriter and uncovered a letter identifying a possible accomplice. Often cryptic, and fluctuating between being actively threatening, passive aggressive, and conciliatory, it was addressed to someone named "Dick", and was signed "Babe".[6]

The letter seemed to suggest that Leopold was "Babe". Not only did the letter imply he had a homosexual lover (it made reference to homosexual sex and "an unavoidable bond between us"), but also that the lover was a partner in crime (it mentioned an "equal footing legally", and that "Babe" had "purposely committed the same tort of which you are guilty"). The investigators quickly identified "Dick" as Leopold's inseparable friend, Richard Loeb. Furthermore, they discovered a .32-calibre Remington handgun among Leopold's things. As Leopold had not obtained a permit for the weapon, it was technically illegal for him to possess. This gave the Chicago police the authority to detain Leopold longer and subject him to additional questioning.

Armed with this new evidence, State Attorney Crowe sent officers to bring Richard Loeb in for questioning, and relocated Leopold from the opulent hotel to the Criminal Court Building. Between the illegal firearm, suspicious ties to Loeb, and conspicuously missing glasses, Nathan Leopold was increasingly looking like their man.

Once Leopold was resettled in the Court Building, Crowe produced the pair of tortoiseshell glasses that Paul Korff had found near the body site. Leopold admitted they were indeed his. However, there was a perfectly reasonable explanation. He had, after all, been hunting in the area on May 17, hastily pursuing some sandpipers across the railway track and down the embankment about 10 to 20 feet (3 to 6 m) away from the culvert. His glasses must have simply fallen out of his pocket. If they needed to corroborate his story, Leopold suggested they contact his hunting buddy, George Lewis. The story was a good one, but Crowe still remained unconvinced. If the glasses had been lying on the hillside for four days, they should have been muddy. Instead, they were surprisingly clean. Deciding to probe further, Crowe asked Leopold what pocket he would have placed his spectacles in, to which the young man answered that they would have been in the left breast pocket of either his coat or vest. Since Leopold said he could not recall stumbling, it begged the question as to how the glasses had fallen out of his pocket in the first place.

"Will you put those in your left breast coat pocket," Crowe said while offering the glasses to Leopold, "and run and bend, and see whether they will drop out?"[7] Leopold obliged, twice. On neither occasion did the spectacles tumble to the floor.

By now Richard Loeb was sitting in a separate room providing an identical alibi to Leopold's. Yet, the revelation of the pair's homosexual relationship led Crowe to doubt the existence of the girls in the story – Edna and May – or indeed that Leopold and Loeb had ever gone looking for girls in the first place. He reasoned that they would have no reason to do so, if they could simply have sex with each other instead.

There was also evidence tying Leopold to the ransom letters. His handwriting, which was easily obtained, matched the writing on the envelope addressed to Jacob Franks. Late the next afternoon, investigators discovered legal notes that Leopold had typed for one of his law classes. Both the legal notes and ransom letter had been composed on the same typewriter. Investigators returned a third time to the Leopold house to search for a portable Underwood typewriter. When asked, the maid revealed that there had indeed been such a piece of equipment in the house. She had last seen it two weeks previously.

Armed with these new revelations, Assistant State's Attorney, Joseph Savage, resumed interviewing Nathan Leopold at 6:30 p.m. on Friday, May 30. Savage asked Leopold about the portable typewriter that had been repeatedly seen at his residence. Leopold replied that he recalled seeing one himself, but that it did not belong to him, and must have been left by one of the boys from his university study group. One by one, Savage contacted the students. All denied ever owning a portable typewriter, let alone bringing it to 4754 Greenwood Avenue. Yet they did remember seeing one in the library while collaborating on school work at the Leopold mansion. The net around Nathan Leopold was rapidly tightening.

At 10 p.m., an Assistant State Attorney agreed to speak with a man who had been waiting patiently on a bench outside the State Attorney's Office in the Criminal Court Building. The man insisted he had important information regarding the Bobby Franks case. He introduced himself as Sven Englund, the Leopold family chauffeur. He stated with utmost confidence that Nathan Leopold could not have committed the abduction and murder of Bobby Franks on May 21, because he hadn't had access to his car. At 12:30 p.m., Englund had seen Leopold pulling into the driveway in his maroon Willys-Knight followed by Richard Loeb in a dark green car.

Leopold had approached the chauffeur complaining that the Willys-Knight's brakes had been squealing for days, and as he did not need the vehicle any time soon, asked Englund to fix the brakes for him. Englund promised he would, and Leopold and Loeb had driven away in the other vehicle. Englund had spent all afternoon repairing the brakes, before finally storing the car in the family garage where it remained until 10 p.m.

The Leopold family had been elated that there was finally strong evidence suggesting their youngest son could not have perpetrated such a foul deed. Of course, none of them were aware of the details of their son's alibi. Unwittingly, Sven Englund had just sealed Nathan Leopold's fate. Crowe now held a silver bullet; the only question was, who would crack first: Leopold or Loeb. Knowing the latter was exhausted and irritable, Crowe decided to start with him.

Crowe confronted the suspect: "Isn't it a fact that Wednesday, May 21st . . . you drove up to that garage, to Leopold's garage, you driving your mother's car, that green Cadillac, he driving the red car . . . and you turned the car over to the chauffeur and got into your car and drove away?"[8]

"No,"[9] Loeb replied, visibly shocked.

"If the chauffeur took the car in and oiled it up, oiled the brakes and fixed it up, that would make an impression on his mind, wouldn't it?" Crowe insisted. "If he says that is a fact, he is a liar or mistaken?"[10]

"Yes," came Loeb's reply, "I would say he was still a liar or mistaken."[11]

But Loeb's resolve had taken a heavy blow, and he could not hold out much longer. Within half an hour, the self-styled master criminal broke down and gave a full confession.

When Crowe was finished with Loeb, he entered Nathan Leopold's interview room. The young man sat calmly smoking a cigarette. Leopold then asked Crowe a "hypothetical" question: if a member of an affluent family had committed a murder, what were his chances of being convicted? Crowe told him he was about to find out. He was charging Nathan Leopold for the murder of Bobby Franks. At first, Leopold replied that Crowe was obviously bluffing. His confidence soon melted away when the State Attorney informed him that Richard Loeb had confessed to the crime. Crowe provided Leopold with the new details Loeb had supplied, just to make sure he understood. "Well," Leopold said, "I am surprised that Dick is talking. I thought he would stand till hell froze over . . . I will tell you the truth about the matter."[12]

Following Leopold and Loeb's confessions, State Attorney Crowe made the clever decision to allow the murderers to lead them to the various crime scenes in chronological order – from the site of Bobby Franks' abduction to the river where Leopold had disposed of the portable typewriter – so the detectives could retrieve additional evidence along the way. By doing so, Crowe ensured that nobody could later accuse the officers of beating or otherwise coercing a confession out of the two wealthy teens.[13]

Ironically, Leopold and Loeb's claim that they consciously chose to perpetrate the murder because they were Nietzschean *Übermenschen,* and thus "beyond good and evil", resulted in them boasting to the mental health assessment team that they were well aware of the concepts of "right" and "wrong", and had killed Bobby Franks purely to transcend them. Their attorney, the legendary Clarence Darrow, correctly concluded this would make mounting a Not Guilty By Reason of Insanity (NGRI) defence impossible. And given the quantity of evidence against them, he was also confident that no jury would acquit his clients on the charges of murder and kidnapping. Leopold and Loeb were going to hang. However, Darrow had one trick left up his sleeve.

On Monday, July 21, 1924, Clarence Darrow stood in court before Judge Caverly, and announced that the defendants wished to change their pleas to "guilty". "The statute provides that evidence may be offered in mitigation of the punishment, and we shall ask, at such time as the court may direct, that we may be permitted to offer evidence as to the mental condition of these young men," continued Darrow, "to show the degree of responsibility they had, also to offer as to the youth of these defendants, and the fact of a plea of guilty as further mitigation of the penalties of this case. With that we throw ourselves upon the mercy of this court and of this court alone."[14]

Despite the protestations of State Attorney Crowe that the testimony of mental health experts was inadmissible unless the defendants had entered an NGRI plea, Judge Caverly overruled him, and the trial proceeded to sentencing. From August 1–12, 1924, Darrow paraded an array of psychologists and psychiatrists onto the witness stand. They offered mitigating testimony ranging from their shared belief that both Leopold and Loeb were emotionally underdeveloped, to the presence of brain abnormalities in both defendants. Infuriated, Crowe fought the process every inch of the way.

In the end, though, none of it mattered. On September 10, 1924, Judge Caverly explained that despite the testimony from the mental health professionals on both sides, he would spare the teens the hangman's noose – precisely because they *were* teens, "in accordance with the progress of criminal law all over the world and with the dictates of enlightened humanity."[15] Instead of sending them to the gallows, Judge Caverly sentenced both Nathan Leopold and Richard Loeb to life imprisonment at Joliet Penitentiary for the murder of Bobby Franks, plus an additional 99 years each for "kidnapping for ransom".[16]

Twelve years into his sentence, 30-year-old Richard Loeb was attacked in the shower by inmate James Day on January 28, 1936. Suffering 58 wounds from a straight razor, Loeb died in the prison hospital that same day.

Incredibly, Nathan Leopold was granted parole in March 1958. He found work as a medical technician at Castañer General Hospital in Puerto Rico. Eventually he married, and settled on the island, earning his master's degree at the University of Puerto Rico where he would later teach and conduct research on leprosy. Leopold died of a heart attack on August 29, 1971. His corneas were donated to a suitable candidate – whether the recipient ever learnt of what those eyes had witnessed on May 21, 1924, remains unknown.

Psycho 1960
The Texas Chain Saw Massacre 1974

The Crimes of Ed Gein

***Psycho* and *The Texas Chain Saw Massacre* each helped to define gruesome new eras for the horror genre. Though very different in style and tone, both movies were inspired by the same killer, the so-called "Plainfield Ghoul": Edward Theodore Gein.**

While Fritz Lang's *M* and Alfred Hitchcock's *Rope* were psychological thrillers centred upon brutal murders, it was only with the release of Hitchcock's *Psycho* that the "slasher" genre arguably began. Long periods of tension in *Psycho* finally erupt when knife-wielding maniac Norman Bates ambushes and stabs a character to death, nevertheless many movie critics contend that it is actually a psychological thriller. *Psycho*'s status as the first slasher movie may therefore be contested, but the "slasher-cred" of Tobe Hooper's *The Texas Chain Saw Massacre* is indisputable. Regardless of whether one awards the honour of "first slasher" to *Psycho* or *The Texas Chain Saw Massacre*, both films were inspired by the same real-life killer: Ed Gein.

From the very opening shot of *The Texas Chain Saw Massacre*, the connections to the infamous Ed Gein case are clear. The film's protagonists Sally Hardesty and her wheelchair-bound brother, Franklin, travel with friends to a cemetery where their grandfather is interred after hearing radio reports of graverobbing in the area. Though they find his grave has been left undisturbed, upon stopping to visit his abandoned house, they stumble into a neighbouring home where they are slaughtered one-by-one by hulking cannibal "Leatherface", named for wearing a mask of human skin. The house is adorned with items made from human body parts, and Leatherface has a variety of masks, including feminine ones with lipstick, which he wears with an accompanying dress.

Gein's connections to *Psycho*'s Norman Bates are subtler and focus more upon his unhealthy relationship with his mother than the harvesting of flesh trophies. While Bates dons his mom's dress and wig to assume her identity, he stops short of Gein's notorious "woman suit". When Bates takes on her identity, he lectures Norman on staying away from women – all of whom are "harlots" – which emulates the beliefs espoused by Augusta Gein, though there is no evidence Ed Gein ever had these dissociative conversations with himself. Certainly, Gein and Bates are both loners inhabiting large empty houses (and both keep their mother's room pristine), but Gein left his farm to do odd jobs while Bates operates a motel on the property. And though Gein dug up the bodies of women who resembled his mother, he did not, contrary to popular belief, actually disinter her corpse and keep it in his house, as Bates did. Nor is there any evidence Ed Gein murdered Augusta (though his brother, Henry, has long been considered a possible victim). Norman Bates, on the other hand, killed his mother and her lover in a jealous rage 10 years before his apprehension.

That both Norman Bates and Leatherface were based on Ed Gein is undeniable. However, these characters borrow different aspects from him, with neither truly mirroring the complex psychology of the "Plainfield Ghoul".

—

Edward Theodore Gein entered the world on August 27, 1906, with a number of disadvantages. A congenital growth on his left eyelid caused it to droop, while his pronunciation of certain words was hindered by a tongue lesion. He also stammered – a condition that may have been exacerbated or even caused by the psychological abuse Gein suffered at home. Sadly, Ed seemed to get the worst of it both at home and school. His puritanical mother, Augusta, ruled over the Gein household in the small town of La Crosse, Wisconsin with an iron fist, dominating her alcoholic husband, George, and their two sons. Having proved inept at farming, tanning, and carpentry, George Gein had been chronically unemployed and intoxicated since February 1902, a mere 13 months after the birth of Ed's older brother, Henry. This left Augusta to provide for the family, working all day at her grocery store, then returning home to cook and clean. While cruel, her constant deriding of George as "useless" seems to have been largely merited. Fiercely religious, Augusta Gein apparently viewed the 30,000-resident town of La Crosse as a Gomorrah of the northwest, and began plotting the family's exodus. In 1914, the Geins relocated to a 195-acre (79-hectare) farm on the outskirts of Plainfield, 90 miles (145 km) northeast of La Crosse. Their new home was a bleak, isolated farmhouse, more than a mile from their nearest neighbour.

At school, Ed was relentlessly mocked by the other children for his physical and verbal afflictions. His somewhat effete manner only made things worse. Even his teachers thought the droopy-eyed boy who chuckled to himself was strange. They weren't wrong. A year before relocating to Plainfield, seven-year-old Ed apparently became sexually aroused at the sight of blood and guts spilling from a hog carcass.[1]

Apart from school and infrequent shopping trips into Plainfield, Ed and Henry were insulated from the "corrupting influence" of life beyond the farm. With her brood in physical and social isolation, Augusta Gein hammered her sons with scripture, denouncing lust and drink as tools of the devil. Ever meek and obedient, Ed tried to avoid girls at school. Even so, Augusta used cruelty to try to suppress his development. On one occasion, she allegedly caught him masturbating in the bath, and painfully twisted his penis, shrieking that it was the downfall of man.

Despite his mother's insistence, Ed found an outlet not in the Bible, but within the well-thumbed pages of pulp magazines and paperbacks. He flooded his imagination with a phantasmagoria of pirates, cannibals, and Polynesian headhunters: a salve to escape his loneliness and suffering. Ed was an average student, with no ambition to better his lot, and he dropped out of school in 1920 after completing the eighth grade.

After years as an invalid, George Gein suffered a heart attack and passed away on April 1, 1940. Henry and Edward had long supported the family by farming and taking on odd jobs – Ed often babysat, apparently preferring the company of children to adults. The brothers had a reputation for being honest, dependable, and hard working. Soon after the bombing of Pearl Harbor in December 1941, Ed was summoned before a draft board in Milwaukee. Medical personnel quickly determined he was unsuitable for military service, and sent him back to Plainfield with a 4F (unfit) classification. At that time, it was the furthest he had ever travelled.

Meanwhile, 42-year-old Henry Gein was growing weary of his life of unmarried drudgery. When in Ed's company, he would sometimes speak ill of their mother or entertain hopes of starting a family of his own. Whatever escape route Henry might have been planning came to an abrupt halt on March 16, 1944, when a wildfire broke out on the Gein property. Numerous causes have been attributed to the blaze over the years, from lightning to arson. Bearing shovels, Ed and Henry ran into the smoke to extinguish the flames. According to Ed, the two became separated and unable to find each other. Once the fire was out, and with Henry still missing, Ed raced off in his car to notify the police, as there was no phone at the house. He returned to the property with the lawmen, reportedly leading them straight to his brother's corpse. A quick investigation of the unsinged remains revealed abrasions on Henry's scalp. On the surface, it appeared Henry had been clobbered to death rather than succumbing to fire. But Ed was convincing during his interrogation, and on May 18 the county coroner recorded the cause of death as "asphyxiation". The local police quickly returned to their dull routine, and nobody seems to have considered the serious probability that Henry was bludgeoned unconscious and left to inhale smoke.

Thirty-seven-year-old Ed now had his mother all to himself, but Augusta had by no means mellowed with age. Marooned in the dilapidated house, she vacillated between obsessively adoring her only living son and angrily denouncing his sinfulness. This emotionally incestuous arrangement proved short-lived. Augusta survived a stroke that left her virtually incapacitated. Ever dutiful, Ed waited on her hand and foot. They managed to share one last Christmas together, before another stroke ended her life on December 29, 1945.

After her sparsely attended funeral, Ed Gein returned home to the Plainfield farm. He boarded up the entry to Augusta's bedroom, which remained a shrine to his mother – forever sealed and pristine. Outside the farmhouse, the winter winds howled. For the first time in his life, Ed Gein was completely and utterly alone.

Part-time sheriff's deputy Frank Worden spent Saturday, November 16, 1957, hunting in the forests of central Wisconsin. Having had little luck, and with the skies slowly darkening on the prairie, he pulled his car into a Phillips 66 gas station. While filling his tank he was approached by Bernard Muschinski, the gas station's owner, who informed him that something strange was going on at the local hardware store, which belonged to Frank's mother. Bernard had seen the company delivery van speed off early that morning, leaving the door locked and the premises vacant. Knowing his mother was scheduled to be working, Frank sped into town and parked outside the family business on Main Street. He used his keys to enter the store, but found no sign of Bernice Worden. Chillingly, the cash register was missing, and a .22-calibre rifle had been removed from its rack and placed on the counter. Nearby, Frank found a receipt for antifreeze. A trail of blood led through the back door, disappearing outside. At once, Frank's mind conjured up the image of a certain droopy-eyed loner. Ed Gein had been popping into the hardware store a little too often recently, even inviting 57-year-old Bernice to accompany him to a roller rink in nearby Hancock. He recalled that Ed had stopped by the previous day, enquiring about the price of antifreeze and asking Frank when he next planned to go hunting.

Frank Worden telephoned his boss, Sheriff Art Schley in Wautoma, who raced immediately to Plainfield with Chief Deputy Arnie Fritz. They entered the hardware store to find Frank pacing. He told them his mother had been kidnapped and that he suspected Ed Gein of abducting her.

In a town of less than 700 inhabitants, it didn't take long for them to find Gein. Officer Dan Chase and Deputy "Poke" Spees drove up to Gein's farmhouse to find the doors locked and nobody home. Heading next door to the Hills', they found Ed sitting in his black sedan with his neighbour Bob, warming up the engine. The officers approached the driver's side window and began asking Ed about his movements throughout the day. The lisping recluse attempted to outfox them, but quickly found himself outmatched.

"Somebody framed me,"[2] he blinked.

"Framed you for what?"

"Well, about Mrs Worden."

"What about Mrs Worden?"

"Well, she's dead ain't she?"

"Dead! How'd you know she's dead?"

"I heard it. They told me in there,"[3] Ed motioned to the Hill house.

Chase and Spees had heard enough. They arrested Ed Gein for the murder of Bernice Worden, and placed him in the back of their patrol car for safekeeping.

Once Sheriff Schley received word of the arrest, he headed up to the old Gein farmhouse at 8 p.m. with Captain Lloyd Schoephoerster of the Green Lake Sheriff's Department. They determined the weakest point of entry was a door to the "summer kitchen" – a shed attached to a wall at the rear of the property – and kicked their way in. They found themselves in pitch darkness, assailed by a rancid odour. As they made their way through the room, torch-beams sweeping over piles of refuse, Schley bumped into a heavy, stinking mass suspended in mid-air. Stepping back, he aimed the light at the object and recoiled in horror. Bernice Worden's nude, headless corpse hung upside down from the rafters. A ragged split ran from her sternum, but there was no dripping blood or dangling innards. She had been gutted like a deer.[4]

Sheriff Schley barely made it outside before heaving the contents of his own stomach into the snow. Schoephoerster hurried to the squad-car radio, reported the gruesome discovery, and requested back-up. They had barely crossed the house's threshold.

Heeding the call, sheriffs, deputies, state troopers, and criminologists gradually assembled at the farmhouse until they had formed a makeshift team of investigators. Like most isolated rural buildings in Waushara County at the time, the Gein residence did not have electricity, meaning they would have to enter its dark confines with only kerosene lamps and torches to illuminate the many horrors they would encounter. Navigating through the summer kitchen, they passed Bernice Worden's inverted corpse and entered Gein's inner sanctum.

From the moment they first set foot in the living areas of the house, it was obvious that Gein was a hoarder of epic proportions. Between the cartons, cans, rags, stacks of comics, and scraps of rotting food, not only was it difficult to avoid tripping over something unpleasant, the stench was almost unbearable. Among the many oddities were coffee cans filled with wads of used chewing gum, a sand-filled basin, and rows of yellowed dentures arranged along the shelves like priceless antiques. A heavy layer of dust blanketed most of the house, leading them to conclude that Ed probably inhabited less than a handful of rooms. The scene was bizarre enough already when Captain Lloyd Schoephoerster picked up a curious-looking bowl from the kitchen table, and held it up to the light to inspect it. To his horror, he realized it was the sawn-off cap of a human skull. This was far from the only household item Gein had fashioned from bones. Beyond an entire collection of bowls, investigators found a pair of skulls adorning his bedposts.[5]

Though he'd made extensive use of human bones, Ed's preferred medium for decoration was clearly female epidermis. Among the many bizarre items in the house were four chairs, whose rattan seats had been carefully removed and replaced with skin. There were also skin waste baskets, lampshades, bracelets, tom toms, and sheaths. A true "artist" of the macabre, Gein had painstakingly fastened enough nipples together to make a belt. Undoubtedly, though, his most shocking creation was a "woman suit" consisting of a tanned vest, leggings, and series of interchangeable masks. Among the clutter, they found individual boxes filled to the brim with noses and other extremities.[6]

The discovery of Bernice Worden's heart inside a plastic bag near the stove gave rise to another sick possibility – cannibalism. Her innards were found wrapped in newspaper tucked away inside an old suit. Crime-scene photographer Allan Wilimovsky subsequently discovered her head when he noticed steam rising from a burlap sack stuffed between two filthy mattresses in the summer kitchen. Ed had jammed a bent nail into each of her ears and fastened a piece of twine to both nails. It was difficult to believe it was intended to be anything other than a decoration to hang from the wall.

But the discovery of Bernice Worden's head was overshadowed by that of a second. Picking up a musty horsehide robe behind the kitchen door, Deputy Arnie Fritz pulled a hefty paper bag from its confines. Inside was a withered skin mask with straw-dry hair still attached to it. Raising it to the light, Fritz heard a cry of astonishment from one of the investigators.

"By God. It's Mary Hogan."[7]

Three years earlier, on December 8, 1954, the plump 54-year-old

German tavern owner had gone missing from her place of business in Pine Grove, seven miles (11 km) north of Plainfield. Finally, Wisconsinites had an answer to this nagging mystery. Yet, the unveiling of Mary Hogan's remains simply invited another question: just how many victims were there?

Ed Gein's first formal interview with law enforcement took place on Tuesday, November 19, between 1:45 and 7:25 p.m. The polygraphist was Joe Wilimovsky, brother of crime-scene photographer Allan. Though Ed was reluctant to discuss the murders, offering curt, dismissive replies, he was eerily candid about his activities with the corpses. He admitted to robbing graves to procure the bodies of recently dead older women, mutilating and shaping them to fit his needs, and even treating the skin with an oil to preserve them.[8] Most of his ideas had come from reading magazine articles about Nazi war atrocities – specifically, the skin-covered interior decorations of the infamous "Bitch of Buchenwald", Ilse Koch – though his cranium collection harkened back to his boyhood fascination with headshrinkers, and his bone bowls were inspired by stories of Vikings drinking mead from skulls. Severely limited in his interactions with other people, a great deal of Ed's inspiration seemed to have come from the pages of pulp magazines. One of the stories he might have happened upon was that of the Danish artist Einar Wegener, who, following a 1929 sex-change operation, had been reborn as "Lili Elbe" and shocked the world.

Eventually, Ed would confess to wearing the dead skin masks, breast vests, leggings, and other parts to roam around the old farmhouse feeling feminine. On some nights, when the mood took him, he would don his "woman suit" and step outdoors to frolic in the moonlight.[9]

An unidentified source, who had been present during the Gein interviews, told the press that Ed "wished that he had been a woman instead of a man. He bought medical books and studied anatomy. He wondered whether it would be possible to change his sex. He considered inquiring about an operation to change him into a woman and even thought of trying the operation upon himself, but did nothing about such plans."[10]

On the morning of Monday, November 25, District Attorney Earl Killeen, Sheriff Schley, Deputy Fritz, and eight assistants, arrived at Plainfield cemetery with shovels and a determination to get the unpleasant work ahead of them over and done with. Although Ed Gein had provided the names of nine graves he had robbed, Killeen decided only to dig up those of Eleanor Adams and Mabel Everson. At this point, nobody was quite sure whether or not to believe Ed's gravedigging stories. However, it was obvious there were more body parts in the old farmhouse than could be accounted for by just the two identified homicide victims, and looking into his claims was an investigative necessity. By 12:30 p.m. Killeen and his colleagues had unearthed both the Adams and Everson graves, only to discover that their coffins had been split open and their remains were either mostly or entirely missing. Turning to the swarm of reporters outside the old wrought iron cemetery gates, Killeen announced the results of their discovery, stating that as far as he was concerned, they had now verified Gein's story.[11]

Two days before, on November 23, Edward Theodore Gein had been admitted to Waupun's Central State Hospital for the Criminally Insane, where he could be assessed by a team of mental health professionals to see if he was fit to stand trial for murder. After interviewing and examining Gein on several occasions, Dr E.F. Schubert wrote a report on his motives:

> "He rather vehemently stated that none of this would have happened if his neighbours had shown some interest in him and would have visited him . . . He stated that he is unable to recall any of the details of the murder of Mrs Hogan and . . . is not clear on many of the details involved in the murder of Mrs Worden . . . he feels that her death was an accident because the gun must have discharged accidentally . . . Much

of the interview was spent in discussing his feelings about his mother. His mother was a very religious woman and his only description of her was that 'she was good in every way' . . . He stated that since the death of his mother he has had feelings that things around him were unreal and at one time, shortly after the death of the mother, he felt that he could raise the dead by will power. He also stated that he heard his mother talking to him on several occasions for about a year after she died . . . He stated that he had violated nine graves and when questioned as to his reasons for doing this, he stated he thought it was because he wanted a remembrance of his mother. He denied any sexual relations with any of these bodies and gave as his reason that 'they smelled too bad' . . . He claimed to have tried to rouse his dead mother by an act of will power and was disappointed when he was unsuccessful. He also admitted this sort of thing with some of the bodies which he had exhumed . . ."[12]

On December 13, a second report by Dr R. Warmington stated:

"The subject is an introverted, odd, withdrawn personality that has had difficulty relating closely to other people . . . The unused parts of bodies were burned or buried and eating is denied . . . The motivation [for murder] is elusive and uncertain, but several factors come to mind – hostility, sex, and a desire for a substitute for his mother in the form of a replica or body that could be kept indefinitely. He has spoken of the bodies as being like dolls and a certain comfort was received from their presence . . . "

A board of specialists conducted a final assessment of Gein on December 18, and determined that his schizophrenia hindered his ability to judge the difference between right and wrong, or recognize the consequences of his actions. He was therefore unfit to stand trial for murder and should be committed to the hospital until such a time that he was deemed able to go to court.

On Thursday, March 20, 1958, an unexplained fire suddenly broke out in the old abandoned Gein farmhouse, reducing it to ashes. When Ed was informed about the strange tragedy, he simply shrugged, "Just as well."[13]

Edward Theodore Gein was finally deemed fit to stand trial for the murder of Bernice Worden on November 7, 1968. Ultimately, Judge Robert H. Gollmar determined that Gein was not guilty by reason of insanity and he was returned to Central State Hospital. He died of respiratory failure on July 26, 1984, at the age of 78.

Frenzy 1972

The Crimes of John Christie and Neville Heath, and the Hammersmith Nude Murders

Alfred Hitchcock's *Frenzy* portrayed a lustful serial killer murdering victims with that most prosaic item of male attire – a necktie. The film presented murder as dark comedy, but there was nothing remotely comedic about the sadistic, manipulative real-life murderers *Frenzy*'s killer was based on: John Christie, Neville Heath, and the unknown killer that the press dubbed "Jack the Stripper".

Alfred Hitchcock's *Frenzy* marked the director's return to murder thrillers and critical acclaim, reaping $12.6 million at the box office. Filmed in colour on a $2 million budget and released in 1972, this final British film in Hitchcock's career begins where his earlier film *The Lodger* ended, with an elusive sex murderer preying upon the women of London.

In the opening scene, a crowd gathered along the River Thames gasps "another neck-tie murder!" as the nude, garrotted body of a young woman floats into view. As if cheekily acknowledging Hitchcock's neglect of his own artistic strengths, a medical doctor commenting on "The Necktie Killer" in a pub flippantly remarks, "Well, we haven't had a good juicy series of sex murders since Christie!"

While the identity of the murderer, greengrocer Bob Rusk, is revealed less than half an hour into the film, suspicion falls upon his friend Dick Blaney. An angry man given to drink, Dick attempts to visit his ex-wife Brenda at her dating agency. Finding the door locked and his knocks unanswered, he leaves, but is spotted by Brenda's secretary when she returns from lunch. When the secretary enters the office to find Brenda Blaney fatally strangled, she assumes the short-tempered Dick is the culprit. The police agree. A fugitive, Dick Blaney seeks the help of his old friend Bob Rusk. Instead, Rusk plants evidence in Dick's belongings and telephones the police, resulting in his arrest, trial, convictions, and imprisonment. Knowing that Rusk is Brenda's murderer, Dick escapes from prison and breaks into Rusk's apartment intent on killing the grocer. Instead, he finds Rusk's latest murder victim lying in bed. Chief Inspector Timothy Oxford – who was suspicious of Rusk and surveilling him – enters to find Dick Blaney standing over the dead woman's body. At that moment, Rusk bursts into his apartment carrying a large trunk. He is caught red-handed, or as Oxford puts it, "Mr Rusk, you're not wearing your tie."

Though *Frenzy* tells the tale of a fictitious London lust killer and his victims, it is an amalgamation of three of the most notorious serial murder cases in the city's history. In 1949, John Reginald Halliday Christie murdered the wife of his neighbour Timothy Evans, then framed him for the crime. Clearly the inspiration for *Frenzy*'s Dick Blaney, Evans was a financially hard-up binge drinker, whose hair-trigger temper only served to further incriminate him. Evans hanged for his alleged crimes in 1950, all the while protesting "Christie done it!" According to actor Barry Foster, who portrayed killer Bob Rusk, Hitchcock also asked him to read two books on the infamously charming British sadist, Neville Heath, in preparation for the role. The film's image of a nude woman's strangled body floating in the Thames was based upon the still-unsolved "Hammersmith Nude Murders", which began with the August 1964 murder of Hannah Tailford and ended with that of Bridget O'Hara on January 11, 1965.

—

In their cramped upstairs flat at 10 Rillington Place – a bedbug-ridden slum in London's Notting Hill district – newlyweds Timothy and Beryl Evans were having a rough time of it. A near-illiterate, Welshman Tim was ever-conscious of marrying above his station and worked 12-hour days as a delivery driver to provide for his family. Beryl, though beautiful, was a terrible homemaker and cook. Having lost her own mother in childhood, she had simply never learnt, let alone mastered, what were then considered the basic duties of a housewife. Tim's mother, Thomasina, and sister, Eileen, often dropped by to help, but became frustrated with Beryl's apparent lack of interest in improving. They voiced their concerns to Tim in no uncertain terms. Already beleaguered, he sought refuge from the domestic turmoil at the "KPH" (Kensington Park Hotel) and the Elgin – his two favourite local pubs – where he became something of a fixture.

Sadly, the domestic tensions heightened in October 1948 when Beryl gave birth to their first child, Geraldine. Though Tim and Beryl were overjoyed at the arrival of their baby daughter, the presence of another mouth to feed only added to Tim's stress. Worse, Beryl was far from a conscientious mother. On Saturday mornings, Eileen would take Geraldine to her mother's home for a proper wash and change of clothes. It was clear Beryl was not managing the infant's hygiene as attentively as she should have. Again, word of this got back to Tim.

Growing up fatherless, with untreated learning difficulties and chronic health problems leading to hospitalization, Tim had overcome seemingly insurmountable disadvantages to cobble together his little family and provide a life for them. Unfortunately, his efforts were undermined by a short temper, which was exacerbated by his fondness for alcohol. His quarrelling with Beryl was loud and near-constant, and 10 Rillington Place apparently had paper-thin walls and floors. Downstairs, there lived a seemingly innocuous older man who was always listening: John Reginald Halliday Christie, or "Reg" to those who knew him.

Balding and bespectacled, Christie grew up in Yorkshire and had been living at 10 Rillington Place with his wife, Ethel, since 1937. A visibly anxious man, his voice rose to little more than a whisper – a result of his exposure to mustard gas during World War I. When he did speak, it was to gossip or announce his disapproval of the growing West Indian population in the neighbourhood. He never mentioned that there were two women buried in his back garden.

In the autumn of 1949, Beryl Evans discovered she was pregnant once again, and twice attempted to induce a miscarriage by taking pills. When her efforts failed, she informed Tim that she planned to have an abortion. A staunch Roman Catholic, he strongly objected. Abortion was illegal in the United Kingdom until 1968, meaning Beryl would have to rely on a "backstreet" abortionist – a risky and potentially fatal gambit. Vexed, Tim and Beryl confided in kindly Mr Christie, who reassured them that he had received medical training before the war, and had terminated pregnancies successfully on several occasions. Nevertheless, he felt morally obligated to let them know that about 10 per cent of patients died as a result of the procedure. Beryl was adamant that she was having an abortion and that their downstairs neighbour was the best man for the job. Tim resisted right up until the evening of Monday, November 7, when Beryl announced that Christie would be performing the procedure the following morning, whether Tim liked it or not. The two rowed ferociously and Tim stormed off to the KPH to drown his sorrows.

When he awoke next to Beryl at 6 a.m., she instructed him to inform Christie that she was ready. If Tim refused, she added, she would simply tell him herself. Resigned to the inevitable, Timothy Evans passed the message to Christie on his way out the front door. He stepped into the early morning bleakness and made his way to his delivery van.

When Tim Evans returned to 10 Rillington Place at 6 p.m., he found Christie waiting for him at the bottom of the stairs. He offered to accompany Tim back up to his flat. Once they were behind closed doors, Christie told him "It's bad news. It didn't work."[1] Tim entered the bedroom to find the curtains drawn and what appeared to be a human form covered by a quilt. He removed the eiderdown to reveal Beryl's lifeless body clad in a skirt and blouse. Blood was trickling from various places on her body. Nearby, baby Geraldine lay sound asleep in her cot. Christie explained that Beryl's stomach had become septic during the procedure, resulting in her being poisoned. Knowing Christie could be in serious legal trouble if his wife's body was discovered, Tim agreed to let the old man keep it in a vacant apartment and then dispose of it in a nearby storm sewer. Christie told Tim it was important that he go about his deliveries as usual the next morning, to avoid drawing attention. He and Ethel would watch over Geraldine.

Before Tim left for work on Wednesday, November 9, 1949, Christie assured him he knew a couple in East Acton who would look after Geraldine. When Tim returned that evening, Christie confirmed the couple would be coming to fetch Geraldine at 9 a.m. the next morning, so Tim should ready the baby and pack her things. He complied, and by the time he had returned from work on Thursday, Geraldine was gone. Christie explained that he had hidden Beryl's body in the drains, and urged Tim to leave the city as soon as possible, promising to transport the baby's high chair and pram to East Acton. Knowing there would be questions from Beryl's family and friends, Evans and Christie concocted a story that she and the baby had gone to live in Brighton.

Selling their belongings, Timothy Evans pocketed £40, and took the night train to Wales on Monday, November 14. He stayed with a paternal aunt and uncle in his ancestral community of Merthyr Vale.

Eventually, Tim's mother, Thomasina, sister, Eileen, and half-sister, Mary, independently knocked on the door of 10 Rillington Place, only to be greeted by Christie. He informed them that Tim had gone to Bristol, and Beryl and Geraldine to Brighton, and refused to let the visitors enter the building. When Mary noted contradictions in Christie's story and kept pressuring him, the usually meek old man became angry and threatening.

Having contacted Beryl's father in Brighton and been informed that he hadn't seen his daughter, Thomasina penned a letter to Tim's aunt saying "I don't know what lies Tim has told you down there, I know nothing about him and I have not seen him for 3 weeks . . . his name stinks up everywhere I go [sic] people asking for money he owes them. I am ashamed to say he is my son."[2] When Tim's aunt read the letter to him aloud, his nerves finally gave way. On Wednesday, November 30, he walked into the Merthyr Vale police station and said "I want to give up. I have disposed of my wife . . . I put her down the drain."[3]

Tim Evans went on to make a statement to the police at Merthyr Vale that Beryl had attempted to self-terminate the pregnancy, threatening to commit suicide when she was unsuccessful. By chance, Tim said he had encountered a man in a cafe who had given him a bottle containing an unlabelled substance that would induce a miscarriage. However, when Beryl took it, she unexpectedly died. Tim had hidden her body beneath a manhole cover, found someone to look after Geraldine, and quit his job before selling his furniture and absconding.

The Merthyr Vale police notified law enforcement in London, and policemen were sent from the Notting Hill branch to investigate the sewers. It took three strong men to lift the manhole cover, but upon examining the drains, they found nothing. When informed of this, Tim gave a second statement to the police, saying his first one had been to "protect a man named Christie".[4] Now suspicious of Christie for not disposing of Beryl's body in the manner he had claimed, Evans gave a recollection of the true story as he understood it – Christie's "botched abortion" account.

Meanwhile, Notting Hill police entered Evans' apartment to find a stolen briefcase, which was filled with newspaper clippings about a recent dismemberment murder – in hindsight, Christie had obviously planted it there to incriminate him. Two detectives from the London Metropolitan Police now had reason to charge Tim Evans with theft, and arrived at Merthyr Vale to arrest him. When Christie was also questioned, he denied everything. He added that the couple upstairs were always loudly quarrelling, and that Beryl had once confided in his wife that she was afraid Tim would kill her one day. Ethel Christie corroborated every aspect of her husband's story.

Yet there was still the puzzle of where Beryl and baby Geraldine were. Having searched every corner of 10 Rillington Place, that night the policemen decided to check the adjacent wash-house, which had recently been refurbished by builders. Shining their torches into the blackness they noticed a large object concealed beneath a pile of boards. Removing the debris, they uncovered the bodies of Beryl and Geraldine Evans – a man's necktie cinched around the child's neck. An autopsy found both victims had died from ligature strangulation. Beryl had genital bruising, but the injuries were attributed to an attempted abortion.

Notified of the discovery by a Detective Chief Inspector Jennings back in London, Tim Evans provided yet another statement on December 2 at Notting Hill station, confessing to the murders. It is important to recall his learning difficulties and illiteracy, and the fact he had just been confronted with the revelation that his 14-month-old daughter was dead – it is likely that he experienced intense guilt. As the author Neil Root points out, Evans' confession was obviously not written down accurately, as the document contains words such as "incurring" which would have been outside his limited vocabulary. Evans would also later say the police interviewers had fed him the information necessary to make his statement fit the known facts.

On January 11, 1950, Timothy Evans was tried at the Old Bailey for the murder of his daughter, though the judge permitted evidence from Beryl Evans' killing to be included. Having entered a plea of not guilty, Tim's defence focused on John Christie as the true culprit. When Christie took the stand, he contrived to send Tim to the gallows, modestly emphasizing his own terrible illnesses, military service in World War I, and work as a War Reserve Policeman to endear himself to those assembled. However, Evans' attorney forced Christie to admit to a criminal history that included convictions for obtaining money through false pretences in 1923, larceny in 1924, auto-theft in 1933, and malicious wounding in 1929. Why the attorney did not place more emphasis on the character of the last charge is unknown, as the "upstanding" Mr Christie had viciously beaten a woman with a cricket bat.

Evans performed poorly on the witness stand, and after just 40 minutes of deliberation, on January 13, 1950, the jury found him guilty of murdering his infant daughter. He was sentenced to death by hanging. After a standard medical inquiry at the magistrate's court judged Evans fit to hang, the prisoner was allowed to speak.

"I say Christie done it,"[5] he stated.

On the morning of March 9, 1950, Albert Pierrepoint executed Timothy Evans by hanging at Pentonville Prison. Five months later, the owner of 10 Rillington Place sold the building to a Jamaican immigrant, Charles Brown, who rented the upstairs and mid-floor flats to his fellow countrymen, much to the Christies' chagrin.

On March 20, 1953, John Christie illegally sub-let his flat to a young couple for £7 and 13 shillings, then disappeared into the streets of London with the cash, never to return. By this time the neighbours hadn't seen Mrs Christie for several months. Charles Brown notified the prospective sub-letters they weren't legally permitted to move in, explaining they would have to take up their grievances with Christie. After Christie moved out, the landlord allowed his upstairs tenant, Beresford Brown, to use the Christies' vacant kitchen. On March 24, while redecorating the space and building some new shelves, Beresford spotted what appeared to be a new section of wallpaper behind a cupboard. To his horror, he soon discovered the paper did not cover a wall at all, rather, a hidden alcove containing three decomposing female corpses.

The police recognized the infamous address immediately, and began a full search of the premises. Noting some loose floorboards in the front room, they pried them up to reveal the near-nude remains of Ethel Christie wrapped in a blanket. Pathologist Dr Francis Camps quickly determined that all four women had been murdered by ligature strangulation. Ethel had been dead for nearly 14 weeks, while the women in the alcove had been killed more recently. They also discovered a tobacco tin containing pubic hair belonging to several women. By the time the skeletal remains of two other female victims were unearthed from the back garden, Christie's name and likeness were already emblazoned across newspapers all over London.

Christie was arrested on March 31 by a police constable on routine patrol, who spotted him gazing out at the River Thames from the south bank near Putney Bridge. A pathological liar, Christie gave numerous contradictory accounts of what had happened regarding his "latest" victims, along with the Evanses. Ultimately, it came to light that with the exception of his wife, Christie had rendered each of the women unconscious before raping them, then strangled them to death. It is widely believed he engaged in post-mortem sex acts with the bodies. His outstanding victims were identified as 21-year-old Ruth Fuerst (killed in 1943), Muriel Eady, 31 (1944), Kathleen Maloney, 26 (1953), Rita Nelson, 24 (1953), and Hectorina MacLennan, 27 (1953).

Convicted of the murder of Ethel Christie on Thursday, June 25, 1953, John Reginald Halliday Christie was executed on July 15 on the same gallows as Timothy Evans three years earlier, and by the same executioner – Albert Pierrepoint. In October 1966, Timothy Evans was granted a royal pardon. The Home Office awarded a monetary sum for miscarriage of justice to his sister, Eileen, and half-sister, Mary, in January 2003.

—

Aside from their shared habit of murdering attractive young women, Neville George Clevely Heath was in many ways the opposite of John Christie. Strappingly handsome with a cleft chin and shock of blond hair, the former Royal Air Force pilot exuded a charismatic confidence that ensured he was always the centre of attention. He was always ready to share heroic tales of his exploits fighting the Nazi *Luftwaffe*, and even though the shrewder punters suspected these were fabricated, they simply shrugged it off. In retrospect, it can be seen that the dashing Heath was a psychopath who possessed a magnetic charm.

On the afternoon of June 20, 1946, Heath was drinking at The Falstaff, a pub on Fleet Street that was a popular haunt for journalists, newspapermen, and everything in between. Looking dapper in his mustard-brown jacket, RAF tie, and grey flannel trousers, the popular pilot was bankrolling this latest binge with a roll of cash – £30 in total – that he'd received in advance to fly a *Daily Mail* journalist to Copenhagen the following morning. Heath didn't actually have a plane – or pilot's licence for that matter – but he possessed an uncanny knack for talking his way into or out of things.

Draining his pint, Heath bid farewell to his audience, and made his way to Mayfair to meet up with boyhood friend, Leslie Terry. The two embarked on something of a pub crawl, even drinking one establishment dry. Terry would later claim Heath had downed 24 pints, but whether he had personally witnessed this feat or simply took Heath at his notoriously unreliable word is unknown. Slowly, the two made their way to the Trevor Arms in Knightsbridge where Heath had a woman waiting for him.

Thirty-three-year-old Margery Gardner would have resonated more with the bawdiness of Weimar Germany or the San Francisco free love culture of the Swinging Sixties, than post-war London. The attractive young woman had left her husband in Sheffield for the London nightlife, where she felt her bohemian soul could finally blossom.[6] An aspiring artist – having written half a novel and worked as an extra in several films – Margery was ill-suited for the domestic drudgery of the industrial north. She had embarked on flings with several lovers since arriving in the capital, and had first encountered the charming Heath in April. Soon after meeting, the couple had indulged an apparently mutual penchant for sadomasochistic sex.[7]

Upon reaching the establishment at the corner of Knightsbridge High Road and Charles Street, Heath apparently decided that Terry's usefulness had been exhausted, ditched him at the Arms, and left for his date with Mrs Gardner. After dining at the Normandie, the couple relocated to the Panama Club, dancing and drinking until midnight, when they took a cab to the Pembridge Court Hotel in Notting Hill. With no night staff on duty, Heath let them in using his key, and the drunken couple stumbled to his room. Once inside, Margery stripped nude and lay face down on the bed. Heath placed a gag between her teeth and bound her wrists and ankles. Next, reaching into his suitcase, he produced a riding crop.[8]

At 2:30 the following afternoon, a chambermaid entered room 4 to find a woman's naked body lying on the bed, her back severely mutilated and her hair caked with blood. Mrs Wyatt, the hotel owner, knew "Colonel Heath" usually slept late, and had wondered when he would finally make his way downstairs. Summoned to his room by the distraught cleaning lady, Mrs Wyatt turned on the lights, took one look at the bloodied bedsheets and trussed corpse, and nearly vomited.[9]

Investigators quickly determined the victim's identity from the wartime ID card lying in the room. However, the extent of the brutality she had endured would not be revealed until Prof Keith Simpson – England's most accomplished pathologist – documented the findings of his autopsy. Margery Gardner had died of suffocation between 12 and 1 a.m. after suffering a series of "appalling" injuries.[10] A total of 17 diamond-shaped lacerations marked her body: nine on her buttocks and back; six on her chest, breasts, and stomach; and two across her face and eyes, all from some kind of whip. The attacker had repeatedly bitten her breasts, nearly severing them. Most horrifically, there was a 7-inch (17-cm) long wound to the victim's genitals, which had apparently been inflicted with a fire poker. Her face and throat were heavily bruised. Though there was evidence Margery Gardner had been gagged, Prof Simpson concluded that her face had likely been forced into a pillow, causing her to suffocate.[11]

By this time, Neville Heath had already taken a train from Victoria railway station to the quaint seaside town of Worthing. Checking into the Ocean Hotel, he had telephoned yet another lover, Yvonne Symonds, and the two had met for lunch. The following morning the shocking news of Margery Gardner's murder broke in the *Daily Mail*. Oblivious, Symonds met with Heath again, who confided in her that he was indirectly connected to the slaying. Heath claimed a male stranger named Jack had asked him if he could use room 4 at the Pembridge Court Hotel for a tryst with a lady friend. The convivial Heath had kindly obliged him. The next day, an Inspector Barrett of Scotland Yard had led Heath to Margery Gardner's body – a sight that Heath characterized as the gruesome work of a sex maniac. In an ill-considered move, he disclosed to Symonds that a fire poker had been protruding from Gardner, and that he believed this to be the cause of her death.

The next day, when the story was splashed across newspapers all over the country, Symonds went to her parents for advice. Afterwards, she called Heath to relay their concern that he was linked to a murder, and he assured her he would drive back to London immediately to cooperate with the investigators.[12]

Instead, he took the train to Bournemouth, arriving that same evening. He stored a hard leather suitcase at the station's cloakroom, taking a ticket with him so he could retrieve it at a later date. Using the ostentatious pseudonym "Group Captain Rupert Brook", Heath then checked into room 71 of the luxurious Tollard

Royal Hotel, which had a view of the ocean. Possibly contemplating suicide, he relocated to room 81 – which had a gas fire – four days later. Rather than keeping a low profile, the habitual charmer struck up conversations with fellow guests, drank at the hotel bar, and even went out dancing. While in hindsight such activities clearly betrayed the foolhardy bravado of a psychopath, as the newspapers still had not printed a photograph of the suspect, "Brook" was free to party and socialize while all of England had their eye out for Neville George Clevely Heath.

On Wednesday, July 3, at 2:30 p.m., Heath ran into 19-year-old Doreen Marshall on the promenade. Wielding his ever-reliable charm, he managed to convince her to accompany him back to the Tollard Royal for tea at 3:45 p.m. Doreen must have enjoyed Heath's company, as she agreed to reconvene with him for dinner. She arrived at the Tollard Royal by cab at 8:15 p.m., wearing a black dress, camel hair coat, and necklace of artificial pearls. When their meal had concluded, they moved to the lounge, and then the writing room, where Heath was served a potent combination of beer, brandy, and gin by a porter he had befriended. At some point, the same porter noticed that Doreen looked agitated. She asked a hotel guest to call for a taxi, but Heath quickly intervened, saying he would escort her back to her hotel, the Norfolk. As the two left the Tollard Royal just after midnight, Heath told the porter, "I'll be back in half an hour."

"No," Doreen quickly countered, "in a quarter of an hour."[13]

When "Rupert Brook" still hadn't returned at 4:30 a.m., the confused night porter went up to the guest's room and knocked gently on the door. Receiving no answer, he slowly turned the door handle and peeked inside. The man was sprawled across his bed in a deep slumber. Strangely, his shoes, set down in front of the door, were caked in sand.

Late the next morning, the debonair "group captain" made his way downstairs, and began regaling the employees of the Tollard Royal with the story of the hilarious practical joke he had played on the night porter – he had used a builder's ladder to climb in through his first-floor window.[14]

Two days later, the manager of the Norfolk rang up the Tollard Royal, and informed them that one of his guests, Doreen Marshall from Pinner, Middlesex, had not been seen since Wednesday, July 3. The young woman had spoken of having dinner with a guest at the Tollard Royal, and the manager was so concerned that he had notified the police. Asking around, the manager of the Tollard Royal quickly learnt that "Rupert Brook" had entertained a woman fitting that description on the night of the disappearance. When the manager asked the intrepid group captain about Doreen Marshall, "Brook" replied, "Oh no. I've known that lady a long while, and she certainly doesn't come from Pinner!"[15] While the manager took him at his word, he urged "Brook" to approach the Bournemouth Police to eliminate himself as a suspect in the disappearance. The young man replied that he would be happy to.

Neville Heath reached Detective Constable Suter of the Bournemouth Police by telephone at 3:30 p.m., perhaps confident he could talk his way out of the investigation, and was asked to appear at the station in two hours to look at a photograph of Doreen Marshall.

Pushing his luck even further, Heath did just that. When shown the picture by DC Suter, he was forced to acknowledge that this was indeed the woman he had dined with – there were too many witnesses to deny it – but offered that she had told him she was leaving town with her sweetheart, an American serviceman.

Just as Heath was leaving the police station, confident in his ability to mislead the police, he saw the missing woman walk in accompanied by an older man. Heath went as white as a ghost, a reaction DC Suter didn't fail to notice.[16] DC Suter introduced "Rupert Brook" to Marshall's father and sister – the latter bore a striking resemblance to Doreen – and Heath immediately regained his composure, loosening his pilot's scarf in the process. As he did, Suter spotted two deep scratches on his neck. The unflappable policeman let the suspect work his charm on the Marshalls, while he furtively flipped through a booklet of "wanted" photos. Upon reaching a photograph of a fugitive named Neville Heath, who bore an uncanny likeness to "Rupert Brook", Suter decided to stall him until Detective Inspector Gates, an experienced interviewer, returned. He convinced "Brook" to wait at the station a little longer to complete a witness statement. DI Gates entered at 6:30 p.m. and spoke to the suspect, after which he announced that "Brook" would be detained for further questioning. Heath, who was wearing just a shirt, claimed to be getting an evening chill and asked if he could first go back to the Tollard Royal to retrieve his mustard-brown sports jacket. Instead, DI Gates went to get it for him, discovering a Bournemouth-London train ticket in the pocket, along with a single fake pearl corresponding with the necklace Doreen had been wearing on the night in question. Most importantly, he found the luggage ticket Heath had been given at Bournemouth West station on June 23.

The investigators immediately retrieved Heath's suitcase and opened it to find a leather riding crop with dried blood on its criss-cross patterned weave, two bloodstained scarves, and numerous items of clothing marked with the name "Heath". Back at room 81 of the Tollard Royal, they uncovered a bloody knotted handkerchief containing two of Doreen Marshall's hairs. Confronted with the evidence, Heath finally admitted the crimes, and was taken into custody by police investigators from London, who charged him with the murder of Margery Gardner.

At 8 p.m., on July 8, a woman walking her spaniel near Branksome Dene Chine, a wooded river valley located a mile (1.6 km) from the Tollard Royal Hotel, found the naked body of Doreen Marshall in some rhododendron bushes, concealed beneath her clothing and some clipped branches. A pathologist determined she had been murdered by two incisions to her neck, while her hands revealed multiple slashes, indicative of defensive wounds. She had been sliced open – thankfully after death – and an unknown foreign object had been thrust into her genitals.[17]

Though Heath casually confessed to both slayings, admitting to his psychiatrist that flagellating women gave him sexual pleasure, he ultimately pleaded not guilty to the murder of Margery Gardner.

His trial for her murder commenced at the Old Bailey on Thursday, September 24, 1946. Adoring female fans flocked to the gallery, hoping to attract the attention of the handsome defendant.[18] Three days later, he was found guilty by a jury after an hour's deliberation, and seemed completely indifferent when Judge Morris sentenced him to hang. While awaiting his execution he sent his mother a number of letters, the last stating, "Well, it wasn't really a bad life while it lasted . . . Please don't mourn my going . . . and don't wear black."[19]

Offered a glass of whiskey on October 16, mere minutes before his execution, Heath quipped, "You might make that a double."[20] Then, walking coolly onto the scaffold he said, "Let's get this over with."[21] Minutes later, he was dead. The famous hangman, Albert Pierrepoint, would later remark that Heath was the most handsome man he had ever executed.

—

Between February 1964 and January 1965, the bodies of six London sex workers were found either in the River Thames, or near its north bank, between the town of Brentford in the west and West Kensington in the east. The victims were all nude or mostly nude, white, and ranged in age from 21 to 30 years. Dubbed "Jack the Stripper" by the press – a sensationalist homage to London's last prolific murderer of sex workers – the offender seemed to stop killing in 1965, and was never brought to justice, though nearly a dozen suspects have been proffered in the years since.

On February 2, 1964, members of the London Corinthian Sailing Club were preparing to launch 40 dinghies into the Thames in Hammersmith, when brothers Harold and George Capon spotted a nude female corpse trapped beneath a chain tethering a pontoon to the dock.[22] Instantly, 50 or more hobby sailors were staring into the water and uttering exclamations. A bystander called 999, and within no time the Thames Division of the Metropolitan Police, including Detective Inspector Frank Ridge and a pathologist, Dr Teare, were speeding towards the scene of the crime. Using a tarpaulin, the police dredged the body from the murky water, and laid it on the bank. It was that of a woman – around 5 feet 2 inches (1.57 m) tall, with brown shoulder-length hair – naked, save for some stockings around her ankles, and a torn piece of underwear stuffed into her mouth. Judging by the maceration of the skin, she had been in the water for 48 to 72 hours. A subsequent medical examination determined that she had died from drowning. The complete absence of restraint marks or signs of violence was peculiar. Soon after the authorities published a photograph of the dead woman's face, she was identified as 30-year-old Hannah Tailford – a sex worker and pornographic model from Northumbria. A known drug user, addicted to purple heart barbiturates, Hannah had recently left her boyfriend and three-year-old daughter, and disappeared. Her blue coat had been found wrapped around the propeller of a police boat at Waterloo Bridge two nights before the discovery of her body.[23]

Five days later, a River Thames police crew found the naked body of another woman, floating face down among the rubbish on the steps of Corney Reach. She was quickly identified as 26-year-old sex worker Irene Charlotte Lockwood. Irene apparently had a well-rehearsed trick of stealing her clients' wallets and fleeing while they washed prior to intercourse, possibly increasing her chances of falling prey to violence.[24] Indeed, a friend and accomplice, Vicky Pender, 22, had previously been found strangled to death in her apartment in Finsbury Park. Like Hannah Tailford, Irene also allegedly participated in secret orgies, allowing herself to be extensively photographed. She supposedly used photographs taken of her and her clients as blackmail, a practice rumoured to have been shared by Hannah Tailford, but never confirmed.[25]

Irene, too, had died of drowning, and again had a notable lack of any physical injuries, save for a post-mortem slash to her chest believed to be from a boat propeller. This latest victim had been four-and-a-half months pregnant at the time of her murder.

On April 24, an assistant groundsman at Beecham's sports ground in Acton, a mile north of the Thames, called the police to report finding a nude woman's corpse on the property. She lay prone on top of a heap of refuse, her black hair cropped in an almost "Beatle"-like fashion. Tire tracks marked the cinder-block road leading to the dump site. This third victim was particularly curious, for the pathologist determined she had been dead for at least 48 hours; yet, her corpse must have been placed there only the previous night or it would undoubtedly have been seen earlier. This time there were signs of violence – the victim had been fatally strangled by the killer twisting her collar, though the clothes themselves were now missing. Fingerprints identified her as 22-year-old Helen Barthelemy: a Scottish-born sex worker who generally associated with and did business in London's black West Indian community.[26]

Helen Barthelemy had last been seen leaving The Jazz Club on Westbourne Park Road, dressed in a high-necked sweater, tight skirt, black leather boots, and a brown coat. Helen had asked a gentleman at the club to watch her handbag for her, implying she intended to return. Whoever had throttled her had then stripped her body. Upon closer examination of the victim, Scotland Yard was amazed to discover their first real evidentiary lead. The victim's flesh was speckled with minuscule specks of black, orange, yellow, and green paint. This meant the offender either worked in or had access to a paint spray operation. However there was an issue with this strong hypothesis: the multiple colours seemed to imply a professional workshop where various types of paint jobs were carried out, yet if the body had been kept there for any period of time, the workshop would surely have to be private.

Three months passed before "Jack the Stripper" would claim his next victim. The strangled body of Mary Fleming, a 31-year-old Scottish sex worker, was discovered at 5:30 a.m. on July 14 by a husband and wife, looking out of their bedroom window. They had been awoken three hours earlier by the squealing of tires in the garage forecourt below, but had not seen anything until first light. Mary's corpse was found with its legs crossed and torso slumped forwards. Specks of paint and dust found on her body were linked chemically to those on Helen Barthelemy. After further analysis of their composition, the lab technicians now concluded that the murderer was likely taking the bodies into – or in the immediate vicinity of – a building where vehicles were sprayed for repair.[27] Strangely, the pathologist was unable to determine a cause of death, and there were no wounds or abrasions of any kind on her body. However, after going door to door, police learnt that a group of painters working a night shift at a business behind Chiswick High Road had heard what sounded like two car doors slamming. Curious, they had looked out of the frosted window to see a shadowy figure standing next to a car. Suddenly alerted that he was being watched, the man had hurried back into the driver's seat and sped away.[28]

The remains of the next victim, Frances Brown (aka Margaret McGowan), were not located until November 25, when assistant civil defence lawyer Dennis Sutton noticed that a rubbish bin lid was missing on the street above the local civil defence centre in Kensington. Sutton spotted it lying on a pile of rubble, wood, and weeds in scrubland behind the car park on Horton Street. He picked it up, revealing a woman's corpse decomposing under the refuse. Whoever had dumped the body had done so only 100 yards (90 m) from the bustling High Street. Standing just over five feet (1.52 m) tall, Frances, a Glaswegian, had been strangled to death. From an investigative perspective, she was perhaps the most intriguing victim, as her testimony in the Profumo Affair – a 1961 political sex scandal – had helped acquit defendant Stephen Ward on a number of charges. As several of the other victims were tangentially connected to the Profumo scandal, one spurious hypothesis was that they were all targets of political assassination.[29]

Frances was the only victim for whom an eye-witness description of her probable killer was obtained. On Thursday, October 22, she and her friend Beryl had been out drinking, and decided to look for clients on Portobello Road. Two cars pulled up to the curb: one customer wanted Frances and the other, Beryl. The women announced they would only go if one car followed the other. The drivers agreed, and Frances and Beryl climbed into their respective vehicles. However, Beryl's driver soon lost sight of Frances'. Beryl and her client conducted their business and he dropped her off safely at the agreed location. Frances did not return.

According to Beryl, the man who picked up Frances "was about 5 feet 8 inches, between 30 and 32 I would say, well-built and he had a full face with big ears, and brown hair. He was a Londoner by his accent and he wore a sheepskin jacket. He had a grey Zephyr, but at Shepherd's Bush we lost sight of it. I think Margaret must have died that night. You see she and I had an arrangement that we would meet afterwards at a club. She didn't turn up."[30] Beryl would later work with the police to provide a sketch of the suspect, and claimed she felt the two clients knew each other.

Last seen climbing into a car on Agate Road, 27-year-old Irish-born sex worker Bridget O'Hara had vanished on January 11, 1965. Over a month later, on February 16, electrician Len Beauchamp was heading to work on the Heron Trading Estate when he spotted a pair of toes with red nail polish poking out from some grass and fern. Bridget had finally been found. She was naked, with abrasions from manual strangulation marking her throat. Like many of the other victims she was small, standing 5 feet 2 inches (1.57 m) tall, with short, dark hair. The sixth confirmed – and seemingly final – victim of "Jack the Stripper", Bridget's body was similarly sprinkled with the tell-tale paint flecks.[31]

Many historians and criminologists also link the 1959 strangulation murder of 21-year-old Elizabeth Figg in Chiswick and that of Gwynneth Rees, 22, in the autumn of 1963 in Mortlake to "Jack the Stripper". Yet, the official victims identified by the police are those killed between 1964 and 1965. Numerous suspects have been suggested, from boxing champion Freddie Mills who committed suicide in July 1965, to members of the Metropolitan Police, and most recently the Welsh serial killer, Harold Jones, who had lived in the Hammersmith area from 1948 to his death in 1971. At this time, however, the true identity of "Jack the Stripper" seems likely to remain a mystery.

The Exorcist 1973

The Possession of "Roland Doe"

Inspired by a secret Catholic exorcism that had occurred in 1949, William Friedkin's supernatural horror *The Exorcist* affected some audience members so profoundly that a new psychiatric term – "cinematic neurosis" – was coined to describe the marked distress the film triggered in some people.

Cinemas across America had never seen anything like William Friedkin's *The Exorcist:* a film that triggered mass nausea to the extent that establishments provided "barf bags" with the tickets, or notified ambulances that they would be screening it in case people collapsed. The severely offensive language, contorted bodies, expulsion of bodily fluids, and (occasionally brutal) under-aged sexualization featured in the movie played a large part in eliciting this reaction, but *The Exorcist* also confronted its audience with a hitherto-unseen level of sacrilege during a time of rapid cultural change.

The plot revolves around 12-year-old Regan MacNeil who, after playing with a Ouija board, is possessed by a malevolent entity. The entity appears to be an ancient Sumerian demon, but at times claims to be the Devil himself. When conventional scientific and psychological methods fail, Regan's mother Chris MacNeil looks to the Catholic church for help and finds Father Damian Karras, a young psychiatrist reeling from the recent death of his mother and experiencing a crisis of faith. Sceptical at first, Karras soon changes his mind when he sees the words "Help Me" erupt in scars on Regan's stomach. Realizing he lacks the experience to handle an exorcism alone, he summons Father Lankester Merrin, who has survived previous battles with invading entities. When Merrin falls dead from a heart attack during the ritual, the enraged Karras offers his body to the entity instead of Regan's. As soon as it begins to take hold of him, he races to the bedroom window and jumps to his death, sealing both his own fate and that of the demon.

Friedkin's film was based on William Peter Blatty's novel of the same name. Blatty's *The Exorcist* drew much of its material from a secret exorcism performed on a male teenager, known only by the pseudonym "Roland Doe", in April 1949.

—

Roland Doe* was born in 1935, in Cottage City, Maryland – a suburb of Washington D.C. – to a government employee named Charles* and his wife Gladys*. The boy grew up an only child in a household that also included his maternal grandmother, but he enjoyed frequent visits from an aunt named Hattie*. Knowing of his love of board games, Hattie taught him to use a Ouija board. A spiritualist from St. Louis, she believed in life after death, and spent a great deal of time communicating with the spirits of the deceased, as well as sharing her knowledge of séance techniques with Roland.[1]

On Saturday, January 15, 1949, 13-year-old Roland was at home with his grandmother when they heard dripping sounds coming from her bedroom. As they puzzled over the cause of the sound, they noticed a painting of Christ on the wall shaking. The strange events continued when Roland's parents came home: they all heard scratching, as if nails were dragging across wood. Assuming they had rodents under the floorboards, the family ignored the sounds and went to bed. Despite setting out poison, the noises continued, and Charles tore up boards and wall panels to no avail. Just over a

* Pseudonyms

week later, Aunt Hattie died unexpectedly, and a grieving Roland took to using his Ouija board regularly, hoping to reach his beloved aunt. Gladys and her mother weren't too concerned by Roland's new hobby, and the family was relieved to find that the scratching sounds had stopped – they assumed the troublesome rodents must finally be dead.

Soon it became apparent, however, that the noises hadn't stopped: they had simply changed form. Roland started to hear sounds in his room as he prepared for bed. To begin with, it was as though squeaky shoes were walking around his bed. This then escalated to feet marching as if to beating drums.[2] His mother and grandmother heard them, too. One day, as all three of them lay on his bed trying to make sense of the noises, Gladys shouted, "Is this you, Aunt Hattie? . . . If you are Hattie, knock three times."[3] Three separate waves of pressure passed through them, each reaching the floor with a thud. As a further test, Gladys asked Hattie to do the same thing with four knocks, and again it worked. Next, they heard a strange scratching coming from inside the mattress. It began to shake violently, and one of the covers rose up above the bed, curling up at the edges as if being held.

For three weeks, the mattress scratching sounds continued nightly. Then, at Roland's school, his desk started sliding around, causing havoc in the classroom. Back in the Doe residence, more random events followed: items flew across rooms, books fell to the floor, and Roland's clothes were found strewn about the kitchen. Roland denied responsibility for these happenings, and his family were compelled to believe him when a heavy armchair he was sitting in suddenly lifted into the air and flipped over, tipping him onto the floor.[4]

Roland became agitated whenever anybody suggested that he might be playing tricks, and stopped going to school to avoid his peers' mockery. His parents decided to consult with a general physician, psychiatrist, and a psychologist. The doctors found nothing out of the ordinary with the teen. Next, the Does approached their

Lutheran minister, Reverend Schulze, and suggested that Aunt Hattie might be the cause of the disturbances. The minister had witnessed several strange happenings with his own eyes: moving furniture, a vibrating bed, and flying crockery. While Reverend Schulze suspected Roland was pranking the family, he kept those thoughts to himself.

Hearing screams emanating from Roland's bedroom one night, the family ran to his assistance, only to watch as a heavy dresser slid towards the door, blocking their exit. One by one, the drawers began opening and closing. In the aftermath, word spread around the small town of the Does' ordeal.

Having heard the family debating whether Roland might be possessed, Reverend Schulze recommended prayer and that they attend Sunday Communion. The minister invited Roland to spend the night at his home, both to give him a change of scenery, and to give the family a break. After prayers, Roland and Reverend Schulze retired to separate beds in the same room. The minister was stirred around midnight when Roland's bed began trembling. The boy, though awake, was lying completely still. Schulze was unsettled, but guided Roland downstairs for a comforting mug of hot chocolate. Returning to the bedroom, Schulze directed the boy into a comfortable chair, and kept a light on. Roland tucked his knees under his chin, feet perched on the seat, and seemed to be in a trance. Then, to his horror, the reverend watched as the chair slowly shifted back against the wall, tipping the child onto the floor. Not knowing what to do, Schulze placed two blankets on the floor and tucked Roland between them. At 3 a.m. he awoke once more, to see both the boy and his blankets sliding across the floor and underneath the bed. The minister shouted for Roland to stop, but the boy said that he was not moving. Roland's body then rose up, repeatedly striking the springs beneath the mattress. Frantic, the minister pulled him out from underneath the bed, only to discover the boy's face was scratched and cut, and his state was near catatonic.[5]

Reverend Schulze was forced to give serious consideration to the possibility that the 13-year-old boy was possessed by a powerful force of unknown origin. Though Roland appeared quite normal in the day, his nights were filled with terror. Long claw marks started to appear on his arms, legs, and torso, seeming to mark out random letters of the alphabet. It was almost as if something was trying to communicate.

Unlike many other Christian denominations, the Catholic church unequivocally believes that demonic possession exists, and that it can only be cured by exorcism. Indeed, prior to the Protestant Reformation, all of Christianity believed in a literal Satan and his ability to inhabit a human body – there were even specific instructions on how to expel him. According to scripture, Jesus himself performed many exorcisms, but eventually Protestants, including Lutherans, repositioned these activities as Jesus simply conforming to local folk beliefs. While Catholics believe in possession, historically the church has only been called upon for consultation on extremely rare occasions. The parents of Roland Doe were Lutherans, but felt the case of their son undoubtedly qualified. It was time to consult a priest.

Charles Doe phoned the local Catholic church, and was invited to attend the following day. When he recounted Roland's story to the priest, Father E. Albert Hughes, the easy-going and personable 29-year-old realized he was completely out of his depth. All he could offer was prayer, holy water, and candles. Gladys called Father Hughes the next morning to say that she had sprinkled the holy water and ignited a candle. However, when she had lit the wick, a flame shot up to the ceiling, forcing her to extinguish it. Later, she had found the bottle of holy water shattered. Father Hughes advised her to try again. Gladys called him back, but before she could explain herself, both were startled by the sound of the telephone stand in the Doe household smashing itself to pieces. The young priest contacted the archbishop of Washington D.C., the Most Reverend Patrick A. O'Boyle, and advised him of the situation.

Father Hughes was given the go-ahead to perform an exorcism, even though he had no experience and was ill-prepared.[6]

Roland was secretly admitted to Georgetown Hospital – a Catholic institution associated with the local university – in late-February to early-March 1949. Aware that an exorcism was about to take place, the mother superior gave strict orders that no records be kept. With Roland strapped to the bed, Father Hughes began the exorcism prayers. Soon, however, the holy man was shouting in pain as his arm was sliced open by a bed spring that Roland had pried loose. The ceremony was over. Father Hughes went on to work at other churches, allegedly never regaining the full use of his arm, and forever haunted by the experience.[7]

After Roland left the hospital, and despite efforts to hush up the incident, word spread, and people became wary of the boy and his family. The Does began discussing whether to uproot their lives and leave. Their decision was hastened when Roland's screams drew his mother to the bathroom. Scratched into his chest in bloody lettering was the name "LOUIS", and on his hip, "SATURDAY".[8]

On Saturday, March 5, Roland and his parents took a train to St. Louis, Missouri, where both Charles and Gladys had relatives. Two days later, the family gathered at a kitchen table in Roland's uncle's house. They were equipped with a homemade Ouija board and the conviction that Aunt Hattie was the cause of all their problems. She seemed to confirm this when a heavy bed reportedly moved across a room before their eyes. That night, the family heard scratching coming from Roland's mattress as he slept. A local Lutheran minister declined to get involved and, as in the case of Reverend Schulze, recommended they seek Catholic intervention. However, Roland's parents didn't want to risk a second attempt at exorcism, and were still convinced Aunt Hattie was at the root of the problem, though were unsure why she would be tormenting them. When frightening occurrences started to happen in relatives' homes whenever Roland slept there, Charles and

Gladys decided they had no choice but to request the assistance of a Jesuit priest.

The family were referred to Father Raymond Bishop, 43, Head of the Department of Education at St. Louis University. After consulting with other members of the faculty, Bishop felt certain that Roland was possessed, and requested the help of Father Reinert, the university president. Father Reinert was hesitant to rush into the situation, and asked Father Bishop to look into the matter himself.

On March 9, Father Bishop was driven to the house where Charles, Gladys, and Roland were staying. They told him all that had happened and answered his questions, but omitted to mention the failed exorcism and wounding of Father Hughes in Maryland. Father Bishop met Roland, and performed a mild form of exorcism – that of a place rather than an individual, sprinkling holy water and blessing each room.

After Roland went to bed, Father Bishop was preparing to leave, when the boy's screams sent the family rushing upstairs. Together, they witnessed Roland's mattress moving back and forth for approximately 15 minutes while the 13-year-old lay motionless upon it. Father Bishop sprinkled holy water over the bed in the shape of a cross and the movement stopped, only to restart when he exited the room. Roland cried out in pain, and his mother raised his pyjama top to reveal a zig-zag pattern of red scratches on his stomach.

The following day, Father Bishop consulted with his friend, Father William Bowdern, the 52-year-old pastor of St. Francis Xavier Church – a stocky, dark-haired chain smoker. Visiting the Doe residence, Father Bowdern also witnessed the strange and troubling phenomena. While Bowdern and Bishop discussed the possibility that Roland was mentally ill, and could have been responsible for the happenings in St. Louis, they began to read up on exorcisms and the three stages of demonic possession: infestation, obsession, and possession. They had already noted the first two stages and vowed to find an exorcist before Roland became possessed. On March 14, Bowdern wrote to Archbishop Ritter – the Ordinary of the Archdiocese – outlining the case and asking him to authorize an exorcism and appoint an exorcist. Ritter eventually chose Father Bowdern to perform the exorcism, despite knowing that he was totally unqualified.[9]

On March 16, Father Bowdern said Mass, confessed his sins, and spent most of the day in prayer, before he and Father Bishop were driven by Walter Halloran, a 26-year-old Jesuit student, to the house where the exorcism would begin. Despite being ordered by Ritter to keep the exorcism secret, Bowdern wanted Bishop to keep a daily diary of events as a reference for anyone who found themselves facing a similar situation in the future. The priests each carried a copy of the 400-page *Roman Ritual*, which spelled out the 21 steps to be followed. The three main prayers were "*Praecipio*" (I command); "*Exorcizo te*" (I cast thee out); and "*Adjuro te*" (I adjure thee).[10]

Bowdern led the procession into Roland's room, with Gladys and an aunt and uncle following directly behind. Each knelt along the sides of the boy's bed as holy water was sprinkled on it, and Halloran was directed to kneel at the foot of the bed. After everyone, including Roland, said prayers, Bowdern began reading the Litany of Saints. Immediately the mattress started to shake. This lasted for two hours, until the final amen, when Bowdern stood and shouted, "*Praecipio tibi*! . . . I command thee!"[11] Whenever Bowdern uttered the word "*dominus*" (Lord) or "*deus*" (God), Roland would scream in pain as additional scratches appeared in his flesh. At one point, the letters "H-E-L-L" manifested on Roland's chest, inverted, seemingly so that the child could read them. "G-O" also emerged on his abdomen and an "X" figure appeared on his leg. Bowdern continued as Roland thrashed about, hitting his pillow and headboard, and babbling with his eyes closed. The priest then threw holy water on him, startling him awake. Roland recounted a dream in which he was fighting a powerful red devil that was preventing him from entering through some gates, above a deep, hot pit.[12]

Bowdern, Bishop, and Halloran stayed until 5 a.m., praying. By this time, Roland had fallen back into a deep sleep. Exhausted, the men rose to leave, when suddenly the boy sat up, eyes clenched shut, and began singing "Swanee River" in a horrific, distorted voice, his arms swaying off-rhythm. Next, he switched to "Ol' Man River". Afraid to leave the boy, the priests stayed until 7:30 a.m. Given that they were sworn to secrecy regarding the exorcism, the three Jesuits had to keep up their daily routines to avoid suspicion, despite their lack of sleep. They guessed that whatever force was at work, it was intentionally depriving them of rest. They were now embroiled in a holy war of attrition.

For four more nights the exorcism continued, with Roland acting in much the same way as on the first, though his behaviour escalated. Teeth bared and snapping, he now spat in the faces of those assembled and bit the hands of anyone who tried to pin him down. He urinated during symbolic parts of Latin prayers – a language that he should not have been able to understand. Roland's voice would fluctuate from deep and menacing to irritatingly high-pitched, interspersed with chilling laughter. He added the songs "The Blue Danube" and "The Old Rugged Cross" to his repertoire, uttering blasphemies so repellent that the priests dared not record them.[13]

Seeing little progress, Father Bowdern thought the time had come to convert the child to Catholicism and prepared a room for Roland and his father in the rectory. He brought in another priest, Father William Van Roo, and they gathered around the bed. As Bowdern started the Litany of the Saints, Roland lashed out, spitting and kicking as the three men wrestled him down. When Van Roo commented that Halloran was being too rough with the boy, the young Jesuit released the boy's arm only to have his nose broken, followed by Van Roo's nose. As they grabbed the boy's fists, they realized that Roland's eyes had been closed for the entire attack. That night, Roland taunted Bowdern mercilessly, laughingly telling him, "I'm in hell . . . I see you. You're in hell. It's 1957."[14] At this point the priest faltered, but then quickly resumed the prayers. Despite days of praying *en masse* with other Jesuits, both the conversion and exorcism proved unsuccessful, and on Saturday, March 26, Roland was returned to his uncle's home in St. Louis.

For the first few days, everything was suspiciously quiet. Then, on Thursday night, Roland came downstairs saying his feet were hurting, and asked everyone to come up to his room. As they watched, the boy sat up in bed, and began moving his finger across the sheets as the bed trembled. His finger traced out the words he spoke. To the best of her ability, his cousin, Elizabeth, wrote down the confused words:

> "I will stay 10 days, but will return in 4 days. If [Roland] stays (gone to lunch) If you stay and become a Catholic it will stay away. [Gertrude] God will take away 4 days after it becomes 10 days God is getting powerful The last day I will leave a sign on my front Fr. Bishop – all people that mangle with me will die a terrible death."[15]

Gladys called Father Bowdern and relayed what had happened. He arrived at the house at 1 a.m. with Father Van Roo. As the priest recited the prayers, Roland asked for a pencil, and began scribbling across countless large sheets of paper. Bowdern realized he had made a mistake: he had permitted Roland to disrupt proceedings and take control. As per Bowdern's instructions, Bishop recorded everything in his diary, including Roland's writings. Most of the words made no sense, and there were strange drawings, too. One of these sketches gave Father Bishop a nasty shock. It was a human face next to the words "Dead bishop".[16] Bowdern was similarly disturbed by the words, "You may not believe me. Then Roland will suffer forever."[17] Bowdern decided once more to convert

Roland to Catholicism. His baptism would have to proceed as quickly as possible – April 1 was chosen as the day.

At 7:30 p.m. on April 1, the family set out for the College Church, as Father Bowdern made his preparations. Waiting at the church door, he was unaware that chaos had erupted in the car, as Roland had tried to take control of the wheel and run the family into a lamp post. Fortunately, his uncle had pulled on the emergency brake just in time. When the car parked in front of the church, Father Bowdern watched as Roland's father and uncle dragged him out in a torn suit, with the child spitting, swearing, and laughing. Directing the men into the adjacent rectory rather than into the church, Bowdern threw a jug of icy water in Roland's face, quietening him enough to drag him upstairs. Rather than the planned baptism at the church font, Bowdern began a more desperate ceremony in a bedroom, from which Roland struggled to get free. Upon the third time of asking Roland if he renounced Satan, the boy quietly said, "I do renounce Satan and all his works."[18] The ceremony took four hours, followed by the usual exorcism prayers. At 11:30 p.m., Roland and his father settled down to sleep.

But from April 2, things took a turn for the worse. As soon as he woke up, Roland smashed a crockery basin and an overhead light. Bowdern decided to perform Holy Communion with the help of Father Bishop and Father John O'Flaherty, a 38-year-old Jesuit, but Roland spat out the piece of host. On the fifth attempt, and after the three priests completed a rosary, Roland swallowed the wafer, and his first communion was complete.

Unfortunately, it seemed to make little difference, as Roland tried once more to attack the driver on his way home, and continued his seemingly demonic behaviour until a few days later, when he was secured in the mental ward of Alexian Brothers Hospital in south St. Louis. His situation failed to improve. When he became particularly violent on Easter Sunday – assaulting several Brothers at the Jesuit hospital – they managed to strap him to his bed and summoned Father Bowdern. As they conducted the exorcism prayers, a deep voice emanated from Roland's mouth, spewing profanities and threatening to kill them. They dubbed this new manifestation the "Devil's Voice".[19]

Father Bowdern and the Brothers returned on Easter Monday to wage spiritual war against the demon. The room had become so cold that Bowdern was forced to wear an overcoat, while Roland's features were now so twisted that he appeared a totally different person. Amidst the chaos of the ensuing exorcism, in which the Brothers managed to make Roland ask for spiritual communion, the "Devil's Voice" told them "That isn't enough. He has to say one more word, one little word. I mean one BIG word. He'll never say it . . . I am always in him. I may not have much power always, but I am in him. He will never say that word."[20] Roland then burst into song, and the Brothers left the room, once again defeated.

On April 18, Father Bowdern had a revelation – the demon had once said something about not responding to Latin, because he only spoke the tongue of the person he had possessed. Bowdern called Father Bishop and Father O'Flaherty and asked them to join him by Roland's bedside at 7 p.m. After Bowdern said the prayers in Latin as usual, he told Roland that he could respond in English. Tracing crosses on the boy's body, he then put a crucifix in Roland's hand. The boy flailed around, managing to throw the crucifix to the floor, before the two Brothers held him still. Roland asked about Latin and O'Flaherty taught him the Hail Mary in Latin – *Ave Maria* – which Roland was able to repeat after 15 minutes. Leafing through a Catholic school reader, Roland suddenly placed it on his head, and it flew across the room, hitting a wall. At 9:30 p.m., Roland asked if he might recite the rosary, and if Bowdern and the Brothers could respond. They agreed, and he was given the rosary beads. He held the crucifix and started to say the Apostles' Creed. Though he faltered, he was swiftly prompted, and continued. The boy sought guidance, claiming he wanted to make a spiritual communion, but then fell into a sleep-like state after complaining that the Christian medals around his neck were burning him.[21]

At 10:45 p.m., Father Bowdern said the final amen, and a voice emanated from Roland that they hadn't heard before. It was rich, deep, and rang out clearly: "Satan! Satan! I am Saint Michael, and I command you, Satan, and the other evil spirits to leave the body in the name of *Dominus*. Immediately! Now! Now! Now!"[22] Bowdern realized that *Dominus* must have been the word the demon had promised Roland would never speak. For the next eight minutes, the boy's body writhed and contorted on the bed as he screamed, then he serenely whispered, "He's gone!"[23] Roland opened his eyes, looked around at everyone, and said he felt fine. Everyone in the room claimed they felt it – the demon had left.

As the Brothers rose from their knees crying and hugging, Father O'Flaherty noticed that Bowdern's face remained unsmiling. Roland relayed to the priests the wonderful dreams he had. He described a beautiful figure, standing in brilliant light, wearing white clothing that looked like chain mail. It appeared to be an angel, holding a flaming sword, and pointing down to a pit where the devil and other demons stood. As the devil surged towards the angel and tried to fight it, the angel had smiled at Roland, then turned back to the devil and said, "*Dominus*".[24] Instantaneously, the devil and demons had disappeared into a cave; the bars on its entrance read "SPITE". Suddenly, Roland said he felt a snap in his stomach. In an instant, he felt happier than he'd felt since January 15.

Roland awoke the next morning and went to Mass and Holy Communion, receiving the host readily. He returned to his room afterwards to sleep. Upon waking, he stood up and rubbed his eyes, saying, "Where am I? What happened?"[25] As if on cue, a loud sound reverberated through the hospital, which was allegedly heard by everyone present. As the Brothers ran to Roland's room the reverberation continued. For Bowdern, this was the sign he had been waiting for: it was over.

After Roland left the hospital, his room was locked, and an

order given that it must never be opened again.[26] The hospital was eventually demolished. The Jesuit community joined in the vow of secrecy: the exorcism and the events surrounding it were never to be revealed to the outside world.

For more than 40 years the secret was largely kept, although the fragmentary stories that did leak out inspired William Peter Blatty's 1971 novel *The Exorcist*, and the film adaptation of the book that followed two years later. A detailed account was finally made public in 1993, in author Thomas Allen's *Possessed*. The book was based on the diary kept by Father Raymond Bishop, but was met with much scepticism. In particular, it was attacked by a Maryland historian named Mark Opsasnick. Interviewing over 100 people who had known "Roland Doe" growing up, Opsasnick learnt that the child was a notorious trickster who delighted in scaring other children – and even his own mother – with elaborate pranks. A classmate recalled that Roland and another boy had spitting contests, developing an uncanny knack for spitting accurately up to 10 feet (3 m) away. If he had used this peculiar talent on the Jesuit priests, they might have concluded the feat could only be demonic in origin. One of Roland's best friends remembered an incident at Bladensburg Junior High School in 1948, in which Roland caused his whole desk to vibrate at a tremendous speed. When his teacher warned him to stop doing it, Roland said he wasn't, and was thrown out of the classroom. Unsurprisingly, Roland is recorded as having detested school.

The boy was even observed by some of the priests using his long fingernails to scratch words into his own flesh. Apparently this did not raise any red flags, and instead was interpreted as yet another manifestation of diabolical possession. Tellingly, one of the Jesuits – a philosophy professor – first tasked with looking into the case by Archbishop Ritter brushed it off, concluding that all of the reported phenomena could be accounted for naturally. In his final report on his investigation in 2000, Mark Opsasnick said of Roland:

"The facts show that he was a spoiled and disturbed only-child with a very overprotective mother and an unresponsive father. To me, his behavior was indicative of an outcast youth who desperately wanted out of Bladensburg Junior High School at any cost. He wanted attention, and he wanted to leave the area and go to St. Louis. Throwing tantrums was the answer. He began to play his concocted game. For his efforts he got a collection of priests . . . who doted over him."[27]

Jaws 1975

The Jersey Shore Shark Attacks, the Sinking of the USS Indianapolis, and the Life of Frank Mundus

Steven Spielberg's 1975 blockbuster, *Jaws*, relied on the invisible suspense conjured by sharks to terrify audiences and reap huge profits at the box office. Audiences might have been even more terrified if they'd known that, six decades earlier, the Atlantic coast of the US really *had* been plagued by a man-eating shark.

Jaws combined a formidable screenplay, strong acting, novel photographic and editing techniques, and an iconic soundtrack by John Williams to create an extraordinarily tense horror movie.

Starring Roy Scheider, Richard Dreyfuss, and Robert Shaw, the movie is set in the coastal New England resort of Amity Island, where the community is preparing for the influx of summer tourists and July 4th weekend. When a young woman's mutilated body is found on the beach, Martin Brody, the chief of police, asks to close the beaches, believing the victim was attacked by a shark. The local mayor, fearful of the impact on the town's tourist trade, disagrees, pushing the theory that she died in a boating accident. When another attack occurs shortly afterwards, the community is forced to accept that a shark with a taste for human flesh is targeting their coastline. This is confirmed by oceanographer and shark expert, Matt Hooper. A bounty is placed on the shark, causing a frenzy as local fishermen try to catch the creature. A man named Quint, claiming to be a professional shark hunter, offers his services, but is rebuffed for charging too much. A tiger shark is soon caught, but Hooper argues that it is not the shark in question, which he believes is a *Carcharodon carcharias* – a great white. This is confirmed when the attacks continue, including an incident where the shark enters an estuary and devours a man.

The town now agrees to hire Quint. He, Hooper, and Brody set out in Quint's boat to hunt the shark. Quint attempts to harpoon the creature with lines attached to barrels, hoping to tire the fish and prevent it diving deep. The shark turns the tables on the hunters by ramming the boat, thereby disabling its engine. After the boat is repaired, Quint tries again, but the shark simply drags the boat backwards through the water. With the boat now sinking, the shark attacks and devours Quint, while Hooper becomes trapped on the seabed in a shark cage. Brody, clinging to the sinking wreckage of the boat, successfully jams a pressurized air tank into the shark's mouth, then shoots the tank, which explodes, blasting the shark apart. Hooper surfaces, and he and Brody swim towards Amity Island.

Jaws was originally a novel by the American writer Peter Benchley. He used a number of sources as inspiration, foremost of which were the Jersey Shore shark attacks of 1916, in which one or more man-eating sharks attacked and killed a number of people that summer. The salty Captain Quint, who engages in a battle of wills with the shark, was modelled on the exploits of legendary shark hunter Frank Mundus, whom the author had personally met. When the book was adapted into a movie, Steven Spielberg made a number of changes to the story, one of which was that Quint was now a survivor of the notorious shark feeding-frenzy that following the sinking of the *USS Indianapolis* in 1945.

—

Twenty-five-year-old Charles Vansant seemed to have the world at his fingertips. Tall, dark, and handsome, "Van" came from one of

America's oldest bloodlines. After graduating from the University of Pennsylvania in 1914, he had taken a position at Folwell Brothers, a brokerage firm in Philadelphia, where his natural charm won him many friends and admirers.

Like many Philadelphians, come the July 4th weekend of 1916, Van wanted to get out of the city to enjoy some sun and surf. Fortunately, the new express train from Philly to Beach Haven could transport Van to the popular resort island off the New Jersey shore in less than two hours. On Saturday, July 1, he met his father Dr Eugene L. Vansant, and sisters, Eugenia and Louise, on the train. The family arrived in Beach Haven just after 5 p.m. Eager for a pre-dinner dip in the ocean, Van asked Louise if she wanted to head to the boardwalk. She agreed. Once they reached Centre Street, he ducked into one of the many bathhouses to change into his swim shorts.

Feet crunching in the sand, Van smiled as a Chesapeake Bay retriever unexpectedly followed him down to the water. He waved to the lifeguard, Alexander Ott – a member of the American Olympic swimming team – who returned his greeting. Van waded into the shallows and spent a few minutes splashing around with the retriever, before swimming out past the breakers. Immersed to his chest, he turned back to his canine companion and tried to encourage the dog to join him.[1]

Meanwhile, on the beach, a handful of sunbathers spotted a large dark object manoeuvring just below the surface. A black fin emerged from the water, rapidly heading in Van's direction. They cried out trying to alert him, but he didn't seem to understand what they were saying. Suddenly, his calls to the dog turned into a piercing scream. Frantically, Van started swimming back to shore, but 50 yards (46 m) from the beach, he began shrieking and thrashing about wildly. Blood erupted in the water around him. Springing into action, Alexander Ott dashed into the surf and seized Van's torso. He dragged him to where the water was waist deep, but the shark was still clinging to Van's leg. Locals John Everton and

Sheridan Taylor ran to help the lifeguard. As soon as the fish's belly touched the sand, it released its grip and disappeared into deeper water. Finally, the three men were able to pull the swimmer ashore. Louise Vansant looked down at her brother's mutilated body, blood pumping from his leg onto the sand. Ott quickly fashioned a tourniquet out of a bathing suit and tightened it around the torn flesh to stop the bleeding.

Charles Vansant's left thigh had been stripped to the bone and there was another large laceration on his right. His father, aided by two other doctors, whisked Charles to the Engleside Hotel, but by 6:45 p.m. the young man was dead. His passing marked the first recorded fatality by shark attack in the history of the eastern United States. Witnesses described the shark as being approximately nine feet (2.7 m) long and weighing around 500 lbs (225 kg), with grey-blue or black colouring and a triangular dorsal fin.[2]

Despite the deadly attack and reports from sailors that they had seen large sharks swimming off the coast, the beaches remained open. Tourist dollars were vital to the local economy, and record profits had been predicted for the summer of 1916. To allay the public's fears, Robert Engle, proprietor of the Engleside, erected a wire net along the shoreline, enclosing the length of the beach.[3] Unfortunately, many other beaches remained unprotected.

Forty-five miles (72 km) north of Beach Haven, in the seaside community of Spring Lake, the opulent Essex & Sussex (E&S) Hotel was enjoying a lucrative summer. One of the bellhops who carried the wealthy elites' luggage to their rooms was 28-year-old Charles Bruder. A popular employee of Swiss extraction, Bruder had recently come into close contact with sharks while visiting California, and had found them almost amusingly timid. As such, he received the news of the Vansant shark fatality with scepticism.

Thursday, July 6, was a scorcher and both Bruder and his friend, Henry Nolan, an elevator operator, had worked up a terrific sweat. When their lunch break came at 1:45 p.m., Bruder and Nolan headed down to the water to cool off. Crossing the boardwalk, they noted the beach was packed with women in swimwear and pretty sundresses.

As the two men neared the bathhouse at the South End Pavilion to change into their trunks, Nolan chuckled, "what if I dove under and came up in front of one of those pretty young ladies with my black swim tights on? They'd think I'm a sea monster, or at least the real Moby Dick."[4] Bruder replied that if Nolan wanted to keep his job, he had better stay clear of the guests' bathing area.[5] The E&S had a strict policy that prevented the staff from mingling with the guests. At that moment, he spotted Mrs Mona Childs – a prominent socialite staying at the hotel – standing on her private balcony, staring through a pair of theatre glasses. She was gazing across the beach. "You're right, Charles," Nolan said, "Mrs Childs would have my head for sure if I swam anywhere outside the employee section."[6]

Bruder and Nolan entered the water with some friends at 2:15 p.m. The south breeze was blowing, chilling the sea, and it wasn't long before Nolan and the others became uncomfortably cold and swam back to the shore to towel off. Bruder, a very strong swimmer, was accustomed to the cold, and took the opportunity to swim out past the lifelines. He was about 130 yards (120 m) from the shore when he started to scream.

A woman spotted a peculiar red shape in the surf, and thinking a canoe had capsized, brought it to the attention of two lifeguards, George White and Chris Anderson. Neither man remembered seeing a canoeist that day, and they realized at once that the red shape was a swimmer surrounded by blood. Climbing into their rescue boat, they seized the oars and began rowing as fast as they could towards the scene. Meanwhile, beachgoers watched in horror as the distressed swimmer was flung into the air, blood spurting from the shredded stump of his right leg. When he landed back in the water, the shark lunged in his direction, tearing off his left foot. By the time the lifeguards reached Charles Bruder, he was ghostly white, his face barely bobbing above the water.

"A shark bit me! Bit my legs off!"[7] he managed to utter. White seized Bruder's arm and pulled him into the boat. It was easier than White had expected – most of Bruder's lower legs had been bitten off. Moments after they'd pulled him aboard, Charles Bruder was dead.

Watching the horror unfold from her balcony, Mona Childs hurried to the E&S switchboard and demanded that the operator relay a message to every hotel along the coast: "Get out of the water!"[8]

When local physicians Dr John Cornell and Dr William Trout arrived at the beach, the manager of the E&S asked that, since Charles Bruder was already dead, they attend to the dozens of women fainting and vomiting into the sand. Dr William Schauffler, who had been staying at the E&S, examined Bruder's corpse. His right leg was completely severed through the shin, leaving the muscle in bloody tatters. The left leg had also been torn off, albeit closer to the foot, leaving only jutting bone. Another chunk had been torn from the left thigh, and there was an apple-sized gouge in the right side of the abdomen. The cause of death was irreversible circulatory shock resulting from the severing of multiple arteries in the legs. Overnight, America was thrust into a shark-attack panic. The gruesome deaths of two athletic young men off the Jersey Shore was more than enough to give people reservations about entering the sea.

On Saturday, July 8, a panel of scientists from the American Museum of Natural History and Brooklyn Museum – Frederic Augustus Lucas, John Treadwell Nichols, and Robert Cushman Murphy – assured the public that the likelihood of being ripped limb from limb by a shark was extraordinarily low. However, they also admitted that the present situation had taken them completely by surprise. Nichols, an ichthyologist (a marine biologist specializing in fish), reminded swimmers that if they stayed within the netted bathing areas, safety from shark attacks was practically guaranteed. However, the strangest twist in the tale was yet to come.

M: A City Searches for a Murderer (1931)

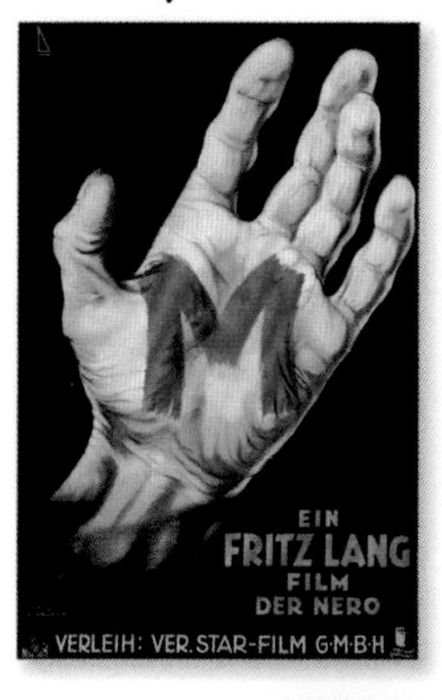

M: Eine Stadt sucht einen Mörder premiered in Berlin on May 11, 1931. It starred Peter Lorre (above) in the role of serial killer Hans Beckert.

The body of the "Cannibal of Ziębice", Karl Denke, after his suicide.

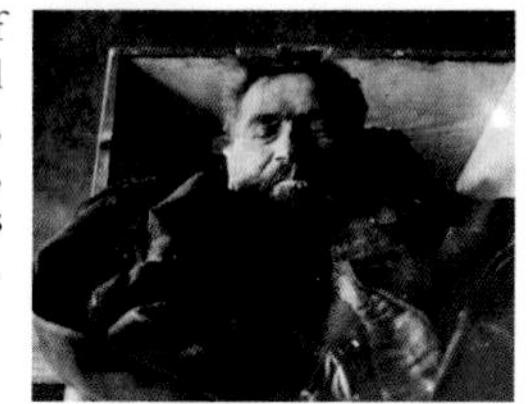

Friedrich "Fritz" Haarmann is escorted to the courthouse in December 1924 to stand trial for multiple murders.

Carl Großmann, the serial killer and cannibal who allegedly stuffed his victims' flesh into sausages.

Haarmann was found guilty of 24 murders. He was executed by guillotine in Hanover Prison in April 1925.

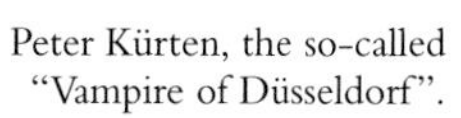

Peter Kürten, the so-called "Vampire of Düsseldorf".

Rope (1948)

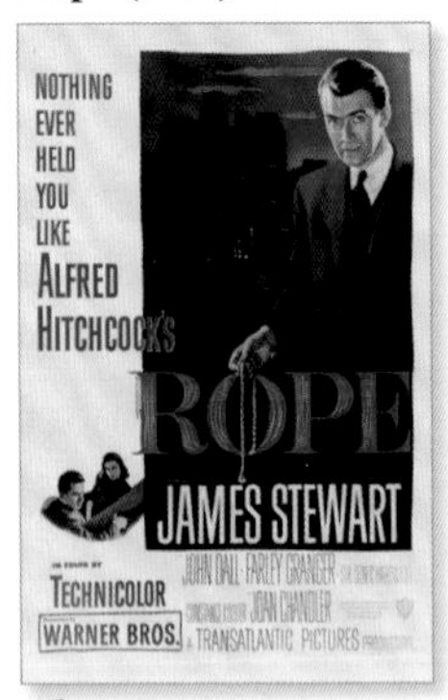

Rope is notable for appearing to have been shot in a single, continuous take. Hitchcock cleverly disguises the various cuts.

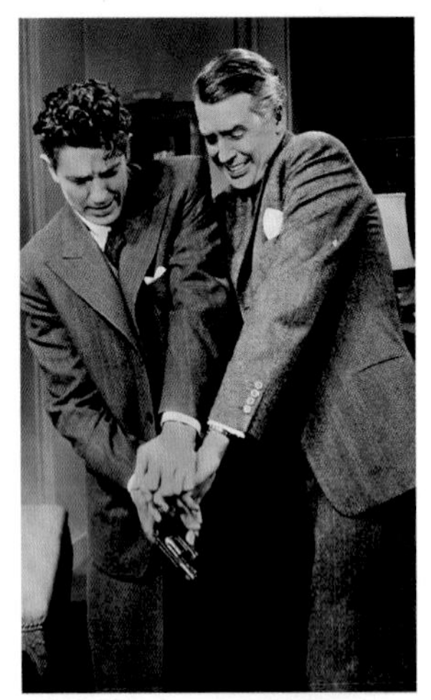

James Stewart (right), in the role of Rupert Cadell, wrestles with Farley Granger (left), who portrays murderer Philip Morgan.

In the film, young intellectuals Shaw and Morgan try to commit the "perfect murder."

Nathan Leopold (left) and Richard Loeb (right), with their attorney, Clarence Darrow.

Leopold's headshot, taken at Illinois State Penitentiary in September 1924.

The two men during their trial at Cook County Courthouse, Chicago.

Fourteen-year-old victim Bobby Franks was Richard Loeb's second cousin.

Psycho (1960) and The Texas Chain Saw Massacre (1974)

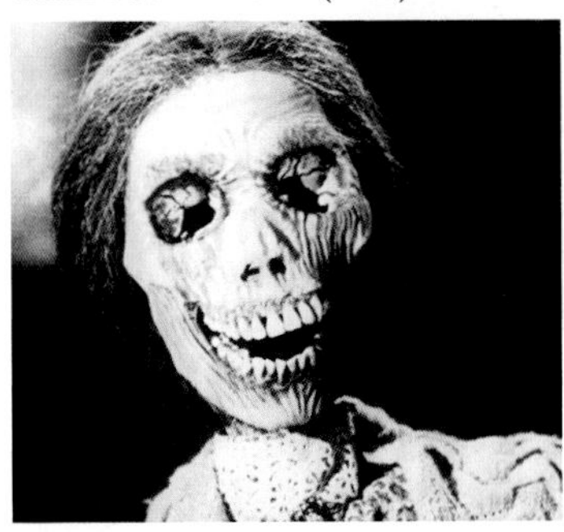

The mummified corpse of Norman Bates' mother in *Psycho*.

Leatherface, the skin-wearing antagonist of *The Texas Chain Saw Massacre*.

The dilapidated mansion inhabited by Bates and his domineering mother.

The isolated farmhouse belonging to Ed Gein, a few miles southwest of Plainfield, Wisconsin.

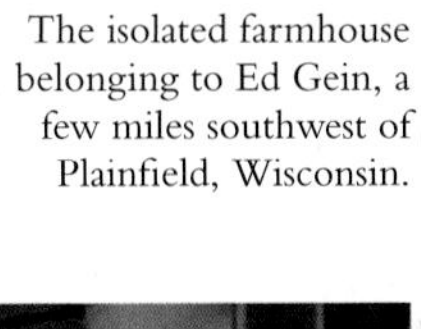

The interior of Gein's house was a stinking shambles, filled with nightmarish relics crafted from human remains.

Gein (right) was eventually found "not guilty by reason of insanity" and confined to a mental institution for the remainder of his life.

Frenzy (1972)

Jon Finch (right) portrays Dick Blaney, a man framed for his wife's murder.

A victim of the "Necktie Strangler" floats down the Thames.

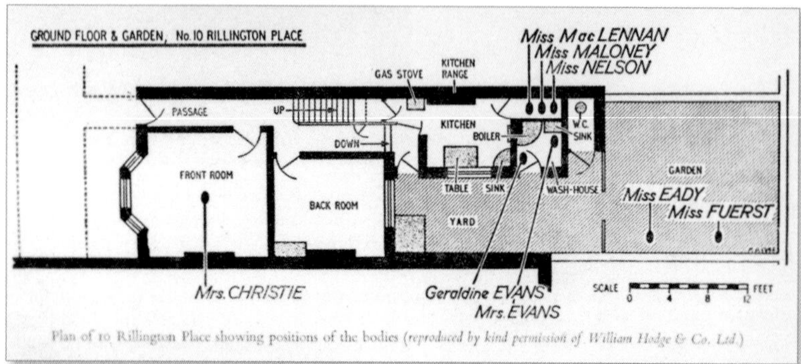

Plan of 10 Rillington Place showing positions of the bodies (*reproduced by kind permission of William Hodge & Co. Ltd.*)

10 Rillington Place (above and left), home of British serial killer John Christie.

Neville Heath, who murdered two women in 1946.

John Christie and his wife, Ethel, whom he strangled to death in December 1952.

Christie arrives at court to stand trial for murder, April 8, 1953.

The Exorcist (1973)

Linda Blair starred as Regan MacNeil, a young girl who is the victim of a terrifying demonic possession.

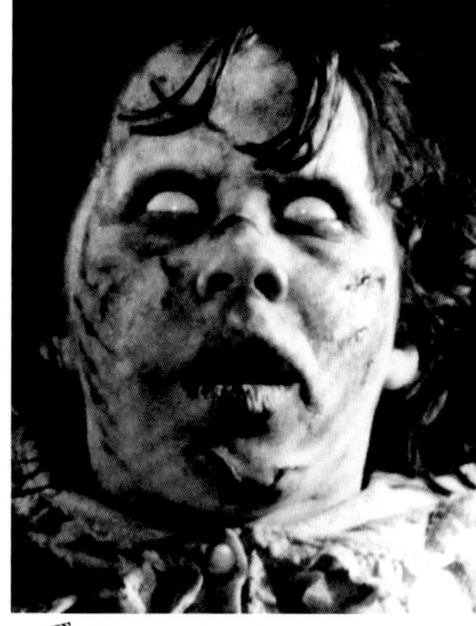

The Exorcist horrified audiences to such an extent that showings were accompanied by warning messages.

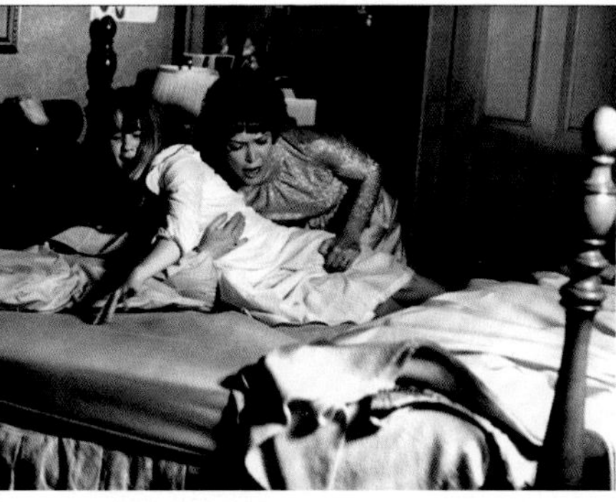

In the film, Regan's possession manifests in numerous ways, such as telekinesis, abnormal strength, and obscene language.

The St. Louis home once occupied by "Roland Doe", the child whose alleged possession inspired *The Exorcist*.

Jaws (1975)

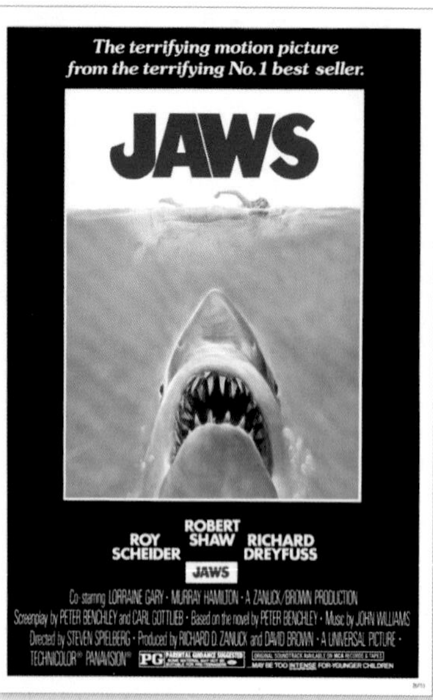

Jaws was released on June 20, 1975. It is often credited as the first "Summer Blockbuster".

The shark's first victim, Chrissie Watkins, is devoured.

Robert Shaw portrays the ill-fated shark hunter Quint, who was heavily based on fisherman Frank Mundus.

The *USS Indianapolis*, which was sunk on July 30, 1945. The survivors were subjected to the largest mass shark attack in recorded history.

The grave of 11-year-old Lester Stillwell, the third victim of the 1916 Jersey Shore shark attacks.

Matawan Creek – this tidal river was the scene of two fatal shark attacks on July 12, 1916.

The Town That Dreaded Sundown (1976)

The original movie poster for *The Town That Dreaded Sundown*.

A crime scene in the movie following an attack by "The Phantom".

Actor Ben Johnson in the role of J.D. Morales, a character inspired by the real Texas Ranger Manuel T. Gonzaullas.

Jimmy Hollis, who survived his encounter with "The Phantom".

Traps set up by one Texarkana resident to guard against the mysterious killer.

The Amityville Horror (1979)

Actors James Brolin and Margot Kidder in front of the stand-in house in Toms River, New Jersey.

Much of the promotional material for *The Amityville Horror* featured the house's distinctive, eye-like windows.

The real George and Kathy Lutz pose while on a press tour in January 1979.

The real 112 Ocean Avenue, seen at the time of the murders in 1974 (above), and today (right). The boathouse can be seen in the foreground.

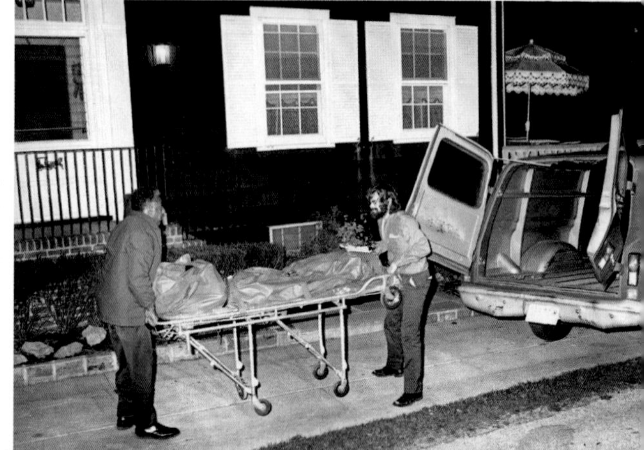

The bodies of the DeFeo family are removed from 112 Ocean Avenue on November 13, 1974.

Unlike the bustling tourist communities along the coast, Matawan, New Jersey, bore a stronger resemblance to typical small-town America. Located 20 miles (32 km) northwest of Spring Lake, nearing the New York state line, and two miles (3 km) inland from Raritan Bay, the alarming headlines about killer sharks barely registered with its 1,200 quiet, hard-working farmers and factory workers. And while Matawan Creek – technically a tidal river running from Lake Lefferts and Lake Matawan to the Atlantic Ocean – had been well-travelled for hundreds of years, it had never seen anything like the events that occurred on July 12, 1916.

It was a hot and sticky summer day, and the boys of Matawan were cooling off at their favourite spots along the creek. At approximately 1:20 p.m., Captain Thomas Cottrell, a retired sailor, was returning from an unsuccessful day of fishing at nearby Keyport. As he crossed the town's trolley drawbridge, where construction workers were making adjustments, he noticed a familiar shape in the water below – dark grey and about eight feet (2.4 m) long – moving upstream with the incoming tide. Struggling to believe his own eyes, he turned to the workmen and knew instantly by the looks on their faces that they, too, had seen the shark. Cottrell raced to the bridge keeper's phone to alert the citizens of Matawan. Unfortunately, nobody believed him, in fact, they openly ridiculed him. "You have a better chance of seeing an elephant cooling off down there than a shark!"[9] one of the patrons of the police chief's barber shop remarked.

Undeterred, Captain Cottrell found a motorboat, and began speeding upriver to warn swimmers about the approaching danger. He reached Main Street, anchored the boat, and raced into Matawan to tell everybody about what he saw in person. His efforts were only met with further derision.

In a terrible twist of fate, Cottrell passed Wyckoff Dock mere seconds before a group of friends, Lester Stillwell, Albert O'Hara, Johnny Cartan, and Anthony Bubblin – all 11 or 12 years of age – arrived for their daily dip. The boys stripped naked and entered the swimming hole at about 2 p.m. Albert was swimming closest to shore when he felt something coarse rub past his leg. Looking down, he saw the tail of an enormous fish in the murky water. At the same time, Johnny saw what appeared to be an "old weather-beaten board"[10] drifting along the surface of the water.

"Hey fellas, watch me float!"[11] Lester Stillwell called out from a deep patch.

Suddenly, a dorsal and tail fin appeared on the "board". It was heading right for him. There was a splash, a scream, and Lester's body jerked violently. The boys looked on in horror as the shark's white-toothed jaws closed around their friend. There was a brief struggle, the brown water turned crimson, and Lester disappeared below the surface.

Frantic, the boys took off towards town, not even stopping to put their clothes back on. Lester needed help. That was all that mattered.

"Shark! Shark! A shark's got Lester!"[12] they shouted as they raced down Main Street.

As they passed 24-year-old Watson "Stanley" Fisher's dry cleaners, his girlfriend Mary Anderson looked out the window and noticed that the boys were naked and genuinely terrified. While Stanley didn't know what to make of the cries of "shark", he knew Lester was an epileptic and likely in trouble. As Stanley headed towards the front door, Mary reminded him that Captain Cottrell had warned of a shark, too.

"A shark here? I don't care!" he replied. "Lester's got the fits. If we don't get to him soon, he'll be finished."[13]

As he stepped onto Main Street, Stanley spotted his friends Red Burlew and Arthur Smith, and told them they needed to follow him to Wyckoff Dock immediately. The three men raced to the creek to find the water had turned blood red. It had been half an hour since Lester's disappearance and they sombrely concluded that they were probably looking to retrieve a body, rather than a living, breathing child.

They pushed a rowing boat into the creek, climbed inside, and began probing the depths with long rods. By this time, most of Matawan was lining the banks, looking on. When the rowing boat method failed to locate Lester, the men quickly changed into their swimming trunks and jumped into the water. Not long after they had entered, Arthur felt something scrape his abdomen, and looked down to see he was bleeding. Stanley was convinced that Lester's body was mired in the deepest point of the watering hole, but his companions decided to give up. Stanley was about to join them when he noticed Lester's distraught parents standing on the bank. He decided to keep looking. Taking a deep breath, he dove below the water and found Lester's body caught on what seemed to be a dark log. Seizing the child, he pulled the boy's body to the surface. As he attempted to make his way to the muddy bank, he felt dagger-like teeth sink into his leg. "He's got me!" Stanley cried, releasing his grip on Lester's body, "The shark's got me!"[14]

The powerful young man kicked and punched the predator, to no avail. Twice he was pulled under the water, and each time he re-emerged fighting. Deputy Sheriff Arthur Van Buskirk joined the fray, thrashing the shark with an oar. Eventually, it released its hold on Stanley, and the terrified onlookers threw him a rope. With the help of a motorboat, Stanley Fisher used what remained of his strength to climb back onto the bank. As Stanley lay on the dock, Dr George C. Reynolds observed a gaping 18-inch (46-cm) gash in the victim's right thigh, with approximately 10 lbs (4.5 kg) of flesh missing.[15] He hastily fastened a tourniquet above the wound to prevent further blood loss, but Stanley did not look like he was going to make it. As his condition was too compromised for a bumpy car ride, they would need to wait for a train to take him to the hospital. Meanwhile, Captain Thomas Cottrell had returned to his mission of patrolling the river in his boat, warning swimmers of the monster in their midst.

At the brickyard dock of the New Jersey Clay Company, half a mile from Wyckoff Dock, brothers Michael and Joseph Dunn of New York City were playing in the creek with their 16-year-old friend Jerry Hourihan from Matawan. Thirty minutes had elapsed since the attacks on Stillwell and Fisher, and in the distance the boys heard somebody shouting warnings, but the only word they could make out was "shark". Jerry and Michael climbed up the ladder and onto the dock in time to see Joseph's head bob in the water about 10 feet away. It looked as if something was trying to drag him under the surface. Suddenly, the water around him exploded with blood. Linking arms, Jerry and Michael formed a human chain, and Michael jumped into the water, grabbing his 12-year-old brother's hand. Amazingly, they managed to wrest Joseph away from the shark, but exhausted themselves in the process. Fortunately, Robert Thress, the superintendent of the brickyard, came to the rescue, along with 35-year-old fisherman Jacob Lefferts, who dove into the water to ensure Joseph could make it to the dock ladder. As they waited by the bottom rung, Captain Cottrell's motorboat whirred into view. Together, they hoisted both Dunn brothers aboard, and Cottrell sped back towards Wyckoff Dock with the injured child.

Upon arriving, Joseph Dunn was taken to a nearby bag factory to be examined by Dr H.S. Cooley, a physician from Keyport. Cooley determined that Joseph's injuries were less severe than Stanley's, and decided the boy could be safely transported by car to St. Peter's Hospital in New Brunswick about 20 miles (32 km) away. When they arrived, as Joseph was being helped out of the car, an enterprising reporter asked, "How did it feel to be bitten by the Jersey man-eater? What happened?"[16]

"I was about ten feet from the dock ladder, when I looked down and saw something dark," Joseph answered. "Suddenly I felt a tug, like a big pair of scissors pulling at my leg and bringing me under. I felt as if my leg had gone! I believe it would have swallowed me."[17]

Dr R.J. Faulkingham observed severe lacerations to the boy's calf muscles and incisions through several of his ankle bones.[18]

Back in Matawan, at 5:06 p.m. the train arrived to take Stanley

Fisher to Monmouth Memorial Hospital. He entered the operating room at 5:30 p.m., but sadly passed away at 6:35 p.m. According to visiting surgeon Dr Edwin Field, the young hero's last words were: "Doc, I found the boy on the bottom; I got Lester away from the shark. Anyhow, I did my duty."[19]

Rain was falling at dawn on July 14 when Lester Stillwell's mutilated remains finally bobbed to the surface. A medical examiner noted:

"The boy's left ankle was chewed off, his left side was mangled from hip to knee, his left abdominal region was ruptured and the intestines herniated and torn open. The intestines were nearly all torn out. The right hip, right chest muscle, left shoulder, as well as several fleshy areas of the body were all eaten away and the flesh between his right hip and thigh was mangled. His face was untouched."[20]

That same morning, 45-year-old animal trainer and taxidermist, Michael Schleisser, and his friend, John Murphy, hopped into a motorboat and headed out from South Amboy, New Jersey to Raritan Bay. After news of the triple attack in Matawan was broadcast across the northeast, many vengeful Americans had embarked on what could only be described as a mass shark hunt. Schleisser and Murphy had read that crowds of Matawan residents were lobbing dynamite and pointing guns at the water, and thought it would be an intriguing sight to behold. Near Sandy Hook Bay, the two men dropped a dragnet off the stern, hoping to catch some fish for breakfast. They were just a short distance away from the mouth of Matawan Creek when their boat suddenly lurched, stalling the engine. Looking over the side of the boat, Schleisser saw a black tail fin caught in their net.

"My God, we've got a shark!"[21]

Perhaps it would have been more accurate to say that the shark had got them. It was dragging the vessel backwards, causing the bow to rise out of the water and waves to lap over the stern. Snatching up a broken oar, Schleisser hit the shark about the head, nose, and gills in an unrelenting barrage. Struggling, the creature further entangled itself in the net, becoming increasingly vulnerable to Schleisser's blows. When the intrepid animal tamer had finally beaten the life out of the shark, he and Murphy flagged down a larger boat, which helped them drag the shark back to South Amboy. The sailors remarked that this was unlike any other sharks they had ever encountered: it was larger and more muscular. Once the creature was lying on the shore, Schleisser took a sharp blade and opened it up in front of the gasping spectators. Calmly, he removed the viscera, organ by organ, until he reached the contents of the stomach: 15 lbs (6.8 kg) of flesh and bone. Two physicians in attendance immediately identified the remains as human.[22]

Schleisser brought the shark back home to New York City for taxidermy, planning to display it at the office of the *Bronx Home News*. Meanwhile, he mailed the bones inside its digestive system to Dr Frederic Lucas at the Brooklyn Museum, along with a description of the shark: "Dark-dull blue, with a white belly, and the mouth, when open, can fit a man's head inside. It has four rows of teeth. It is 7½ feet in length and weighed 350 lbs."[23] Lucas confirmed the bones were "parts of the left radius and ulna [lower arm bones] and one of the anterior left ribs, all human."[24]

Dr John Treadwell Nichols would later identify the shark as a young *Carcharodon carcharias* – a great white shark. While debate continues to rage as to whether Schleisser's catch was indeed the "Jersey Man-Eater", the fact remains that there were no further shark attacks in the area. The events of July 1916 would forever change the way scientists and the general public alike viewed the propensity of sharks to feed upon human prey.

Joseph Dunn was released from St. Michael's on September 15 with both legs intact. He had received hundreds of "get well" cards from all over the country, including one from President Woodrow Wilson himself. He was determined to reply to all of them. When asked how he was coping after his brush with death, the boy answered, "Four other people got killed by that shark, and I think the least I could do is feel fortunate I am able to live my life."[25]

—

One of the most memorable scenes in *Jaws* occurs when the grizzled shark hunter Quint relates, in a chilling monologue, his experiences as a survivor of the *USS Indianapolis* during World War II. Though Quint was a fictional creation, partly based on the famed shark hunter Frank Mundus, the sinking of the *Indianapolis* was all-too-real.

The *USS Indianapolis* was a heavy cruiser, laid down by the New York Shipbuilding Corporation on 31 March, 1930, and launched on November 7, 1931. Known affectionately to its crew as the "Indy", the ship was fortunate to be at sea when the Japanese attacked the US Naval base at Pearl Harbor, Hawaii, in December 1941. Unlike much of the US fleet, the *Indianapolis* was unscathed, and went on to participate in military operations against Japanese forces in Papua New Guinea, the Aleutian Islands, Western Carolines, Mariana Islands, and Okinawa.

The ship's most notable role in defeating Imperial Japan occurred in July 1945, when the captain and crew were entrusted with a top-secret mission of paramount importance. They were to transport enriched uranium – and other components necessary to assemble a nuclear bomb – to the island of Tinian. The US military had perfected this new weapon, and the time had come to use it. Leaving Pearl Harbor on July 19, the *Indianapolis* arrived at Tinian on July 26, setting a new nautical speed record. All of the pieces were now in place to create "Little Boy": the infamous atomic bomb that would devastate the Japanese city of Hiroshima on August 6, 1945.

With its mission complete, the *Indianapolis* departed for Guam, where it swapped out a number of crewmen who had completed their tours of duty, replacing them with a fresh crop of sailors.

On July 28, the vessel left Guam, sailing for the Philippine island of Leyte where the new crew members were to receive training. Unbeknownst to the *Indianapolis*' captain, Charles B. McVay III, the Japanese submarine *I-58* was lurking in the Philippine Sea.

Around midnight on July 30, the crew of the *I-58* spotted the *Indianapolis*. The submarine fired a Type 95 torpedo into the ship's starboard bow and another into the middle of the ship, devastating the vessel.[26] The *Indianapolis* had become top-heavy over the course of the war owing to the continued addition of equipment, which made the fatally wounded ship unstable. Within 12 minutes, the damaged cruiser rolled over, its stern lifting into the air, before quickly disappearing into the depths. The nearest land was 280 miles (450 km) away.

Roughly 300 sailors went down with the ship, but the survivors – just under 900 men – spilled into the ocean. Among them was Seaman Don McCall:

"They tell you to throw your life jacket in first, then jump in and get your life jacket. I looked over [the ship's rail] and there were too many guys who didn't have a life jacket. I decided when I got there, I was going to have one. I strapped mine on before jumping overboard and went through the Navy procedure, holding on to the collar when you hit the water. It felt like my legs were going down and my top was going up. When I hit the water, fuel oil and sea water went down my throat. I was gagging and spitting and trying to swim away from the ship. I finally threw up and got rid of most of it, but then when I ran out of air, I stopped and looked back at the ship, and it was going down."[27]

According to Seaman Lyle Umenhoffer, the oil-slicked waters presented another danger: "When I looked down at myself, I noticed I was covered in this oil and the first instinct is to get away from it, you know, because if it catches on fire then you are really in trouble."[28]

The severity of their predicament became immediately apparent when they discovered that there was a serious shortage of lifeboats, life jackets, and rations – some crew members were apparently able to salvage a paltry amount of spam and crackers from the wreckage. The distress signals transmitted by the *Indianapolis'* radio operators before the vessel sank went unanswered.

The surviving crewmen faced hypothermia in the cold, night-time waters, only to suffer dehydration and sunburn with the arrival of dawn. "It was very miserable because of the sun burning the skin, one could not escape it. It was like having your head in a hole in the middle of a mirror, with all this sunlight being reflected and burning your face," said Signalman Paul McGinnis, "so hot, it was miserable – like hell. You couldn't wait for the sun to go down. When the sun went down it was a relief. Then it would get cold and you would start to shiver, and you couldn't wait for the sun to come back up."[29]

Aside from starvation, dehydration, and the elements, the Pacific Ocean harboured another danger: "There were a lot of sharks. So many," crew member Tony King recalled, "I'd see them swimming below me."[30] Once the attacks began, they were as unrelenting as the scorching heat. "All the time, the sharks never let up. We had a cargo net that had Styrofoam things attached to keep it afloat. There were about 15 sailors on this, and suddenly, 10 sharks hit it and there was nothing left," explained Boatswain's Mate Eugene Morgan. "This went on and on and on."[31]

Being desperately thirsty and surrounded by undrinkable water proved too much for some of the sailors to handle. "Others . . . drank so much [salt water] that they were seeing things," said Machinist's Mate Granville Crane. "They'd say, 'The Indy is down below, and they're giving out fresh water and food in the galley!' And they'd swim down, and a shark would get them. And you could see the sharks eating your comrade."[32] Worse, this salt-induced madness made those suffering from it every bit as bloodthirsty as the sharks encircling them: "Men began drinking salt water so much that they were very delirious. In fact, a lot of them had weapons like knives, and they'd be so crazy, that they'd be fighting amongst themselves and killing one another."[33] There were also those whose salt-addled minds caused them to commit suicide.[34]

Even after the ship failed to arrive as planned on July 31, errors at headquarters meant the alarm still was not raised. Three and a half days after the sinking, at 10:25 a.m. on August 2, a PV-1 Ventura plane on a routine patrol spotted what remained of the *Indianapolis'* crew floating in the ocean below. The aviators immediately dropped life rafts and a radio transmitter into the waters. Within hours, a mass rescue operation was underway. Meanwhile, the stranded sailors continued to be ripped to pieces by sharks. In the end, just 316 of the 1195 crew members survived. To this day, the *USS Indianapolis* tragedy remains the single greatest loss of life at sea in American naval history.

While acknowledging that "there is ample evidence that distress messages were keyed by radio operators [on the *Indianapolis*] and possibly were actually transmitted on at least one (500 k.c.) and possibly two frequencies,"[35] the navy added, "no evidence has been developed that any distress message from the ship was received by any ship, aircraft, or shore station."[36]

In need of a scapegoat, in November 1945, the Navy court-martialled Captain McVay, who had managed to survive the ordeal, accusing him of failing to order his crew to abandon ship and failing to sail in a zig-zag pattern that would have reduced the risk of being hit by an enemy torpedo. He was convicted on the second charge – even though the captain of the Japanese submarine testified that it would not have saved the ship. However, despite the Navy's best efforts to blame Captain McVay, he was found to have not been in dereliction of duty. The survivors of the *Indianapolis* did not fault McVay for the tragedy, but some of the families of the dead bombarded him with hate mail and harassing phone calls. On November 6, 1968, 70-year-old Rear Admiral Charles McVay III walked out onto his back porch holding a toy sailor in one hand and a revolver in the other, and shot himself in the head.

By the end of the 20th century, declassified documents revealed that naval command had not only knowingly sent the *Indianapolis* into harm's way, but that three separate distress messages had been received and ignored: one commander was drunk, another was sleeping, and a third believed it to be a Japanese trick.[37]

The United States Congress passed a resolution exonerating Charles McVay for the loss of the *USS Indianapolis* in October 2000, and on December 20, 2018, its crew were collectively awarded a Congressional Gold Medal.

—

In *Jaws*, the shark hunter Quint is hired to catch the man-eating great white that is plaguing Amity Island. He exudes confidence in his pursuit, seemingly viewing the hunt as a game. This makes his subsequent demise in the jaws of his quarry all the more shocking. Like other elements of the movie, the character of Quint was based in reality. He was inspired by a legendary Long Island fisherman named Frank Mundus.

Frank Louis Mundus was born in the seaside resort of Long Branch, New Jersey in 1925, and grew up near the ocean in Point Pleasant. As a boy, he suffered a bone-marrow infection after breaking his left arm, permanently withering the limb. When his father, Anthony, started working as a steamfitter, the Mundus family moved to Brooklyn, New York, where his mother, Christine, operated a boarding house. On doctors' orders, Frank regularly went swimming in the ocean to rebuild the strength in his left arm. Thus began his life-long love affair with the sea.

At the age of 19, he started a charter fishing business out of nearby Brielle on the mouth of the Manasquan River. He named his first boat *Cricket*, because he bore a striking resemblance to Jiminy Cricket from the Disney film *Pinocchio*, released five years earlier. Frank supplemented his income building docks and crewing on tugboats. He soon met 20-year-old university student Janet

Probasco on the boardwalk, and literally swept her off her feet, taking her on a motorcycle journey. The couple married in 1946, and in January 1947 their first daughter, Barbara, was born. Soon after, Frank acquired *Cricket II*: a custom-built, 42-foot-long vessel that he would famously captain until his death. It also became the family home.

In 1951, the Munduses relocated with *Cricket II* to Montauk on the South Fork of Long Island, NY. While Frank took tourists fishing for mackerel and bluefish, Janet would spend her days pushing little Barbara around the shore in her pushchair. "We never had two nickels to rub together in those days," Janet would later say, "but we had it all."[38] That same year, Frank helped to retrieve *The Pelican*: an overloaded party boat that had capsized during a squall, resulting in 45 deaths. By securing the upturned hull and preventing it from sinking, Frank enabled the authorities to recover a number of the victims' bodies, which otherwise would have been lost following the tragedy.[39]

At the time, the Montauk fishing community consisted of two sub-cultures – blue-collar types who were angling for bottom fish to feed their families, and middle-class members of the American *literati* such as Ernest Hemingway and S. Kip Farrington, whose lofty macho aspirations led them to seek only giants, such as marlin, tuna, and swordfish. During a charter fishing trip, Frank observed his customers' excitement when he snared a mako shark and recognized a marketing opportunity. Posting a sign reading "Monster Fishing" by *Cricket II*, Frank Mundus successfully re-branded himself as an adventurous leviathan-hunter, clad in a safari hat, diamond-studded gold earring, and sporting a shark-tooth dagger with a jewel-encrusted hilt.

Frank's income dramatically improved, and the Munduses moved into a small ocean-side house, where they had two more daughters: Patricia in 1957 and Teresa in 1961. Janet was instrumental in helping to run the Mundus "Monster Fishing" empire: delivering bait, grinding and canning bunker for chum, sanding

Cricket II, booking charter reservations, accounting, helping to advertise, crafting shark-tooth jewellery, and representing the company at nautical shows.

Though Frank would catch seven great white sharks over the course of his lifetime, in 1964, he obtained legendary status by spearing one that weighed 4,500 lbs (2,041 kg), using only a hand-held harpoon. He claimed it was 17-and-a-half feet (5.3 m) long. By this time, he had earned the nickname "Monster Man", and it wasn't long before Frank was taking future *Jaws* author, Peter Benchley, out to sea, where Benchley observed his trademark method of harpooning sharks with lines fastened to barrels to exhaust them.[40]

"I respect white sharks, but I'm not afraid of them," Mundus would later state. "Whenever one got away, I felt that he had won the game. This is where I respected him. After all, it is just a game we're playing."[41]

Ten years after the successful cinematic adaptation of Benchley's *Jaws*, in August 1986, Frank Mundus and colleague Donnie Braddick caught a 17-foot (5.2-m) long, 3,427-lb (1,554-kg) great white off Montauk using only a rod and reel. By 1991, Frank had retired to Hawaii at the age of 65. His days of hunting aquatic monsters were now behind him.

"I had a lot of close calls. Probably too many close calls," Frank reflected. "I was lucky and didn't have any injuries. The only accidents on my boat happened to customers and were not shark-related: they were two broken ankles and some fish-hooked fingers."[42] In his older years, Frank's attitude towards his former finned rivals softened markedly, and he campaigned for shark fishermen to release their catches.

On September 6, 2008, Frank Mundus returned to Honolulu after summering in Montauk, and immediately suffered a heart attack. Four days later, he died of resulting complications, aged 82. He had spent his last night in Montauk aboard *Cricket II*.

The Town That Dreaded Sundown 1976

The Texarkana Moonlight Murders

The Town That Dreaded Sundown **is set in the city of Texarkana, where a masked gunman known as "The Phantom" is targeting teenagers in lovers' lanes, leaving a trail of corpses in his wake. But the film's lurid plot is no work of pulp fiction. In 1946, the Texarkana "Moonlight Murders" shocked this rural community to its core.**

Released two years after *The Texas Chain Saw Massacre*, Charles B. Pierce's *The Town That Dreaded Sundown* managed to come far closer to mirroring a particular series of real murders. Though critically panned at the time of its release for blending comic relief with graphic portrayals of violence, as we approach the second quarter of the 21st century, it is considered to be among the most influential horror movies of all time.

Operating on a shoestring budget of $400,000, with the final fifth of the script yet to be written when filming began, and cast members showing up on set hungover after partying all night, incredibly, Pierce's slapdash southern slasher grossed $5 million at the box office. Filmed and set in the area around Texarkana, Arkansas, *The Town That Dreaded Sundown* features a masked gunman attacking and murdering teenagers on lovers' lanes in 1946. After the first double-homicide, famed Texas Ranger Captain J.D. "Lone Wolf" Morales arrives in the community to team up with local lawman Deputy Norman Ramsey. Morales dubs the masked assassin, who Ramsey spotted fleeing a crime scene, "The Phantom" and vows to track him down, culminating in an explosive finale on a train.

Unlike Hitchcock's thrillers and *The Texas Chain Saw Massacre*, which used real-life murderers as the basis for fictional antagonists, there really *was* a masked killer dubbed "The Phantom" gunning down couples in Texarkana in 1946. Growing up in Arkansas, Pierce had been terrified by the killings as a child and sought to transfer that dread to the big screen. His cult classic begins with a chilling warning: "The incredible story you are about to see is true, where it happened and how it happened. Only the names have been changed."

—

On the evening of Friday, February 22, 1946, James and Robert Hollis picked up their dates in their dad's Plymouth and drove to downtown Texarkana's Strand Theater to watch a horror movie. The Strand was a quaint structure at the corner of Main and West 3rd Street, only two blocks west of the Texas-Arkansas state line that bisects the strange little city. Little did Jimmy and his date, Mary Jeanne Larey, know that by the night's end they would step into a horror story of their own.

After *House of Dracula*'s climactic finale in which the ceiling collapses on Frankenstein's monster, burying him beneath the debris, the two couples stepped out into the Texarkana night. Jimmy dropped Bob and his date home. Alone with Mary Jeanne at last, he turned the car north towards Richmond Road. By the time they reached a nearby "lovers' lane" – an unpaved rural road – it was 11:45 p.m. Though Jimmy had assured his father he would return the car by midnight, the couple spent the next ten minutes kissing in the light of the half moon.

Suddenly, a harsher invasive light blasted through the driver's side window. Turning from Mary Jeanne, Jimmy saw a figure shrouded in a ghostly white mask standing by the door: torch in one hand, pistol in the other.

"I don't wanna kill you, fella," a voice growled through the mask, "so do what I say."[1]

The gunman ordered Jimmy and Mary Jeanne out of the Plymouth through the driver's side door. They stood shivering in the cool night air as he silently looked them over.

"Take off your goddamn britches,"[2] he barked suddenly at Jimmy.

Instinctively, Jimmy resisted, but removed his trousers reluctantly when Mary Jeanne begged him to comply. A vicious pistol whipping then sent him careening to the ground, fracturing his skull. The sound of the blows was so jarring that Mary Jeanne thought he'd been shot. The hooded man now turned his attentions to the 19-year-old woman. Terrified, she rifled through Jimmy's trouser pockets to get his wallet. When Mary Jeanne showed the assailant there was no cash, he became furious and denounced her as a "liar", instructing her to retrieve her purse from the Plymouth. There was no purse. Mary Jeanne felt something heavy strike her head, dropping her to the dirt road. As she started to rise, she thought she heard the masked man's voice ordering her to run. Dazed, she stumbled towards the ditch, but the voice directed her towards Richmond Road. As she fled, she could hear the attacker angrily kicking Jimmy's semi-conscious form over and over. Staggering along the dirt road, she came upon an old-model car parked facing the Plymouth. Desperate for help, she stopped to peer inside. It was empty. The frightened teen had only just resumed running when the hooded figure intercepted her. He asked her why she was running. Mary Jeanne, confused, replied because he had told her to. He slammed the weapon against her head once more, sending her sprawling. Then, climbing on top of her, he pinned her to the ground. She felt her mind instinctively go numb as her assailant sexually assaulted her. She had no idea how much time passed. When he had finished, the masked man returned to Jimmy Hollis' crumpled form.

Battered and bleeding, Mary Jeanne ran. Half a mile (0.8 km) down the road she spotted a farmhouse and began frantically banging on the front door. As she waited outside for a reply, a car cruised by towards Richmond Road. She shouted at it for help, to no avail. Having had no luck with the front door, Mary Jeanne circled around to the back, where her constant hammering finally woke the residents. Seeing the bloodied young woman trembling in the porch light, they offered shelter and telephoned the sheriff's office.

By this time Jimmy Hollis had regained consciousness and managed to limp to Richmond Road. He didn't have to wait long before a passing motorist slowed down to attend to him. When the motorist learnt of his plight, he sped off without him to notify the authorities.

Sheriff Walt Presley of Bowie County wasted no time getting to the scene. He attempted to interview both Mary Jeanne Larey and Jimmy Hollis, but the latter kept slipping in and out of consciousness. Presley decided to give priority to their medical treatment, and directed his focus to the crime scene while an ambulance whisked them to Texarkana Hospital. There, Jimmy was found to be in critical condition with multiple skull fractures, while Mary Jeanne required stitches for her lacerated scalp. Back on the lovers' lane, investigators located the Plymouth, Jimmy's trousers, and the bloodstained patch of road where he had been savagely beaten. There were no other vehicles.

Eventually, Sheriff Presley was able to interview both James Hollis and Mary Jeanne Larey. As Mary Jeanne's description of the empty old car parked on the lovers' lane differed from the one that had passed the farmhouse, the sheriff hypothesized that the offender had fled the crime scene in the latter, travelling north to Richmond Road. Interestingly, while both victims described the perpetrator as standing six-feet (1.8-m) tall and wearing a mask fashioned from a pillowcase with eye holes cut in it, Jimmy thought he was a white male under 30, while Mary Jeanne swore that he was black. In 1946, laws mandating segregation were still in place in both states comprising Texarkana, and the racial tension was palpable. Perhaps for this reason, Sheriff Presley never publicly commented on that aspect of her description.

Though 24-year-old Hollis survived his ordeal, he received three months of medical treatment and missed half a year's work.

Plagued by nightmares, Mary Jeanne Larey moved to Oklahoma to live with some relatives, never to return.[3]

In Texarkana, bad dreams gave way to an ever-worsening reality on the rainy morning of March 24. It was 8:30 a.m. when an unidentified driver approached a stationary 1941 Oldsmobile near Rich Road. He simply assumed its occupants were stuck in the mud and could use some assistance. As he approached the vehicle, he looked through the glass to find two corpses caked in blood.

Sheriff Presley arrived with Jackson Neely Runnels, the chief of police on the Texan side of the city. They identified the bodies of Richard Griffin, 29, and 17-year-old Polly Ann Moore in the rear of the vehicle. Moore was lying prone on a blanket covering the backseat with a gunshot wound to the back of her head. Beside her, her purse was open and empty. Griffin had been similarly executed, his body kneeling on the floor between the front and back seats, and his head resting on overlapping hands. Both victims were fully clothed. Like Moore's purse, Griffin's out-turned trouser pockets hinted at robbery. There was significantly more blood outside the vehicle, located 20 feet (6 m) away in the dirt – a surprising piece of evidence given the heavy rainfall – indicating they had been shot to death in the open. Whoever had executed them had clearly then bundled their bodies into the back of the Oldsmobile. Unfortunately, onlookers ghoulishly descended upon the crime scene before police had the opportunity to properly secure it. Between the downpour and trampling feet, potentially useful pieces of evidence, such as tyre tracks and footprints, were obliterated. While it was a common media practice at the time to deny any occurrence of sexual assault to protect both the victim and a general sense of decency, memos circulated among the Texas Rangers indicated that Polly Ann Moore had been raped.[4]

The masked killer struck again before dawn on Sunday, April 14, though his grim handiwork would remain undiscovered until sunrise. G.H. Weaver was driving northeast along North Park Road to Prescott with his wife and son when he spied the lifeless form of a young man lying on the north shoulder. Summoned to the crime scene, police determined that the victim had been shot through his right hand, the same bullet continuing to strike him in the left side of the face. When he had turned to escape, the gunman had fired twice more, striking him through the back of his left shoulder and head. Not far from the body, Sheriff Presley came upon an address book, and surreptitiously pocketed it without notifying his colleagues.[5]

The victim was quickly identified as James Paul Martin, a 16-year-old resident of Kilgore, Texas, who had returned to his hometown of Texarkana on Friday to stay with a friend, Tom Albritton. On Saturday afternoon he had asked Betty Jo Booker – a 15-year-old friend he'd known since kindergarten – for a date later that evening. She had reluctantly agreed.[6] A saxophonist in The Rhythmaires jazz ensemble, Betty Jo had performed at a VFW (Veterans of Foreign Wars) dance that night, and was seen leaving with James between 1:30 and 2 a.m.

Having failed to return home, and with her suitor's bullet-ridden body found lying on North Park Road, Betty Jo became the subject of an intense search by police and local volunteers. As James Martin's car was nowhere to be seen, it seemed reasonable to conclude that once they found one, they would find the other. The clothed corpse of Betty Jo Booker was eventually discovered behind a tree in a wooded area by several of her friends around noon. She was lying supine in the leaves with her right hand tucked into the pocket of her fully-buttoned coat. She, too, had been shot in the left side of her face and again in the heart. Oddly, Betty Jo was found on Morris Lane, more than two miles (3.2 km) from Martin's body. Tom Moore of Morris Lane informed police he had heard a gunshot at around 5:30 that morning.[7]

James Martin's vehicle was finally located close to the main entrance to Spring Lake Park. The key was still in the ignition. The vehicle was a mile and a half (2.4 km) from the Martin crime scene and more than three miles (4.8 km) away from Betty Jo's body; there was no way of knowing which victim had been killed first. Ballistic evidence – either "a handful of .32 calibre shells" or "six cartridge cases and four projectiles"[8] – was found deposited around the outside of the car. A slug and casing recovered from near James Martin's body were eventually matched through forensic ballistics to the same pistol that was used in the March 24 double-murder. The weapon in both cases was strongly suspected to be a .32 Colt semi-automatic handgun. Furthermore, a latent fingerprint recovered from the steering wheel was processed at the FBI lab in Dallas and found to belong to neither of the victims, nor the owner of the vehicle, James' father. Unfortunately, it was of insufficient quality to be compared to the samples on the FBI's fingerprint file; while it could potentially be matched to a specific suspect, it could not be cross-referenced against prints of known offenders. Like Polly Ann Moore, the same FBI office determined Betty Jo Booker had been raped. Strangely, her E-Flat alto saxophone was missing – it was located several months later, in brush around 140 yards (128 m) from where her body had been found.

In isolation, the first double-murder had barely raised an eyebrow in a hard-bitten town like Texarkana. Once it became clearer that the same gunman was responsible for the Martin-Booker slayings, the citizens went into full blown panic. Overnight, the commercial supply of guns, ammunition, and home security devices could not keep pace with the demand. It became local custom to telephone even dear friends before paying them a visit, mitigating the risk of being shot dead by a paranoid homeowner. On April 16, the *Texarkana Daily News* ran a front-page story on the murders – "Phantom Killer Eludes Officers as Investigation of Slayings Pressed" – giving rise to the moniker by which the murderer is still known to this day. Even with the summer heatwave, the homes of many Texarkanans remained barricaded. Like a town suddenly besieged by a malevolent force in a spaghetti Western, Texarkana desperately needed a solution.

It seemed to arrive in the form of Manuel Trazazas "Lone Wolf"

Gonzaullas: a Mexican Civil War veteran turned Texas Ranger, specializing in forensic ballistics and graphology, and wielding pearl-handled pistols. Surrounded by fawning reporters and flashing cameras, Gonzaullas boldly swore to stay in Texarkana until the Phantom was brought to justice. However, he soon gained a reputation among local lawmen for spending more time courting publicity than actually tracking down the murderer. Despite his risky but clever plan to position teenage couples at known lovers' lanes, with armed lawmen waiting in the brush, the endeavour was ultimately fruitless. In August, Gonzaullas drafted a (conveniently) confidential memo excusing himself from remaining in Texarkana along with his entourage of Texas Rangers. By that point there hadn't been a murder resembling the Phantom's in three months.

The last had occurred at 8:30 p.m. on the night of Friday, May 3, at a rural property ten miles (16 km) northeast of Texarkana. Housewife Katie Stark had gone to bed early, and was lying in her evening clothes, the farmhouse interior darkened by the moonless night. In the living room her husband Virgil was resting his sore back while thumbing through the *Texarkana Gazette* and listening to the radio. Suddenly, a strange noise came from outside. Katie asked her husband to turn the radio down, but was answered by shattering glass. Thinking Virgil had dropped something, she bounded out of bed and hurried into the living room. Virgil stood up from his armchair, a look of shock on his face, before falling back into his seat, leaking blood. He had been shot through the window. Horrified, Katie ran to the phone fastened to the kitchen wall, lifted the receiver, and cranked the handle twice. She felt something strike the left side of her face. Blood and teeth splattered and scattered across the kitchen floor. Perhaps to ground herself in the ensuing chaos, she managed to retrieve a single gold-filled tooth, before beating a hasty retreat.[9] Katie dashed through the master bedroom, down a hallway into another bedroom, then through the living room. She burst out of the front porch door and into the yard. Darting across Highway 67, she reached the home of a neighbour, A.V. Prater, who met her wild knocking on his door with a rifle. Realizing she was injured and in trouble, he fired a warning shot into the inky night. Then, accompanied by another neighbour, Elmer Taylor, they drove Katie to Michael Meagher Memorial Hospital in Taylor's sedan. Throughout the journey, she sat slumped in the front seat, bleeding profusely and struggling to stay conscious. Upon arriving at the hospital, it was determined she had been shot through the face. Fortunately, she would survive.

While the attack on the Starks is commonly considered to be the last of the so-called Moonlight Murders, there is reason to doubt it is connected. Certainly, whoever fired the shots that killed Virgil Stark and wounded his wife targeted a male and female, but this violence was directed at an older married couple in their own home, rather than more youthful victims in the pseudo-privacy of a parked car. The Starks were hit with .22 calibre bullets, whereas the previous homicide victims were killed with .32s that were scientifically proven to have been fired by the same pistol. Furthermore, Virgil Stark had been carrying on an affair with a married woman whose husband had recently returned to the area from World War II.[10] Not only did this mean there was at least one other person residing locally with a motive to harm Stark, it may also account for the deviations in the modus operandi.

Three days after the Stark attack, the partially dismembered body of a vagrant named Earl McSpadden was discovered on railroad tracks about 15 miles (24 km) north of Texarkana in Little River County. Though McSpadden was already dead, his corpse had been mutilated by a passing train at 5:30 a.m. Observing the body, Dr Frank Engler noted defensive wounds on McSpadden's hands indicating "the victim had struggled with an assailant armed with a knife," and had suffered "a deep wound two inches long on the left temple which was serious enough to have caused death."[11] Despite the complete lack of any physical or behavioural evidence linking McSpadden's death to the killings in Texarkana, his timely demise gave rise to a number of oft-repeated popular speculations.

In one scenario, McSpadden was the "Phantom Killer" himself, who, wracked with guilt, decided to put an end to his miserable existence. Another theory holds that he was the Phantom's last victim: murdered either because he knew too much or as an elaborate means for the gunman to fake his own death. While none of the investigators gave much credence to McSpadden's death being related to the Phantom, it goes a long way to explaining the dramatic escape-by-railway finale to *The Town That Dreaded Sundown.*

Since 2003, the denizens of Texarkana gather every Halloween season in Spring Lake Park to watch *The Town That Dreaded Sundown.* And while it is not impossible that the "Phantom Killer" is among them, even if he was as young as 18 in 1946, he would be more than 90 years old at the time of this writing.

The Amityville Horror 1979

The Haunting of 112 Ocean Avenue

The story of the "Amityville Horror" is a complex one: a multiple homicide, followed by a supposed haunting, followed by a book about the haunting, followed by a film based on the book (and several remakes). Whatever truly happened in this Long Island home, the stories about it are both compelling and bizarre.

In 1979, an indie film lambasted by critics and initially conceived of as a made-for-TV movie, shocked Hollywood by making $86 million at the box office. Not only was *The Amityville Horror* the second most financially successful picture that year, it remained the highest grossing independent film until 1990. Directed by Stuart Rosenberg, it stars James Brolin and Margot Kidder as newlyweds George and Kathy Lutz. Seeking a suitable home in which to raise Kathy's three children, the family move into a large, suspiciously well-priced home in Long Island: the scene of a horrific mass murder a year earlier and built on an Indian burial ground. Individually, at first, and then collectively, the Lutzes are worn down, terrified, and turned against one another by a paranormal presence inhabiting the structure. Eventually, they are forced to abandon the dwelling altogether to avoid losing their lives and their sanity.

Arguably the first truly popular haunted house movie in cinematic history, *The Amityville Horror* was largely successful due to a clever marketing campaign, Academy-Award-nominated soundtrack, and stellar performances by the ensemble cast. But perhaps most crucially: it was a "true" story, based on the book of the same name by Jay Anson, which detailed the alleged experiences of the Lutz family in December 1975. Though the brutal murders that occurred at 112 Ocean Avenue in 1974 are a matter of historical record, what really occurred when the Lutzes later moved into the home is a topic still mired in controversy. What follows is their story as they recounted it to Jay Anson.

—

When the newlywed George and Kathy Lutz saw the $80,000 asking price for a beautiful three-storey colonial house on Long Island's south shore, they knew something was amiss. After treating them to a tour of the residence, the estate agent pre-empted their question. Just over a year earlier, Ronald "Butch" DeFeo had murdered his mother, father, brothers, and sisters inside the Amityville home while they slept.

The Lutzes were not fazed. With three children from Kathy's first marriage and a half-Malamute, half-gold retriever, Harry, to make space for, they weren't particularly concerned by the house's dark past. Not only did they decide to take it, but they also bought some of its contents: dining room furniture, a girl's bedroom set, a television chair, and even items from Butch DeFeo's bedroom. Kathy, a Catholic, arranged for her priest Father Frank Mancuso* to visit and bless the house on moving day: December 18, 1975.

Father Mancuso awoke that winter morning with an ominous feeling. Before heading over to 112 Ocean Avenue, he had lunch with some clergymen friends from nearby Lindenhurst, just east of Amityville. When he innocently told them which house he would be blessing, they became concerned and informed him that it was the site of the DeFeo massacre. Father Mancuso was entirely unfamiliar with the tragedy. Though his friends advised him not to go,

* Pseudonym

he told them that he wanted to keep his promise to the Lutzes. He arrived at 112 Ocean Avenue at 1:30 p.m., donned his stole, and entered the dwelling. He raised his vial of holy water, flicked it once, and uttered the standard blessing.

"Get out!"[1] a man's voice suddenly boomed from immediately behind him.

Startled, he turned around to find himself alone in the room. Having felt uneasy about the situation all day, Father Mancuso hastily finished the blessing and left the building. He bid farewell to George, Kathy, and their children – Danny, 9, Chris, 7, and Missy, 5 – and sped off. When he next caught sight of himself in the mirror he noticed dark smudge-like marks under his eyes. He could not seem to wash them away. That night, while driving home from his mother's house along the Van Wyck Expressway, the priest felt his Ford being pushed onto the shoulder by an invisible force. Suddenly, the right door and hood flew open, shattering the windshield. Then the car stalled. Father Mancuso phoned for a mechanic, but no matter what the man did, he simply could not get the car to start. Father Mancuso was eventually driven home by a fellow priest, who later called him saying, "Do you know what happened when I dropped you off? The windshield wipers began to fly back and forth like crazy. I couldn't stop them! I never turned them on, Frank!"[2] For some reason, Father Mancuso chose not to tell George or Kathy Lutz about these troubling events.

Meanwhile, George was beginning to have peculiar experiences of his own. On moving day, he had chained his dog, Harry, to the fence in the backyard. While rigging up a stereo system he had purchased from the DeFeo estate, he heard pained howls coming from outside. Danny sprinted in through the front door and told him Harry was in trouble. Rushing into the backyard, George was amazed to see that his beloved pet had somehow leapt over the fence and was slowly strangling on his chain. George managed to free him, but couldn't understand how Harry's predicament was physically possible. In any event, it had been a tiring day, and the Lutz family was ready for bed.

At 3:15 a.m., George awoke to the sound of somebody knocking on the front door. Before he had the chance to investigate, he heard another loud rapping, only this time coming from the sewing room. He entered the room with its large windows overlooking the backyard and Amityville River. At once, he saw a shadowy figure moving down by the boathouse next to where Harry was tied up. The canine sprung to his feet, barking at the shape. George rushed downstairs and out of the back door, snatching up a wooden board as a makeshift weapon. Upon reaching Harry, he discovered that the shape was actually the boathouse door swinging in the wind. George was absolutely certain he had locked it.[3]

In the days following the move into 112 Ocean Avenue, George found himself uncharacteristically moody and unproductive. No matter how much wood he burned in the fireplace or what the temperature said on the thermostat, he seemed completely unable to shake off the cold. George Lutz awoke at exactly 3:15 a.m. on the following two nights, driven by an overwhelming compulsion to check the boathouse.

Aside from becoming short-tempered with the children, Kathy Lutz didn't experience anything particularly odd until the morning of December 22. While sitting in the breakfast nook writing out a list of people to buy Christmas presents for, she felt the gentle embrace of an invisible female presence. Suddenly, the children began calling her to the second-floor bathroom. Hurrying up the steps and into the room, she was shocked and disgusted to find a black slime-like substance coating the inside of the toilet bowl. When nine-year-old Danny rushed to his parents' bathroom to get bleach, he discovered their toilet in a similar condition, emitting a wretched odour. The first-floor toilet was in a similar state. No matter how rigorously Kathy Lutz scrubbed the porcelain, what chemicals she used, or how many times she flushed, the strange discolouration would not go away. Equally bizarre was the sickly unexplained smell of perfume pervading Missy's bedroom. In an effort to air out the house, George went to open the sewing room window, and noticed thousands of houseflies clinging to the inside of the pane – an unusual occurrence in a Long Island December.[4]

Once again, George awoke at 3:15 a.m. that night with a nagging urge to check downstairs. When he reached the ground floor, he found the 250-lb (113-kg) front door wide open, hanging from a single hinge. Oddly, when he called a locksmith to fix it, the man seemed suspicious of him. That same day, Kathy had noticed all three of the Lutz children were uncharacteristically sleeping on their stomachs – the same position in which the murdered DeFeos had been discovered. When she entered her bedroom's walk-in closet, the silver crucifix on the wall was hanging upside down and a sour smell lingered on the air.

By December 24, Father Mancuso was bedridden with fever and fixated on a room he had seen while at 112 Ocean Avenue – it was full of boxes and looked out onto the boathouse. Overwhelmed by a desperate need to warn the Lutz family about the room, he phoned the residence at 5 p.m. and George answered. The room in question had once belonged to Butch DeFeo's murdered brothers, Marc and John. George confirmed it was now Kathy's sewing room and enquired why Father Mancuso thought the family needed to avoid the space. Suddenly, the phone connection was broken by a jarring static which made further communication impossible, and spurred both men to hang up. Despite repeated attempts by Lutz and Mancuso to call each other back over the following days, the phones did not ring on either end. Mancuso's illness worsened.[5]

Like clockwork, George Lutz awoke at 3:15 a.m. on Christmas morning, rousing Kathy with his touch. She recalled a vivid dream in which Butch DeFeo was systematically slaughtering his family in their beds. Particularly, she claimed to know exactly how his mother, Louise DeFeo, had died. George held his terrified wife until she calmed enough to drift back to sleep. Then, as he had many nights before, he quietly slipped outside to check the boathouse. To his relief he found the boathouse door locked and Harry in good health. Turning around to head back to the house, he froze. Five-year-old Missy stood at her bedroom window staring directly at him. Behind her, a pig's face glowered with unblinking red eyes. George sprinted back into the house and bounded up the stairs. He found Missy sound asleep on her stomach, the rocking chair in her room tilting back and forth ever so slightly.[6]

Later that morning, George and Kathy confided many of their chilling experiences to each other, and discussed whether there was something wrong with their new home. Deciding to take Father Mancuso's advice, they warned the children to stay away from the sewing room. When Chris and Danny wondered aloud whether it was because their parents were hiding Christmas presents, Missy corrected them: "I know why we have to keep out. Jodie's in there."[7]

At 9 p.m., Kathy was en route to the children's playroom to prepare Missy for bed, when she heard a voice coming from her daughter's first-floor bedroom.

"Isn't the snow beautiful, Jodie?"[8]

Kathy opened the door to see her daughter sitting in the little rocking chair watching flakes of snow fall gently past the window.

"Who are you talking to Missy? An angel?"[9]

"No Mama," Missy said, looking over to a corner of the room. "Just Jodie."[10]

Kathy followed her gaze, but saw only toys. She asked if "Jodie" was one of Missy's new dolls.

"No. Jodie's a pig," the child replied. "He's my friend. Nobody can see him but me."[11]

The next morning, December 26, Kathy found herself making another list in the breakfast nook, when she caught a familiar whiff of perfume and sensed the same invisible female presence. Only this time, she felt the entity's body against her own, its arms gently winding around her waist. When she demanded to be left alone, it relinquished its hold, placed a comforting hand on her shoulder, then disappeared, leaving only its dizzying fragrance in the kitchen. The Lutzes spent the remainder of the day at a family wedding.

Early in the afternoon of December 27, Kathy was in the basement arranging canned goods when she heard the doorbell ring. George opened the door to Kathy's Aunt Theresa, a former nun turned mother-of-three. Apparently, she'd decided to pay them an unexpected visit. George gave her a tour of their new home. Strangely, the ashen-faced woman refused to enter the sewing room and playroom, saying they were "bad places". Despite having come all the way to Amityville on the bus and walking the rest of the way to the house, Aunt Theresa stayed for just half an hour before departing. Kathy returned to stacking cans in the basement closet. When one of the shelves collapsed under the weight, she realized the basement wall was essentially a plywood facade. She called for her husband. Taking stock of the situation, George tore out the shelves. Then, pushing on the plywood, he and Kathy watched in astonishment as it swung inwards, revealing a secret room. Painted entirely in red, the room totalled no more than 20 square feet (1.85 square metres) and had a peculiar smell, which George claimed he recognized as blood.

The next day, George Lutz decided to check out The Witches' Brew: a local watering hole. As he enjoyed a cold beer, the bartender remarked that George was "a dead ringer for a young feller from around here . . . He's away now. Won't be back for a while. Maybe forever."[12] When George said he had recently moved into 112 Ocean Avenue, the barman dropped a glass.

That evening, George Lutz walked into the living room to put some more wood on the fire, and tripped over a four-foot (1.2 m) ceramic lion, falling face first into the logs and banging his leg. Earlier in the day, Kathy was sure she had seen the statue – a Christmas gift for her husband – move ever so slightly towards her, but hadn't told him. Upon examining his injury the following morning, Kathy found tooth marks around his ankle.[13]

On December 28, George hobbled to his van to run some errands. He had decided to learn more about the DeFeo case, and stopped off at an office for *Newsday*, Long Island's most popular newspaper. Looking through microfiche related to the murders, he found a photo of Butch DeFeo and realized he bore a striking resemblance to the killer. Even more alarming was the revelation that the coroner had determined the DeFeos had been shot dead at approximately 3:15 a.m. – the exact time George had been waking up nearly every night since moving into the scene of the massacre.

Back at the house, Kathy could hear the window in the empty sewing room opening and closing, but dared not open the door.

The next day, the Amityville Historical Society informed George Lutz that before the European conquest, the Shinnecock Indians had used his land as a colony for the physically and mentally ill. Furthermore, a 17th century Amityville settler named John Ketchum, who had been expelled from Salem for witchcraft, had resided a mere 500 feet (150 m) from 112 Ocean Avenue and was rumoured to be buried on the property.

George and Kathy spent New Year's Eve indoors, warming themselves by the fireplace. Exactly one minute after the clock struck midnight heralding 1976, Kathy glanced into the flames and screamed. Following her gaze, George saw a white-cowled demonic face manifesting in the soot against the red brick. Half of its dreadful visage had been blown away, as if hit by buckshot at close range. At 1 a.m., they decided to go to bed. They had only been asleep for five minutes when suddenly a tremendous gale blasted their window open, blowing the blankets off their bodies. The bedroom door slammed shut, yet they could still hear the wind howling in the hallway. George tore open the door and was shocked to see the doors to the sewing and dressing room wide open, while Missy's door remained conspicuously closed. He rushed into the dressing room to close the yawning windows, then did the same to the ones in the sewing room. Kathy found Missy sound asleep in her bed with her windows locked and undisturbed. The only thing moving was the rocking chair. Upon entering the room, George approached the chair – it stopped moving immediately.[14]

The rest of New Year's Day was relatively uneventful – George drove to his office and back, Kathy read to Missy, and Danny and Chris played outdoors in the freshly fallen snow. After the children had gone to bed, George and Kathy lingered in the living room until about 10 p.m. When they turned off the light to head upstairs, they saw two beady red eyes glaring at them through the living room window. George flicked on the light and they disappeared, but he was determined to confront the creature. Racing outside, he came face to face with . . . nothing. However, upon scouring the area with a torch he made a horrific discovery: a trail of cloven hoof-prints led around the house, resembling those of a large swine.[15]

As the Lutz family moved through January 1976, the occurrences at 112 Ocean Avenue became even stranger. In the light of day, they tracked the hoof-prints to the garage and found the entire door had been nearly ripped from its frame. Kathy's third kitchen encounter left her unconscious on the floor, squeezed hard around the waist by spectral hands. Upon returning to the Witches' Brew bar, George learnt that the bartender had once been employed to serve drinks at a party hosted by the DeFeos, and while working in the basement, had also stumbled upon the red room. Afterwards, he had been haunted by nightmares of animal sacrifice.

Soon a fog stinking of human faeces began creeping from the secret chamber, and the lion statue made its way onto the dining room table. George was repeatedly startled awake in the middle of the night by the sound of a marching band playing downstairs. On several occasions, George reported that Kathy levitated from her bed as she slept, either drifting towards the window or transforming into a haggard crone when George helped her down.

Increasingly troubled, George decided to contact a young medium, Francine. On January 7, she visited the house. Francine spoke of an elderly couple in the home who were "lost spirits"[16] and likely former residents of the property. Furthermore, she said 112 Ocean Avenue had been erected on a burial ground, that the body of a murder victim was buried in the basement, and that the house needed to be exorcised. When she left, George noticed the banister on the first-floor landing had been torn out.

Brandishing a silver crucifix, the Lutzes attempted to bless their own house and were assailed by a chorus of disembodied voices commanding them to stop. By January 9, green slime had begun seeping from the walls and keyholes. Despite routine checks to ensure the windows were closed and locked, they continued to blow open all over the house. On January 11, a storm shattered the glass in ten windows on the first and second floors, destroying their locks and latches. Strangely, it also managed to rip the locks from the metal frames in the playroom and sewing room doors. Though the entire house was drenched in rainwater, every member of the Lutz family somehow managed to sleep through the disturbance.

Jodie the pig began to use Missy to relay messages. When he reappeared at Missy's bedroom window, Kathy put a chair through it.[17]

The paranormal activity reached a crescendo on the night of January 13. Chris and Danny's beds began sliding back and forth in their room, drawers opened and closed all over the house, and a terrified George found himself unable to move as he was trampled unconscious by phantasmal hooves. He awoke to find Chris and Danny screaming by his bedside. They told him that a faceless monster had appeared in their bedroom and tried to grab them. As if on cue, Harry the dog started growling in the direction of the staircase. Breaking his strange paralysis, George hurled himself out of bed, nearly bowling over his two sons. He hurried through the door to the foot of the stairs and looked up. There, standing on the top step, was a towering figure in a white cloak – the same horrific demon he had seen manifest in the fireplace – pointing its finger directly at him. George sprinted back into the bedroom, and ordered his frightened family outside and into the van. After 28 days at 112 Ocean Avenue, the Lutzes had finally had enough.

They reached Kathy's mother's house soon after. Safe at last, they unburdened themselves: telling her about the strange and unnerving things they'd seen, heard, and suffered through over the past month. That night they went to bed at 10 p.m., safe in the knowledge that nothing untoward would ever happen to them again.

George and Kathy Lutz apparently awoke to find themselves floating above the bed. They dashed to the top of the stairs, only to see green-black slime slowly oozing up the steps towards them. Fearing that whatever they had encountered at 112 Ocean Avenue would follow them for the rest of their lives, the Lutzes moved across the country to Southern California. When the tale of the Amityville haunting became public, journalist Marvin Scott gathered a group of psychics, parapsychologists, and occult experts to spend a night at 112 Ocean Avenue on February 18, 1976.[18] Among them were Ed and Lorraine Warren: the famed demonologist and clairvoyant. The event was to be filmed for New York's Channel 5. Beginning at 10:30 p.m., the ensemble held three séances, with most in attendance reportedly experiencing noxious and highly disturbing phenomena. Among the guests' many vague pronouncements, Lorraine Warren was unequivocal: "Whatever is here is, in my estimation, most definitely of a negative nature. It has nothing to do with anyone who had once walked the earth in human form. It is right from the bowels of the earth . . . It doesn't have to stay here, but I think it's a resting place."[19]

As more and more of the Lutzes' experiences were inevitably embellished and distorted by the media, George and Kathy agreed to let scriptwriter Jay Anson publish the definitive account of their experiences in his 1977 best-seller *The Amityville Horror.* Anson listened to 45 hours of cassette recordings in which George and Kathy recounted their harrowing tale. He interviewed several other people involved, including Father Mancuso, who unbeknownst to the Lutzes had been suffering strange and terrible physical and mental afflictions since first setting foot in 112 Ocean Avenue. According to Anson, not only did their stories match, but they also unknowingly repeated many documented phenomena associated with the paranormal including cold spots, heightened sensitivity to animals, retrocognition, and poltergeist activity. It all seemed so real.

Unfortunately, for the millions of people who read Anson's 1977 paperback and watched the various cinematic portrayals, the so-called "Amityville Horror" has since been mostly debunked.[20] To begin with, none of the property's subsequent residents have reported any supernatural phenomena whatsoever. In an amusing irony, *Newsday*, the same Long Island publication mentioned in the book, found absolutely no evidence to support the Lutzes' claims of having consulted neighbours, officials from the Catholic diocese, or police.[21] Sceptical organizations and publications conducted investigations into the Lutzes' claims, chipping away at their deception. In an interview for *Skeptical Inquirer*, James and Barbara Cromarty, who bought 112 Ocean Avenue immediately after the Lutzes' departure, stated that the house still retained its antique locks, hinges, and doorknobs: all items the Lutzes claimed had been destroyed and replaced, sometimes repeatedly.[22]

The Cromartys filed a $1.1 million lawsuit against George and Kathleen Lutz, Prentice Hall (the publisher of the 1977 book), and Jay Anson, for damages resulting from loss of privacy.[23] The unsuspecting couple had moved into the home with their children three months before *The Amityville Horror*'s publication. Unsurprisingly, in its wake, a steady stream of tourists flocked to the property, taking photographs and video, and even ringing the doorbell to speak with the new homeowners.[24]

In July 1978, Ronald "Butch" DeFeo's lawyer, William Weber, told the Associated Press he had met the Lutzes soon after they had moved out of the property. Together they had "created this horror story over many bottles of wine that George was drinking. We were creating something the public wanted to hear about."[25] The Lutzes attempted to sue Weber for $1 million, along with a handful of other people and organizations, but during the 1979 trial, Judge Jack B. Weinstein threw the case out of court. Before doing so, he stated "it appears to me that to a large extent the book is a work of fiction."[26]

William Weber counter-sued the Lutzes and Jay Anson for fraud and breach of contract – "in layman's terms, stealing [his] ideas"[27] – claiming George and Kathy had agreed to collaborate with Weber on a book that would have been titled *Devil on My Back.*[28] They settled out of court for $2,500 plus $15,000 for services related to the film and book.[29] In May 1988, Weber appeared on *A Current Affair*, saying "We took real-life incidents and transposed them. In other words, it was a hoax."[30] Despite sticking to their story publicly, the Lutzes were essentially compelled to admit as much over the course of their many trials.[31]

As for the ominous hoof-prints – on New Year's Day 1976, there was no snow in Amityville.[32]

Poltergeist 1982

The Seaford Poltergeist

The 1982 blockbuster *Poltergeist* brought haunted houses right up to date, transporting the horror from a crumbling Gothic mansion to an everyday suburban home that every audience member could relate to. Director Tobe Hooper and screenwriter Steven Spielberg found all the inspiration they needed in the strange story of the Herrmann family of Seaford, Long Island.

In 1982, Tobe Hooper, director of *The Texas Chain Saw Massacre*, and Steven Spielberg, the visionary behind *Jaws*, joined forces to create the supernatural horror movie *Poltergeist*. Nominated for multiple Academy Awards, *Poltergeist* thrilled audiences and critics alike with unforgettably creepy scenes and groundbreaking special effects, earning more than $120 million at the box office.

Whereas most haunted-house films involve a family moving into a mysterious dwelling, the Freeling family in *Poltergeist* have long been living an idealistic life in their Orange County home. That is, until their little daughter Carol Anne starts waking up in the middle of the night to talk to a television screen filled with static. After she ominously announces "they're here", household items begin to bend, break, and fly across the room with seemingly no explanation. When a tree in the backyard smashes through the window and attacks Carol Anne's brother, and then she herself is engulfed by a black hole that appears in her closet, a trio of parapsychologists from the University of California arrive at the home. They inform the Freelings that their house has been invaded by spirits known as poltergeists. Spiritual medium Tangina Barrons comes to the rescue, and after explaining a complex demonology to the family, tells Carol Anne's mother, Diane, that she can still save her daughter. Intent on rescuing her child, Diane tethers herself to a rope and jumps into another dimension, from which she successfully retrieves the girl. The Freelings relocate to another home nearby, only to be confronted by more terrifying paranormal encounters. Discovering that the entire housing development was built on a graveyard by an unscrupulous land developer, they flee the area entirely.

Interestingly, both *Poltergeist* and that other legendary haunted-house movie, *The Amityville Horror*, were inspired by events that occurred in Long Island family homes. Though *The Amityville Horror* pre-dated *Poltergeist*, the events that inspired this Hooper-Spielberg collaboration actually happened nearly 18 years before the Lutz family moved to Amityville. Moreover, while *The Amityville Horror* was marketed from the outset as being a "true story", *Poltergeist* did not resort to that marketing technique – though it very well could have done. Instead, it allowed its audience to trace the origins of the story themselves, back to February 3, 1958 at 1648 Redwood Path. The tale that transpired in this nondescript suburban home almost single-handedly introduced the modern world to the term "poltergeist".

—

It would have been hard to find a more conventional family than the Herrmanns of Seaford, Long Island. The head of the family, 43-year-old James Herrmann – a former Marine Corps Sergeant who had served in the Pacific theatre during World War II – was a strict Catholic, an employee of Air France, and an auxiliary policeman for his community. His wife, Lucille, 38, was a housewife, who had once been head nurse at St. Luke's Hospital in Manhattan. The Herrmanns had two children, 13-year-old Lucille

(Lucy), and James Jr (Jimmy), 12. They lived at 1648 Redwood Path, a three-bedroom family home located a mere four miles (6.4 km) northwest of 112 Ocean Avenue – the house that would later belong to the Lutz family and form the scene of the so-called "Amityville Horror". However, unlike the Lutzes, who moved into the area nearly two decades later, the Herrmanns were the original residents of their home. They had lived there for five years, and nothing particularly untoward had happened. That was, until Monday, February 3, 1958.

It began as another unremarkable winter day. The temperature was just dipping below freezing. At around 3:30 p.m., Lucille Herrmann was sitting in the living room with Lucy and Jimmy. Suddenly, they were startled by a series of loud popping noises sounding in rapid succession throughout the house. Wondering what was going on, Lucille and the children went from room to room, only to discover caps had seemingly exploded off bottles all over the house. In the bedroom, an uncapped bottle of holy water had tipped over, leaking its contents all over the bureau. Bottles of medicine and shampoo were found opened and lying on their sides in the bathroom cabinet, along with a bottle of liquid starch in the kitchen and a gallon container of bleach in the cellar. In Jimmy's bedroom, a ceramic Davy Crockett doll and model ship had been broken in various places.[1]

Lucille called her husband at work to relay the strange happenings. While James Herrmann was concerned, he reasoned that since no one had been hurt, he would look into the matter when he arrived home. Taking the Long Island Rail Road back to Seaford, he checked the various rooms in the house and consulted with his family, but could find no natural explanation for the bottle popping.

At 3:30 p.m. on Thursday, February 6, the exact same thing happened again, with a third incident occurring on Friday. It wasn't until 10:15 a.m. on Sunday morning that James Herrmann witnessed it first-hand. To his astonishment, he found the bottle of holy water again spilling onto the bedroom floor, and caps missing from bottles of starch and turpentine. Forty-five minutes later, while standing in the bathroom doorway talking to Jimmy, who was brushing his teeth, James observed two bottles near the sink suddenly and simultaneously move in different directions. The first slid 18 inches (46 cm), shattering in the sink, while the second glided more than a foot and then toppled onto the floor. Now as puzzled as his wife – he could no longer deny that something strange was happening – he swiftly made a telephone call to the Nassau County Police.

Officer James Hughes arrived shortly after, and had just begun questioning the Herrmanns when he was interrupted by popping sounds coming from elsewhere in the house. According to a police report by 32-year-old Nassau County Detective Joseph Tozzi, Hughes entered the bathroom to find that the same two bottles – shampoo and medicine – had tipped over again, with their caps blown off. During the next few days, the popping activity became more frequent and extreme. On Tuesday, February 11, Detective Tozzi was assigned to investigate the case full-time. That same day, a perfume atomizer flew off Lucy's dresser.

On Thursday, February 13, Tozzi sent five of the affected bottles for physical and chemical analysis at a police laboratory in Mineola, New York. Meanwhile, the chaos continued, with the holy water falling onto its side once more on Saturday, February 15. Touching the bottle, James Herrmann felt warmth, and had an epiphany. If the bottles were warm, someone must have been holding them. Dashing through the house to handle the other popped bottles, he was disappointed to find them all at room temperature.

James' cousin, Marie Murtha, decided to pay the family a visit later that Saturday. Around 7:40 p.m. she was sitting in the living room watching television with Jimmy and Lucy, who were seated on the couch. Marie saw a porcelain statuette tremble on the coffee table next to the sofa, before it suddenly flew into the air and landed on the rug. The Herrmanns were faced with a terrifying prospect: was their home haunted?

News of the seemingly paranormal activity at the Herrmann residence soon hit the New York papers, and was wired to media outlets across the United States. Reporters flocked to 1648 Redwood Path to interview the family and hopefully catch sight of something supernatural. Letters began pouring in from citizens all over the country. One, from a Mrs Helen Connolly of Revere, Massachusetts, explained that she had dealt with a similar problem in her own home, only rather than bottle caps and figurines, heavy items of furniture had moved across her rooms. Ultimately, she had discovered that the cause was a strong downdraught coming from her chimney, and had fixed it with a metal chimney cap. As this contraption only cost $9, the Herrmanns decided to try it out.

The first of many religious figures to descend on the scene was Father William McCloud of Seaford's Church of St. William the Abbot. On Monday, February 17, the priest arrived to bless the Herrmann residence. After assuring the family he had filed a request to perform a formal exorcism, Father McCloud walked from room to room reciting, "O heavenly Father, Almighty God . . . we humbly beseech thee to bless and sanctify this house . . . and may the angels of thy light dwell within the walls,"[2] while flicking holy water and encouraging the good spirits to drive out their malevolent counterparts.

The following day, a well-dressed stranger in a blue wool suit strolled into the Herrmanns' home without speaking a word and began looking around, as if making detailed observations. The family had become accustomed to strangers visiting them unannounced, and presumed he was simply another journalist. When he entered the dining room he collapsed to his knees, spending the next 10 minutes in prayer. Explaining that he was a "holy man" from the hamlet of Moriches – a 45-minute drive east on Long Island – he declared that everything was now alright, and that the Herrmanns had been forgiven. He left without elaborating.

Unfortunately, neither chimney caps, holy water, prayer, nor proclamations of forgiveness had any effect whatsoever. On the very next day, Wednesday, February 19, Detective Tozzi was in the basement with James, Lucille, and Lucy Herrmann when they heard a crash upstairs. Rushing up to the ground floor, Tozzi found a broken porcelain figure on the floor of the vacant living room. The statuette had previously stood on a small table next to the sofa, approximately 10 feet (3 m) away. Jimmy was sitting in the adjoining dining room diligently finishing his homework. Given the house's notoriously creaky wooden floorboards, Tozzi stated that he would have heard Jimmy's footsteps if he had moved from his seat.[3]

Responding to one of Detective Tozzi's theories, the Radio Corporation of America sent a team to search for abnormal radio waves around the property, but they found nothing out of the ordinary. Similarly, the Long Island Lighting Company erected an oscillograph – a tool to measure oscillations in electrical current – in the Herrmanns' basement. Three incidents occurred inside the home while the device was present, but the oscillograph failed to detect any atypical vibrations corresponding with the timing of these events.

Oddly, one far-fetched explanation came from a respected physicist. Robert Zider, a specialist in the acceleration of high-energy particles at the Brookhaven National Laboratory in central Long Island, visited the Hermann home and produced a willow dowsing rod. Walking around the house, he announced that there were streams of water flowing under the structure and into a basin, where they had likely frozen. Whenever an aeroplane passed overhead, its vibrations struck the ice, which somehow sent an electromagnetic surge back up the streams underlying the Herrmann residence, shaking its foundations. James and Lucille politely thanked him for his assistance.

February 25 was a very important date in the Herrmanns' ordeal. The strange incidents began at 7:30 a.m., when an 18-inch (46-cm) plaster statue of the Virgin Mary soared across the room and crashed into a mirror frame. Both objects sustained mild damage. One proposed explanation for the activity was that a nearby well had become unstable and was causing tremors, and the Seaford Fire Department sent a crew to investigate. They determined that the well was in excellent condition. But the firefighters weren't the only investigators to show up at 1648 Redwood Path that day.

Dr J. Gaither Pratt and Dr William Roll of Duke University's Parapsychology Lab had heard about the paranormal activity in Seaford, and travelled all the way from North Carolina to offer their services. James Herrmann was becoming increasingly exasperated and told them he would take whatever help he could get. The duo proved immediately useful, noticing some glaring errors in Tozzi's report of the case. After interviewing Officer Hughes, they learnt that, in reality, only one bottle had toppled over in the bathroom while he was present. Where Tozzi's report stated that Jimmy and his mother "actually saw"[4] the bleach bottle leap out of a box and crash on the floor, upon questioning the Herrmanns, Dr Pratt clarified that this was totally inaccurate. Moreover, though Hughes swore that he had previously inspected the bathroom and seen the bottle standing upright, he had failed to consider the possibility that it might have been tampered with after he had left the room.

Noting that 12-year-old Jimmy was present for 50 of the 67 documented incidents, Pratt and Roll wondered if the young boy was unconsciously emitting psychic energy that resulted in objects being flung about – a case of "recurrent spontaneous psychokinesis" (RSPK). "If correctly reported," they wrote, the incidents could not "be explained as easily performed, simple pranks."[5]

By the end of February, the Herrmanns were receiving up to 75 phone calls and 25 letters a day. The most frequent suggestion was that the family was being plagued by a "poltergeist" (German for "noisy ghost") – a generally non-malevolent prankster spirit from European folklore. Some scientists who contacted them believed poltergeists were real, but rather than being of supernatural origin, their activity stemmed from natural forces that humanity did not yet comprehend. Other correspondents instructed the Herrmanns to burn sulphur to get rid of "ghostlys" or urged them to communicate in a friendly manner with the visitors from outer space who had "come for America's good".[6]

Strangely, while the parapsychologists were staying at 1648 Redwood Path, carefully monitoring and interviewing the Herrmanns, there wasn't a single incident of poltergeist activity. Pratt and Roll concluded that the psychological atmosphere must have been disturbed by the influx of reporters, serving to neutralize Jimmy's "RSPK". They returned to North Carolina on February 28. Almost immediately, on March 2, the poltergeist activity resumed.

Despite the veritable circus of "experts" who were parading in and out of the Herrmann residence, contacting them by mail, or offering advice over the telephone, each and every one of them failed to apply the principle of Occam's razor: essentially, that the simplest solution is most likely the correct one. One letter, penned by an "F. Brill" and sent to *LIFE* magazine, rather than the Herrmanns, cut straight to the core of the issue. Published on April 7, 1958, it read:

> *"Sirs: Either a 'slick little trixter'* [sic] *dwells at 1648 Redwood Path in the town of Seaford, L.I. or our scientists are bypassing a power which, if consciously controlled, might be developed to greatly aid the wrecking business . . . I can't help feeling James Jr. is bored at school."*[7]

Though dozens of professionals remained convinced that paranormal events were occurring, two outsiders were sceptical. Dr Karlis Osis was a 40-year-old Latvian-born psychologist and member of the Parapsychology Foundation. Having closely followed the Herrmann case, he made several keen observations. The first was that of the more than 70 reported poltergeist incidents, none had occurred between the hours of 1 and 6 a.m. – when the Herrmann children were tucked up in bed. His second observation followed from the first: whenever poltergeist phenomena *did* occur, and Jimmy was supposedly in bed, the event always happened either in his room or very close to it. After looking into the boy's history, Osis established that Jimmy was a member of his school science club, where he might have learnt about chemical reactions. Armed with this knowledge, all Jimmy would have to do was introduce reactive substances into the bottles and then wait. The rest could be achieved by simple sleight of hand; as any police officer, psychologist, or criminologist could attest, there are often enormous discrepancies between what people *think* they see and what *actually* occurs. Osis also drew attention to a frightening incident that had occurred in the Herrmanns' basement, in which a 120-lb (54-kg) bookshelf suddenly toppled over, after which Jimmy was observed breathing heavily. Osis speculated that the child was engaging in a campaign of domestic sabotage, motivated by an adolescent urge to rebel against the authority of his disciplinarian Catholic father.[8]

On Thursday, May 15, Osis revealed his conclusions to the media. Unfortunately, his measured analysis did not sell nearly as well as paranormal sensationalism. His conclusions were buried amidst a landslide of quotes from Tozzi and the Herrmanns, who believed the house was haunted, along with Dr Pratt's claims about Jimmy's supposed RSPK.

The other person who believed that the media were being outfoxed by a 12-year-old boy was the renowned 43-year-old stage magician Milbourne Christopher. A master of sleight of hand, Christopher harbored sneaking suspicions about what was actually going on in the Herrmann household, and asked Tozzi if he would be allowed to investigate. Surprisingly, James Herrmann adamantly refused to let a magician into his home – a strange position, for even though James was a deeply religious man, he was certainly intelligent enough to understand the difference between an entertainer and a sincere practitioner of witchcraft. Undeterred, Christopher simply gathered his information from second-hand sources, then boldly claimed he could replicate each and every one of the poltergeist's tricks. He pointed out what he believed were obvious flaws in Detective Tozzi's investigation, such as stating that Jimmy could not have been responsible for the flying figurine in the living room because Tozzi was in the basement with the Herrmanns, and they would have heard him walking around. Apparently, Tozzi had never considered the possibility that the child might have secreted the figurine in his pocket or among his books *before* seating himself at the dining room table and had then thrown it from one adjoining room to the other.

When journalists attempted to interview Christopher, they were plunged into a state of confusion as objects flew through the air and bottle tops began blowing off – the magician was showing that he could convincingly recreate what was occurring at the Herrmann residence. Predictably, Milbourne Christopher's impressive, ghost-refuting displays received even less attention than Osis' deductive reasoning. The Seaford poltergeist was now a "cash cow" – one too sacred to be slaughtered on the altar of truth. Subsequent studies of the media coverage revealed widespread gross distortions in the chronology, narrative, and basic facts surrounding the case. It was also revealing that the Herrmanns refused to take polygraph tests. James Herrmann's excuse was that he was concerned the results might make Jimmy appear to be the guilty party.

In the end, regardless of whether it was a "noisy ghost" or misbehaving child, the Seaford poltergeist ceased its activities on March 10, 1958, never to resume them again.

A Nightmare on Elm Street 1984

Sudden Unexplained Nocturnal Death Syndrome

Sleep brings no solace for the teenagers in Wes Craven's 1984 classic *A Nightmare on Elm Street*. Instead, it brings the terrifying figure of serial killer Freddy Krueger with his hideously scarred face, manic leer, and bladed gloves. The movie convincingly suggested that dreams could kill – an idea that, incredibly, was inspired by a series of real unexplained deaths.

From the expressionistic style of *M* to the unsettling imagery of *The Exorcist*, many horror movies make great use of surrealism. However, it was not until Wes Craven's classic *A Nightmare on Elm Street* that horror movies truly graduated to the horrifically surreal.

In the film, the teens of suburban Springwood, Ohio are plagued by recurring nightmares featuring Freddy Krueger – a hideously burned sadist with a glove of sharpened blades, who taunts them and threatens them with murder. Incredibly, whenever he attacks them, they awake to find actual physical damage to their clothing and bodies corresponding to what transpired in their dreams. During a sleepover party in March 1981, Rod Lane looks on in horror as his sleeping girlfriend Tina Gray is viciously slashed to pieces by a seemingly invisible killer. Rod is arrested for the murder, but as he languishes in a holding cell protesting his innocence, his friend Nancy Thompson experiences an elaborate nightmare in which Krueger burns her. Awakened by the pain, she is shocked to find a scorch mark on her flesh. When Rod is found hanged in his cell – murdered by Krueger in a dream – Nancy shares her dreams with the adults at his funeral. Taken to a sleep clinic by her mother, she nearly falls prey to Krueger, but manages to wake up, dragging his signature hat out from her dream and into reality. Upon seeing the filthy fedora, Nancy's mother confides to her that Fred Krueger had once been the notorious "Springwood Slasher" – a serial child murderer who escaped justice on a technicality. Forming a vigilante mob, the parents of Elm Street barricaded Krueger in his home and burned him alive. Realizing that Krueger's ghost was now seeking revenge against those parents by slaughtering their children in their dreams, Nancy tries to do everything in her power not to fall asleep, lest she become Krueger's next victim. Eventually, she concocts a plan to draw Krueger out of the dream world into reality, where he is physically vulnerable and unable to exercise his magical powers. After a final battle in which she bests Krueger, Nancy returns to her life – and Elm Street – before the carnage Krueger wrought, as if everything had just been a bad dream. Confused to see all of her slain friends living and breathing again, carrying on as if nothing ever happened, she climbs into her boyfriend's convertible, only to realize that she's not only still asleep, but that Freddy Krueger is alive and still exercising complete control over "reality".

The inspirations behind *A Nightmare on Elm Street* and Freddy Krueger are legion, ranging from peculiar happenings in the real world, to songs, religions, and director Wes Craven's own childhood traumas. The greatest inspiration, however, was a series of unexplained deaths that occurred in the United States in the 1970s and 80s – deaths that, bizarrely, seemed linked to horrific bloodshed that took place on the other side of the world.

—

When great empires – or more recently, global superpowers – clash, invariably innocent people are caught in the middle. Such groups are usually left with two options: pick a side, or be crushed between the weight of opposing forces. Such was the lot of the Hmong people of Laos: an ancient and impoverished minority group inhabiting the country's hills and mountains in near-perfect seclusion. Though the Hmong had largely avoided the unprecedented violence that scarred the first half of the 20th century, during the decolonization struggles of the 1950s, war eventually found them.

The first sign of real trouble came in May 1954, when the armies of the waning French Empire, futilely trying to cling on to their colonies in southeast Asia, were decisively defeated by the communist forces of the Viet Minh in northern Vietnam. At the subsequent Geneva Conference, delegates from the triumphant Democratic Republic of Vietnam (DRV) and the humiliated French Republic were joined by those from both sides of the Cold War – the United States and United Kingdom representing capitalist democracy, and China and the Soviet Union representing communism. After two and a half months of negotiations, on July 21, an agreement splitting Vietnam along the 17th Parallel was signed by the DRV, France, China, the Soviet Union, and the United Kingdom. The non-communist government in southern Vietnam rejected the agreement on principle, because it divided the country, while the United States abstained, promising not to interfere. Effectively, what had formerly been French Indochina was divided into four countries: North Vietnam, South Vietnam, Cambodia, and Laos.

Looking back, the Geneva Accords were far from a clean break, rather, they were an open wound guaranteeing future bloodshed. The DRV had never seriously entertained halting its troops at the 17th Parallel; they were simply buying time. Similarly, French presence in the region was quickly replaced by American influence and open support for the virulently anti-communist Republic of Vietnam, as South Vietnam was now known. The result was the Vietnam War, a conflict that would spill over into both the newly formed kingdoms of Laos and Cambodia, claiming millions of lives.

Predictably, communism blossomed in Laos. The Pathet Lao organization, which had formed years earlier at Viet Minh headquarters, began receiving aid from the DRV in their combined communist struggle against the ruling Laotian monarchy. As with South Vietnam, the Americans believed it was of paramount importance to prevent Laos from becoming a communist state. Furthermore, the DRV was secretly smuggling troops and weapons into South Vietnam through Laos and Cambodia, circumventing the 17th Parallel – a route that became known in the United States as the "Ho Chi Minh trail". While the DRV were utilizing the Ho Chi Minh trail as early as 1959, by the mid-1960s – with American troops now fighting communist guerillas in South Vietnam to prevent the country from falling – this supply line had arguably become the most crucial strategic component of the DRV's military effort. While the United States could bombard communist targets in Laos from the air, the Geneva Accords made it illegal for them to put troops on the ground.

Enter the CIA. As early as 1960, they had been capitalizing on historic tensions between the minority Hmong hill dwellers and the lowland Lao majority, persuading the former to aid them in their secret struggle against the communist forces in Laos. The promise of resources and a salary in an area completely bereft of opportunity proved particularly enticing. Dubbed "Operation Momentum", the CIA trained and equipped 10,000–30,000 Hmong – including young children – in neighbouring Thailand, forming a task force called the Special Guerilla Unit (SGU). Their primary centre of operations was a secret CIA military base called Long Tieng, hidden in a valley 3,100 feet (940 m) up in the mountains. At first, the SGU simply collected intelligence about communist forces, but gradually their role expanded to rescuing American pilots who had been shot down by the enemy, and eventually engaging in full-blown combat. The toll exacted on the Hmong population was significant. During this "Secret War" and its fallout, more Laotian Hmong purportedly lost their lives than the 58,000 American soldiers killed in Vietnam.[1]

When the Vietnam War finally ended in defeat for the South

Vietnamese and their American allies on April 30, 1975, the few remaining US personnel were transported back home. But the Hmong people of Laos had nowhere to go. General Vang Pao – a CIA recruiter and the only Hmong to attain such a high rank in the Royal Lao Army – took stock of the situation, and made arrangements with the CIA to evacuate as many Hmong from Long Tieng to Thailand as possible. On May 13, using only three aeroplanes, American pilots evacuated the 3,500 Hmong whom Pao deemed most likely to be executed by the rapidly advancing communists. The next day, Pao made his own exodus by helicopter. The flights then abruptly stopped. The Hmong were left leaderless, demoralized, and with little time to spare. Incredibly, some 40,000 set off for Thailand on foot, carrying their children and possessions on their backs. The forces of the Pathet Lao conquered Long Tieng the next day.

On May 29, the first group of refugees arrived at the town of Hin Heup, about 46 miles (74 km) from the Thai border, only to find it barricaded. When they attempted to displace the barriers, the Pathet Lao guardsmen opened fire, killing more than 20 Hmong and injuring close to 100. Despite the efforts of the Pathet Lao, by the year's end, tens of thousands of Hmong had fled to Thailand. Countless others died, either from the perils of a long journey through the wilderness, or at the hands of vengeful communists.

In December 1975, the Laotian monarchy, headed by King Sisavang Vatthana, was overthrown by the Pathet Lao and the communist Vietnamese army, in a civil war that would claim anywhere from 20,000–60,000 Laotian lives. The Kingdom of Laos was renamed the Lao People's Democratic Republic, and military units and advisors from Vietnam were admitted into the fledgling communist state. In total, 300,000 Laotians fled the country.[2]

Within two weeks of marching into Long Tieng, the Pathet Lao commanders began disarming all Hmong who remained and sending them to "re-education" centres. There, they were forced to attend "seminars" where they performed gruelling tasks as atonement, ridding themselves of capitalist ideology. Officers were compelled to confess all the dates on which they had attacked their conquerors, to list the numbers of communist troops they had "murdered", livestock they had slaughtered or stolen, and provide an overview of the amount of property damage they had caused. Then, based upon the quality and quantity of their "crimes", the commanding Pathet Lao officer would determine the duration of an individual's "seminar". In some cases, it might last the rest of their lives. If the commanding officer doubted a captive's confession, he punished the group as a whole by reducing their rations. Within six months, these "seminars" left all of the prisoners weak and emaciated. Most were worked to death or died of malnutrition. Public servants and leaders were subjected to the same "re-education" programs.

But not every Hmong fighter submitted or fled. Knowing full well what fate awaited them under the new government, rebellious bands of Hmong, dubbed the "ChaoFa", continued to wage guerilla war against the armies of Vietnam and the ruling communists. Dubbing these rebels "American collaborators",[3] the Pathet Lao published an article in 1977 that vowed to wipe them out "to the last root".[4] When conventional warfare proved insufficient, the communists resorted to a deadly cocktail of bombardment, scorched-earth tactics such as burning Hmong villages or spraying their crops with defoliants, and chemical warfare. The effects of the latter were particularly nightmarish – when exposed to nerve gas, Hmong victims would initially feel their noses starting to run and chests tighten as cholinergic crisis set in, resulting in paralysis from muscular contraction. Struggling to breathe, they were seized by gastrointestinal pain, before vomiting and losing control of their bowels. Within minutes their muscles began to jerk uncontrollably before giving way to full epileptic seizure and death.[5] Those who survived suffered permanent neurological damage resulting in exhaustion, impaired vision, insomnia, and heart palpitations.

General Vang Pao estimated that between 1975 and 1978, 50,000 Hmong refugees were murdered using poison chemicals supplied by the Soviet Union, while 45,000 others succumbed to starvation, disease, and enemy bullets while attempting to reach Thailand.[6]

By 1981, 35,000 of those who had reached Thai refugee camps had been resettled in America. The culture shock these Hmong experienced cannot be overstated. In only a few years, they had gone from slash and burn agriculture – subsisting on rice, vegetables, and occasionally, wild boar skewered in the jungle – to 24-hour fast-food drive-throughs, monolithic supermarkets, electric toothbrushes, and an endless litany of sitcoms blasting from television sets. Though they were now free from persecution, for years the lives of the Hmong had been dominated by fear and death. Somehow, this nightmare seemed to follow them across the ocean to America, shifting shape, yet maintaining its malevolent character.

One Hmong who left his ancestral homeland was Yong Leng Thao. In July 1980, the 47-year-old relocated to Portland, Oregon with his wife, Xiong You, and their eight children. Less than a year later, on January 8, 1981, Thao was watching television after midnight. When he finally decided to turn in, he climbed into bed beside his wife, causing her to stir, but within seconds, the couple had drifted off to sleep. When Xiong woke again, it was to the sound of a man struggling to breathe. Panicking, she rolled over to rouse Thao, and gasped. He was dead.

When Multnomah county medical examiner Dr Larry V. Lewman looked down on the middle-aged Asian man lying on his autopsy slab it was like déjà vu. Only three days earlier, Xiong Tou Xiong, a seemingly healthy 29-year-old Hmong male, had died in his sleep under comparable circumstances. In both cases, despite detailed autopsies, toxicology tests, and microscopic tissue examinations, no cause of death could be determined. Completely at a loss, Lewman wrote "pending" on the report under "cause of death".[7]

Soon after, Lewman discovered two additional inexplicable Laotian refugee deaths had occurred in the past nine months. "All were very, very similar. They were restricted to males, all relatively young who died during their sleep." Lewman conceded, "I don't know what we've got."[8] But the doctor was determined to find out. Picking up the telephone, he decided to contact medical officials in other jurisdictions with significant Hmong and southeast Asian refugee populations. In the city of St. Paul, Minnesota, home to 8,000 Hmong, there had been four unexplained nocturnal deaths. Lewman also found cases in Seattle, Washington; Des Moines, Iowa; and Orange County, California. On February 17, another sleeping Hmong death was reported across the Mississippi from St. Paul in Minneapolis. By this time, Dr Lewman had documented 13 instances of unexplained sleep death among Laotian refugees in the USA since 1978. Los Angeles Hmong spokesman Kuxeng Yongchu pegged the number even higher: "There have been 19, 20, very similar deaths, and we have never had any legitimate explanation."[9]

Epidemiologist Dr Tom Prendergast first became aware of the problem when he began receiving phone calls from reporters in Minneapolis and Portland enquiring whether there had been any strange, unexplained deaths of Hmong men in Orange County. What he found were 20 clear cases of seemingly healthy refugees who were "either found dead in the morning or were observed during the night to be making some gurgling noises and in a collapsed state from which they could not be revived."[10] The first known case, the mysterious nocturnal death of Ly Doua, dated back to 1977. Crunching the numbers, Prendergast came to the startling conclusion that in the United States "half of all deaths of Hmongs [may] have been caused by this."[11] By September 1981, the Center for Disease Control had identified 35 cases.[12]

One theory floated by the baffled medical community was that adapting to the tremendous culture shock, combined with wartime trauma, may have been a key factor in the Hmong sleep fatalities. "I wish there had not been the political disaster and the warfare situation and we could remain in our native village. If we could have, I don't think this would have happened to my husband," Xiong You said, "However, I do not blame this country."[13] Having suffered terribly under the communists, the most popular explanation among the Hmong themselves was that it was a side effect of their exposure to chemical nerve agents. This hypothesis was undoubtedly bolstered by the support of General Vang Pao, now living peacefully in Missoula, Montana.

Likely responding to the nocturnal death in Des Moines, Republican congressman Jim Leach of Iowa called for a federal inquiry into both the sleep deaths and long-term effects of nerve gas on human biology. However, Dr Lewman remained unconvinced: "It just doesn't make sense to me. Nerve gas doesn't act this way. There's no evidence . . . Secondly, if it was nerve gas, why does it affect only males, and why only during the night? And if nerve gas doesn't affect people right away, [and] it takes four years, it's not very effective [as a weapon]."[14]

Rather, Lewman countered with a bold yet convincing hypothesis: Hmong men may have been unexpectedly dying in their sleep for aeons. Only now that the phenomenon had been exported to the west had it become subject to scientific analysis.

"We do see sudden, unexplained death in younger people every year, maybe four, five, six in a population of a million," Lewman explained. "But four out of 2,000 [refugees in Portland] is way out of whack. We don't know whether this occurs in the native country to this extent."[15] Dr Vu Dinh Minh, a Vietnamese physician who had worked with the Hmong perhaps more than any American medical professional, noted that "it seems relatively clear now that the mechanism is cardiac."[16]

Fortunately, one unnamed Seattle Hmong lived to tell the tale, and subsequently spent a great deal of time being examined in a laboratory. According to Dr Prendergast, "When he arrived at the hospital he was found to be in ventricular fibrillation. The heart muscle was contracting without effecting normal beats, just sort of quivering . . . With appropriate treatment, the patient survived and went on over the next several weeks to develop the typical electrocardiogram pattern of a person who had suffered a heart attack."[17] Prendergast hypothesized that the attacks entailed fluctuations in heart rhythm, such as spasms, which came and went so rapidly that autopsies would be unable to observe any permanent damage. If true, emergency cardiopulmonary resuscitation accompanied by additional medical care might save lives.

Meanwhile, Dr Lewman was familiarizing himself with a similar condition in the Philippines known as *bangungot* (nightmare) syndrome. Filipinos believed *bangungot* was preceded by terrible nightmares and resulted from falling asleep after eating a large meal. The nation's medical doctors had a more specific hypothesis: the men had likely died by overdosing on large quantities of polypeptides, a toxin found in fish sauce.

In mid-1983, both the Hmong affliction and *bangungot* were being linked with a Japanese disease called *pokkuri* – an onomatopoeia for "snap", as in "sudden" – which causes an estimated 500–1,000 sleeping deaths in Japan annually.[18] As in the Filipino and Hmong populations, *pokkuri* seemed to occur without warning in apparently healthy young men. Dr Ikuo Ishiyama of Tokyo University was sceptical of the role external toxins played in *pokkuri*, citing autopsy results. A specialist in forensic medicine, Ishiyama had discovered multiple incidences of tissue death in the heart muscles of those who had succumbed to *pokkuri*. He proposed that this resulted from depleted myoglobin, an iron- and oxygen-binding protein, which was causing coronary artery spasm.[19]

By this time, the phenomenon had been christened "Nocturnal Death Syndrome" in the West. A number of southeast Asian refugees had come forward to report that incidences *had* occurred in their ancestral communities long before they had made their way to America. In the wake of this new revelation, both the culture shock and nerve gas hypotheses were discarded. As of July 10, 1983, the unexplained nocturnal deaths of 72 southeast Asians had been recorded in the United States. Today, Sudden

Unexplained Nocturnal Death Syndrome (SUNDS) is understood as a multifactorial medical disorder to which East Asians are genetically predisposed, attacks of which sometimes encompass "night terrors".[20]

—

By the time a medical explanation for the sudden nocturnal deaths crystallized, they had long since caught the attention of filmmaker Wes Craven, who had read about them in the *L.A. Times*. Craven seems to have misremembered key details, though, saying, "none of these men were related by family or locale, though they all had similar events happen to them; they would have a disturbing nightmare that was beyond anything they'd experienced before; they would tell their families about it; and they would attempt not to sleep, because they were too frightened to go back to sleep. And in each case, when they did go back to sleep, they died."[21]

At some point, while ruminating on possible causes for the deaths and thinking "What if the death was a result of the dream? What if the dreams were actually killing these men? And what if they were all sharing a common frightening dream?"[22] Craven heard Gary Wright's 1975 pop hit "Dream Weaver". With its inexplicably sinister synth intro – which directly inspired the music of *A Nightmare on Elm Street* – and chorus lyrics "Dream Weaver, I believe you can get me through the night",[23] Craven went from "constructing a villain that existed only in dreams"[24] to one that could weave and alter the very fabric of them. He also recalled experiencing a nightmare as a child, and, upon waking, begging his mother to accompany him back into his dreams to protect him.[25] This wasn't the only childhood trauma that would have an influence on Craven's movie.

The iconic villain who would eventually star in Craven's *A Nightmare on Elm Street* first took shape on a dark night in Cleveland, Ohio in the early 1950s. Eleven-year-old Wesley Earl Craven and his older brother, Paul, were asleep in their bedroom on the second story of their apartment when the future filmmaker was roused by a noise from outside. Rubbing his eyes, Wesley climbed out of bed and made his way over to the window to see what was going on in the street below. An ominous stranger in a slouch hat and overcoat was standing outside the entrance staring directly at him. When this shadowy figure began walking towards the front door, the frightened child woke his big brother. Seizing a baseball bat, the two boys crept out of their apartment and into the hallway to meet the intruder. They found it empty. "The guy was probably just a drunk," Craven later admitted, "but I never forgot it . . . the potential that existed for an adult to take amusement from terrifying you. So that guy got the paradigm vote when it was time to create Freddy."[26]

Though the man in the slouch hat never appeared again, young Wesley was terrorized time after time by a boy who "got his newspapers on the same corner" and beat him up "quite regularly during one particular year. I finally stood up to him and he vanished."[27] The bully's name was Freddy.

Many years later, around 1982, Craven read a story in *Scientific American* that argued "the two most clashing colours to the human retina were this particular green and red. I wanted this costume that [would be recognized] if [Freddy] changed into any other thing in the room."[28] For this reason, Freddy's trademark sweater bore red and green stripes. Finally, the name "Elm Street". This particular street name was derived from a tree-lined stretch of Potsdam, New York, where Craven attended film school. Perhaps surprisingly, the street's name is actually never spoken in this classic horror.

The Serpent and the Rainbow 1988

The Strange Tale of Clairvius Narcisse

After the massive, unanticipated success of *A Nightmare on Elm Street*, director Wes Craven's next foray into the horror genre, *The Serpent and the Rainbow*, moved away from the "slasher", instead tackling zombies and the paranormal. Inspired by the book of the same name by Dr Wade Davis, Craven's movie exploited the torrid imagery of Haitian voodoo, with its zombies, rituals, and magic.

In *The Serpent and the Rainbow*, anthropologist Dr Dennis Alan receives funding from a pharmaceutical company to travel to Haiti, in search of a drug rumoured to be used in voodoo rituals for the creation of zombies. The company hopes to learn the chemical formula so that it can be repurposed as an anesthetic. Dr Alan arrives to find Haiti in revolutionary turmoil, with protesters challenging the power of the notorious dictator "Papa Doc" Duvalier. Alan soon encounters zombies and voodoo priests, but is repeatedly urged to leave the island under threat of violence by Captain Dargent Peytraud of the *Tonton Macoute* – a special-ops branch of Duvalier's paramilitary force. Following a bizarre dream, Alan comes to suspect that Peytraud is a practitioner of black magic, with the power to steal his enemies' souls and transform them into zombies. Alan comes close to acquiring the zombie-creation drug from a man named Mozart, but is abducted, tortured, and framed for murder by the *Tonton Macoute* in an effort to make him return to America.

Eventually, the *Tonton Macoute* forcibly place Alan, unconscious, on an outbound plane. To his surprise, upon waking, he discovers

Mozart has sneaked onto the aircraft. Mozart gives Alan the drug, on the condition that he spreads word of him in the US so that he can become famous. Upon returning to America, Alan is praised for his success by the pharmaceutical company, but Peytraud continues to inflict terror on him using black magic. Forced to journey back to Haiti to confront his foe, Alan is blasted with zombie powder, killed, and buried in an undead state in a graveyard. Rescued by an ally, Alan uses new-found magical abilities to defeat Peytraud at the central *Tonton Macoute* office and send him to hell. The film ends with the now-liberated people of Haiti celebrating the news that Duvalier has fled the country.

Craven's film is loosely based on the highly controversial, nonfiction book *The Serpent and the Rainbow: A Harvard Scientist's Astonishing Journey into the Secret Societies of Haitian Voodoo, Zombies, and Magic* by the Canadian ethnobotanist and anthropologist Dr Wade Davis. Published in 1985, this best-seller details Davis' adventurous research into voodoo and toxicology in Haiti.

—

Wade Davis was pursuing his undergraduate studies at Harvard when he first caught the attention of his professors. The strapping Canadian anthropologist not only had a keen intellect, he was obviously intrepid – he had successfully traversed the Darién Gap, a 150-mile (240-km) stretch of roadless, hazardous rainforest between Panama and Colombia. After graduating, Davis took a two-year break from studying, but returned to Harvard to pursue his master's degree under Dr Richard Evans Schultes. A professor in anthropology, Schultes was a remarkable and eccentric figure in his own right, having once vanished into the Amazon rainforest for 12 years while taking a semester off from teaching in order to gather medicinal flora.[1]

One afternoon in 1982, the now 28-year-old Davis was summoned to Professor Schultes' office. Schultes passed him the address of a New York psychiatrist named Dr Nathan Kline, and asked Davis if he would be able to leave for Haiti within two weeks. Kline was a polarizing figure among academics. His research in psychopharmacology proposed that many (if not most) mental afflictions had neurochemical origins. Ultimately, this approach would result in nearly 80 per cent of patients at American psychiatric facilities being prescribed medication and released onto the streets.

Davis arrived at Kline's apartment in East Manhattan two nights later, and met the bespectacled 66-year-old, along with Kline's colleague, Professor Heinz Lehmann – a former head of psychiatry at McGill University. Lehmann was a pioneer of the pharmaceutical drug chlorpromazine, which was the first successful treatment for schizophrenia.

"We understand from Professor Schultes that you are attracted to unusual places," Lehmann smiled. "We propose to send you to the frontier of death. If what we are about to tell you is true, as we believe it is, it means that there are men and women dwelling in the continuous present, where the past is dead and the future consists of fear and impossible desires."[2]

Kline and Lehmann expounded the medical field's difficulties in accurately diagnosing death, walking Davis through a history of accidental live burials and surprise reanimations on the mortuary slab, dating from Roman times to the present. Lehmann explained there were currently only two means of diagnosing death: a combination brain scan/cardiogram – expensive and yet still fallible – or the lengthy process of waiting for the onset of putrefaction. Next, Kline showed Davis a death certificate, written in French and dating from 1962, for a man named Clairvius Narcisse.

"Our problem is that this Narcisse is now very much alive and resettled in his village in the Artibonite Valley in central Haiti," Kline revealed. "He and his family claim he was the victim of a voodoo cult and that immediately following his burial he was taken from his grave as a zombie . . . Voodooists believe that their sorcerers have the power to raise innocent individuals from their graves to sell them as slaves. It is to prevent such a fate that family members may kill the body of the dead a second time, sometimes plunging a knife into the heart of the cadaver, sometimes severing the head in the coffin."[3]

Kline told Davis that Clairvius Narcisse was merely one of several "zombies" – a body without character or will – that his former student, Dr Lamarque Douyon, had encountered while working in Port-au-Prince, Haiti. However, Kline emphasized that the Narcisse case was particularly curious because Narcisse had been officially pronounced dead at the American-directed Albert Schweitzer Hospital – a thoroughly professional institution that kept meticulous records – at 1:15 p.m. on May 2, 1962. Narcisse's death had been witnessed by his sister, Angelina, and he had been buried the following morning in a cemetery north of his family village of L'Estère. A concrete slab bearing his epitaph was placed over his grave 10 days later.

In 1980, 18 years after Clairvius had been buried, Angelina was approached by a man claiming to be her deceased brother, and who knew intimate family details, at a market in L'Estère. The man told her that their younger brother had hired a sorcerer to turn him, Clairvius, into a zombie, following a land dispute between the two men. After his death, Clairvius had been unearthed from his grave, bound, and transported north, where he was forced to work on a sugar plantation alongside other zombies. Two years later, Clairvius claimed, the zombie master had been killed, breaking whatever spell he had wielded over them. Afraid of his sibling's wrath, Clairvius had then apparently spent 14 years roaming Haiti, until learning of his brother's recent death, upon which he had decided to return to L'Estère.

The story made headline news all over Haiti, and in 1981, the BBC produced a brief documentary on the case. Both Dr Douyon and the BBC went to elaborate lengths to confirm that the "zombie" really was Clairvius Narcisse, and were completely convinced, as were the residents of L'Estère. Relating the story to Davis, Kline compared the shunned state of zombies in Haiti to lepers: if it was a fraudulent claim, where was the benefit to the claimant? Narcisse's future had, to all intents and purposes, been destroyed.

Kline and Lehmann believed, largely through anecdotal evidence, that there was a Haitian folk-poison that caused people to "die", only for them to rise again and live out the rest of their days in a stupefied state, as zombies. Thirty years earlier, when Kline himself had been in Haiti, he had heard rumours of a powder that turned people into zombies and had tried, unsuccessfully, to obtain a sample. According to an elderly *houngan* (voodoo priest), the powder was sprinkled on the ground at the entryway to a victim's house, and absorbed through their feet. This induced "death", which then required a separate antidote to "resurrect" the victim.[4]

What excited Kline and Lehmann was not the prospect of creating zombies – neither man believed that zombification, in the Western sense of the term, was actually occurring – but that the properties of such a drug could be repurposed, in the form of a revolutionary anaesthetic. After all, they reminded Davis, most surgery-related deaths did not result from the procedure itself, but from the administration of these highly volatile drugs. A substance that lowered the metabolic state of a patient to the extent that they could medically be misdiagnosed as dead, but still be alive, would be perfect for these procedures. Naturally, it would have to be followed by the equally mysterious antidote. Dr Douyon had even sent Kline and Lehmann a sample of what he believed to be zombie powder. Unfortunately, lab studies had determined it to be ineffective.[5]

"What we want from you, Mr Davis, is the formula for the poison," Lehmann stated. Wade Davis was tasked with travelling to Haiti, tracking down the voodoo practitioners who had created the zombies, obtaining the drug and its antidote, learning how they prepared and employed it, and then returning to the US with samples to be tested in a laboratory. It was a tall order. In return, they offered to cover his expenses, and put him in contact with both Dr Douyon and the BBC filmmakers. Davis enthusiastically agreed. Kline handed him an envelope containing an airline ticket to Port-au-Prince, cash, and a polaroid photograph of Clairvius Narcisse. By April, Davis was on an aeroplane, headed for Haiti. And he had already formulated an idea of where to begin.

Within two days of landing in Port-au-Prince, Davis visited a man named Marcel Pierre, who had been referred to him by the BBC. The same organization had also called Marcel "the incarnation of evil". A known *houngan*, the scar-faced Marcel met Davis in a *hounfour* (voodoo temple), behind his drinking establishment, the Eagle Bar. The two successfully negotiated a price for Davis to watch Marcel prepare the "zombie powder", and procure a sample. Though Marcel put together an elaborate concoction, Davis mistrusted the *houngan*.

Having conducted some botanical research before leaving the United States, Davis hypothesized that an infamously potent psychoactive plant, *Datura* – the so-called "holy flower of the north star" – was almost certainly an ingredient in the powder. Not only was the plant topically active (its poison works on contact with the skin), but three species grew in Haiti, the seeds having been brought over by slaves from Africa. According to a book Davis had consulted at Boston's Botanical Museum, one of these species, *Datura stramonium*, was known as the "zombie's cucumber" by Haitians. Marcel had not incorporated *Datura* into his preparation – Davis felt this was a dead give-away. He was sure that the dark-green powder Marcel had prepared was a sham.

Next, Davis went to visit Kline's former student, the Haitian-born psychiatrist Dr Lamarque Douyon, at his office. Douyon had completed his psychiatric residency under Dr Lehmann at McGill University, and, observing the effects of psychotropic drugs on human subjects there, had been reminded of the tales of zombies he had heard as a boy. Utterly convinced that "zombie powder" existed, he had procured a vial of white powder from Marcel Pierre. This was the ineffective substance he had sent on to Dr Kline.

"Zombies cannot be the living dead. Death is not merely the loss of bodily function, it is the material decay of the cells and tissues," Douyon told Davis. "One does not wake up dead. However, those who have been drugged may revive."[6] When Davis asked Douyon if he had any idea what ingredients went into the powder, the psychiatrist casually listed a number of animals rumoured to be included, along with *Datura*. Both men agreed that the zombie cucumber had to be the main ingredient in the mixture. When their conversation concluded, Douyon passed Davis a copy of a legal document detailing Article 249 of the Haitian penal code, which specifically prohibited the use of zombie powder to produce a near-death-like-state, and stipulated that if such a victim was buried the crime would be classified as murder.[7]

Shortly afterwards, Davis met with the "zombie" Clairvius Narcisse, who recounted his experiences. They were largely in keeping with what Dr Kline had already told him. Narcisse even pointed to a scar on his right cheek, which he claimed was caused by a coffin nail during his burial. He also provided a vital scientific clue: he had been conscious but immobile on his deathbed, and had heard his sister crying and the doctor declare him dead. During his burial, and in the time after, he had an out-of-body experience in which his soul hovered over his grave.[8]

After Clairvius had been buried for three days, a motley band of men accompanied by a *bokor* – a male voodoo priest who practices black magic – had descended on his grave. Upon calling his name aloud, the ground suddenly opened, and he had heard drumming and the *bokor* singing. Eventually, he was resurrected, disinterred, whipped, bound, gagged, and enslaved on a plantation outside Ravine Trompette by a *bokor* named Josef Jean. Throughout this period, he had felt a profound sense of unreality, as if everything was moving at a slower pace, and that he had no will or control. Years later, he had been freed when one of the captive zombies murdered the *bokor* using a farming tool. It wasn't until later that Narcisse discovered his brother had put a spell on him on Sunday,

April 29, 1962. This sorcery had made him queasy and weak, causing him to visit the hospital late on Tuesday, and rendering him "dead" the next day. After escaping, Narcisse had avoided his brother, travelling south to live in St. Michel de L'Atalaye for eight years. When his brother died, he had returned to his home village of L'Estère, only to find himself far from welcome.

Narcisse ended their conversation with some cryptic remarks about having been taken for eight days of judgment by a powerful cabal he dared not name: "They are the masters of the country, and they do as they please."[9]

Travelling to L'Estère to get the account of Narcisse's sister, Angelina, Davis learnt that Clairvius was apparently a disreputable character. Allegedly, he had impregnated numerous women throughout the Artibonite Valley only to abandon them. This meant he had fewer financial obligations than others, a situation that gave him material benefits – such as putting a tin roof on his home – that more honourable men could not afford. He also refused to loan even small amounts of money to family members. For as long as Angelina could remember, Clairvius had been at odds with their brothers, sometimes coming to physical blows. After their parents died, he had refused to split the land with his brothers, as was Haitian custom. Thus, his death was hardly mourned by his family or community. To the contrary, it had allowed them to get on with their lives and take over his fields. Unsurprisingly, when this "dead man" returned to L'Estère in 1980, he had been told to leave, and subsequently sought police protection.[10]

Davis learnt that another documented zombie – a woman named Francina "Ti Femme" Ileus – was also disliked in her community. She had a reputation for swindling, dishonesty, and swearing at strangers for no reason. Later, Davis befriended a knowledgeable Haitian man who provided him with a vital clue: "In the belly of the nation there is something else going on. Clairvius was not made a zombie by some random criminal act. He told you he was judged.

He spoke about the masters of the land. Here he did not lie. They exist, and these are the ones you must seek, for your answers will only be found in the councils of the secret society."[11]

In the three weeks since receiving the counterfeit zombie powder from Marcel Pierre, Davis had learnt that Marcel was a member of the *Tonton Macoute* – a militia that swore allegiance to Haitian dictator François "Papa Doc" Duvalier and his son and successor, Jean-Claude "Baby Doc" Duvalier. Named after a cannibalistic Haitian bogeyman, the group had killed between 30,000–60,000 Haitians and raped countless others.[12] Marcel had used his position of power in the organization to coerce *houngans* into revealing their secrets to him. Though they had complied, he was subsequently poisoned; a fate which he had survived, albeit with horrible scarring.[13]

Davis met up with Marcel again at the Eagle Bar and told him that the powder had not worked. The two men became embroiled in a heated argument, during which Marcel exclaimed that if Davis did not think he made deadly poisons, he should drink one of Marcel's concoctions and see.

"Marcel, it is not a question of whether or not you make good poison," Davis said coolly. "I know that you can. That is why I came a thousand miles to get it. All I am telling you is that what you made me is worthless . . . You may think that the money I paid you is a lot, but for me it was nothing, for it wasn't my money. To my backers it was so little money that they will not even notice that it's gone. But if you send me back to New York with that useless powder, you will lose the potential to make thousands and thousands of dollars from us in the future."[14]

The scarred *houngan* got the message, and within a few days, met up with Davis once more to show him how to gather ingredients and prepare the *real* poison. On a moonless night, Marcel and his assistant, Jean, led Davis up to a graveyard north of Saint-Marc. There, they unearthed a child's coffin, which they brought back to the Eagle Bar, burying it in front of Marcel's *hounfour* (temple).

The next morning, Jean took the child's bones out of the casket and placed them on the ground next to a grill. Opening a sack, Marcel's assistant also removed two colourful lizards, both recently slaughtered; a dried flattened toad which Davis took to be a bouga, with a shrivelled polychaete worm entangling its leg; two marine fish; and the plants *Albizia* and *Pois gratter.* While Jean waited for the animals and child bones to roast on the grill, he ground pieces of a human tibia into a tin cup using a metal grater. Once the animals had become oily and the child's bones were nearly charcoal, he removed them from the grill into the mortar along with the fragments of tibia and the plants. He then ground the ingredients into a powder using a pestle. Finally, they buried the powder in the child's coffin outside Marcel's *hounfour*, saying it would be ready in three days.

Later, as Marcel Pierre and Wade Davis chatted over a plate of rice and beans at the Eagle Bar, Marcel instructed the young anthropologist on how to properly apply the poison. While it could be sprinkled in a crucifix formation in a victim's doorway, it could also be secreted inside their shoes, or scattered down their backs. In short, the substance was topically active – confirming Davis' initial presumption. However, Marcel was adamant that only the power of a *bokor*'s black magic could resurrect a zombie, and the closest thing to an antidote was a substance that protected against the powder. He ground and mixed this mostly floral counteragent – consisting of *Aloe vera*, *Guaiacum officinale*, *Cedrela odorata*, *Capparis cynophallophora*, *Amyris maritima*, *Capparis*, seawater, crushed mothballs, cane liquor, perfume, shaved animal bones, talc, match heads, sulphur powder, and a mysterious solution known as *magie noire* (black magic) – into a green ammonic liquid for the anthropologist. Davis noted that Jean and Marcel had been rubbing this substance all over their bodies while mixing the poison.

Three days later, the zombie powder was ready. Marcel dug it up and handed it to Davis in a sealed jar. On the evening before he flew back to the United States, Davis stumbled upon an entire field of *Datura* plants in the Artibonite Valley. So far, this part of his hypothesis seemed to have been incorrect – there still did not appear to be any *Datura* in Marcel's "real" zombie powder. Either way, Davis would soon find out.

On April 11, 1982, Wade Davis arrived at New York's Kennedy Airport carrying a tin suitcase filled with dead lizards, tarantulas, a polychaete worm, and two marine fish, all preserved in alcohol; dried flora; necklaces made of seeds; a jar of poison powder covered in red satin; two rum bottles filled with the supposed antidote; human tibia bones; a skull; a dozen powders; and a cardboard box full of herbs, which covered a duffle bag containing a live bouga toad.

When he failed to contact Dr Kline, Davis caught the next flight to Boston, where he dropped off the animal specimens with the experts at the Museum of Comparative Zoology, and took the plants to the Botanical Museum.

A few days later, the zoological experts informed Davis that the bouga toad stores vast amounts of venom (bufotenine) in the paratoid glands on its back. According to Marcel, the function of the polychaete worm was simply to enrage the toad. Placing the two live creatures together in a jar served to agitate the toad, heightening the potency of its poison. This dried toxic compound was so lethal that if half a gram touched someone's skin it would instantly triple their blood pressure, potentially causing heart failure. Apparently, human subjects exposed to bufotenine experienced fiery sensations, convulsive muscle spasms, a severe headache, long-term paralysis, nausea, a prickly feeling in the face, breathing difficulties, hallucinations, delirium, and purple skin. These effects in themselves would seem to account for Clairvius Narcisse's reported hypertension, bluish complexion, paresthesia (prickling of the skin), and acute state of confusion.

Next, Davis visited the laboratory where he had dropped off the fish specimens, and learnt that they were two varieties of blowfish. Their skin and internal organs contained vast reservoirs of tetrodotoxin, a fatal neurotoxin 500 times more potent than cyanide. A lethal dose could fit on a pin-head. Inside B.W. Halstead's

Poisonous and Venomous Marine Animals of the World, Davis found a summary of the effects of tetrodotoxin poison [*italics* added by Davis]:

> "The onset and types of symptoms in puffer poisoning vary greatly depending on the person and amount of poison ingested. However, symptoms of *malaise*, pallor, dizziness, *paresthesias* of the lips and tongue and ataxia develop. The *paresthesias* which the victim usually describes as a *tingling or prickling sensation* may subsequently involve the fingers and toes, then spread to other portions of the extremities and gradually develop into severe numbness. In some cases the numbness may involve the entire body, in which instances the patients have stated that it felt as though *their bodies were floating.* Hypersalivation, profuse sweating, extreme weakness, headache, *subnormal temperatures*, decreased blood pressure, and a rapid weak pulse usually appear early. Gastrointestinal symptoms of nausea, vomiting, diarrhea and epigastric pain are sometimes present. Apparently the pupils are constricted during the initial stage and later become dilated. As the disease progresses the eyes become fixed and the pupillary and corneal reflexes are lost . . . Shortly after the development of paresthesias, respiratory distress becomes very pronounced and . . . the *lips, extremities, and body become intensely cyanotic.* Muscular twitching becomes progressively worse and finally terminates in *extensive paralysis.* The first areas to become paralyzed are usually the throat and larynx, resulting in aphonia, *dysphagia*, and *complete aphagia. The muscles of the extremities become completely paralyzed and the patient is unable to move.* As the end approaches the eyes of the *victim become glassy. The victim may become comatose but in most cases retains consciousness, and the mental faculties remain acute until shortly before death.*"[15]

At once, Wade Davis realized this single ingredient *alone* could account for the vast majority of Narcisse's symptoms. More to the point, it might result in a person being erroneously declared dead. He found two blowfish-related cases in Japan where this exact thing had occurred. In fact, if a person in Japan died from blowfish poisoning, they were typically left to lie beside their casket for three days before burial, just to make sure.

Excited, Davis notified Kline immediately, and sent the dried blowfish powder to Professor Leon Roizin at the New York State Psychiatric Institute so it could be tested on rats. Davis chose not to reveal the origin or nature of the poison to Roizin. When Davis visited Roizin for the results, the psychiatrist demonstrated the effects of the powder on an extremely aggressive rhesus monkey. Within 20 minutes of exposure, the violent primate sunk into a nine-hour-long catatonia. "Some pretty odd drugs have passed through this laboratory," Roizin remarked. "This without doubt is the most peculiar."[16] Davis asked Roizin about the potential pharmacological uses of the powder. "Perhaps cardiovascular surgery," he replied. "It is curious how the heart remains unaffected while the body is totally anesthetized. Also in psychiatry, it might be of use treating something like psychotic excitement."[17]

While Davis was receiving accolades from Dr Kline and a slew of other scientists and academics, he was all too aware that the puzzle of the Haitian zombie was far from solved. Firstly, he had yet to find the elusive antidote that would theoretically bring the subject back from their lowered metabolic state. Moreover, Davis felt he had missed a crucial anthropological point. Pharmacology certainly explained why the subject believed they had died, but Davis remained clueless as to how the pervading voodoo culture allowed the victims, perpetrators, and Haitian public to view this poisoning as "zombification" and the poisoned as "zombies".

With Kline requesting more samples of the zombie powder, and Davis' own curiosity about voodoo peaking, the young anthropologist returned to the Caribbean in July. Having obtained an initial sample of zombie powder, Davis had little difficulty finding more. Though the poison provided to him by other *houngans* consisted of ingredients that had not been present in Marcel's concoction, and several of Marcel's additions had been missing, they nevertheless *all* contained blowfish, a bouga toad and worm, and *Albizia lebbeck* – which was known to cause a tingling sensation.

Davis learnt that when a zombie is removed from its grave it is always fed a paste consisting of potato, cane syrup, and *Datura*. This revelation sent his mind reeling. His preliminary hypothesis that *Datura stramonium* was involved in the zombification process had been correct, but not in the manner he had assumed. Rather than the "zombie's cucumber" plunging the victim into the low metabolic state, the psychotropic served two specific functions in the aftermath. Firstly, *Datura stramonium* contained the chemical atropine which could act as an antidote to tetrodotoxin. Perhaps more importantly, while tetrodotoxin acted upon the victim's physiology, the highly psychoactive *Datura* would activate or enhance the victim's psychosis immediately after their resurrection. For Wade Davis, the pharmacological mystery had now been solved.

However, he still longed to understand how Haitian voodoo culture led people to interpret the near-fatal drugging and revival of a person as zombification, and how and why a particular victim was chosen.

Recalling Clairvius Narcisse's references to being judged by the "masters of the land", Davis learnt through one of his *houngan* contacts about secret societies called *Bizangos*, which conducted voodoo rites. Though much of the peasantry swore the *Bizangos* were evil and cannibalized children, Davis repeatedly insisted to his contacts that he wished to attend a *Bizango* gathering. His wish was finally granted – to his surprise, he was generally treated hospitably and wowed by a cavalcade of pageantry, hypnotic drumming, dancing, singing, and chanting.[18]

Shortly before Wade Davis left Haiti, he was introduced to Jean-Jacques Leophin: a powerful *Bizango* president. Leophin explained to him that the *Bizangos* were forged by the Makala nations in Africa long before they ever encountered Europeans. They had been created to keep order in the community. Anybody who belonged to a *Bizango* fell under its protection, as did their families, effectively meaning that the *Bizango* watched over everyone. One way to offer protection was by punishing sowers of discord. Through a complex process, these troublemakers would be brought before the *Bizango* to be judged for violating the "seven actions". If found guilty, it could result in their "death" and resurrection as a "zombie". Leophin explained that these seven actions were: (1) material greed at the expense of one's family and dependants, (2) showing disrespect to one's fellow man, (3) speaking ill of the *Bizango*, (4) taking another man's wife, (5) gossiping and defaming the character of others, (6) hurting one's own family, and (7) unjustly preventing another person from working the land. At last, Davis now understood why Clairvius Narcisse and Ti Femme had been made into zombies. They had lived their lives in contravention of the "seven actions", and been punished accordingly by the *Bizango*.

Far from being underground criminal enterprises at odds with the state, the *Bizangos* and the Duvalier dictatorship relied on each other; in fact, the official government of Haiti needed the *Bizangos*' support far more than the *Bizangos* needed the government's.

"Imagine what would happen if some invaders landed in some remote corner of [Haiti's] Department of the North-West," Leophin mused. "They would be dead before they left the beaches. Not by the hand of the government. It is the country itself that has been prepared for such things since ancient times . . . The people in the government in Port-au-Prince must cooperate with us. We were here before them, and if we didn't want them, they wouldn't be where they are. There are not many guns in the country, but those that there are, we have them."[19]

With that revelation, everything now seemed to make sense. To Davis, it was clear that voodoo was not a niche culture hiding in the shadows of an apparently westernized Haitian state. Haiti was voodoo, and voodoo was Haiti – a little piece of Africa dislodged and cast into the Caribbean by the transatlantic slave trade. It is for *this* reason that Haitians viewed a person made dormant by tetrodotoxin and revived with *Datura* as a zombie rather than a victim of poisoning. They did not interpret the world through the sceptical lens of western science. Rather, their perspective was based on the proud traditions that their ancestors had carried across the Atlantic with them, when, centuries before, they had been torn from their homelands.

The Silence of the Lambs 1991

Ted Bundy,
The Green River Killer,
Gary Heidnik,
Ed Kemper,
Jerry Brudos,
Dr Alfredo Balli Trevino,
Andrei Chikatilo,
and The Monster of Florence

Jonathan Demme's *The Silence of the Lambs* introduced cinema audiences to the fictional serial killers Dr Hannibal Lecter and "Buffalo Bill". In reality, both characters are fusions of multiple real-life murderers, hailing from places as far afield as Russia, Mexico, the Western United States, and Italy.

Based on the eponymous 1988 novel by author Thomas Harris, *The Silence of the Lambs* is generally regarded as the most successful psychological horror film of all time. Released in 1991, Jonathan Demme's critically acclaimed serial killer classic grossed $272.7 million at the box office, garnered seven Academy Award nominations, and became only the third film in history to win each of the "Big Five" categories: Best Film, Best Director, Best Actor (Anthony Hopkins), Best Actress (Jodie Foster), and Best Adapted Screenplay (Ted Tally). A mere 20 years after its release, the U.S. Library of Congress declared it "culturally, historically, or aesthetically significant" and worthy of preservation by the National Film Registry. A superb screenplay and unforgettable performances by Jodie Foster, Anthony Hopkins, and Ted Levine elevate the film to the level of high art.

The film centres on a deranged serial killer who is abducting young women in the American Midwest, shooting and skinning them, then dumping their mutilated bodies into rivers across the United States. Despite the best efforts of the FBI's Behavioral Science Unit (BSU) to bring the perpetrator to justice, the crudely named "Buffalo Bill" continues to elude them. Seeking insight into the killer's psychology, BSU head Jack Crawford sends star FBI trainee Clarice Starling to consult with Dr Hannibal "The Cannibal" Lecter, an incarcerated psychiatrist with a genius-level IQ and penchant for torturing and devouring people whom he deems vulgar.

Starling forms an unlikely bond with the psychopathic savant, who provides her with mentorship and cryptic clues to help track down "Buffalo Bill". Eventually she comes to realize that Lecter knows the killer's true identity.

When the daughter of an influential U.S. senator is captured by Bill, a desperate Starling and Crawford concoct a fake offer to have Lecter transferred to a nicer facility in exchange for information. He agrees. But their efforts go terribly awry when Lecter's psychiatrist, the self-important Dr Frederick Chilton, secretly exposes the charade to Lecter, hoping to undermine the FBI and learn Buffalo Bill's identity from Lecter himself. While investigating a murder in Belvedere, Ohio, Clarice inadvertently stumbles into Bill's lair.

Meanwhile, Lecter escapes and disappears. Lost in the darkness of Buffalo Bill's basement, Starling manages to take down the killer and rescues the kidnapped girl. At the film's finale, while attending her FBI graduation ceremony, Starling receives a phone call from Dr Lecter, who assures her he has no plans to pursue her and ends with "I'm having an old friend for dinner."

The notion of an intelligent and incarcerated serial killer working with law enforcement to help apprehend another serial killer was derived from Ted Bundy's meetings with detectives

Dave Reichert and Bob Keppel, who wanted his help in catching the "Green River Killer". Retired FBI profiler John Douglas has frequently boasted of being the inspiration for Jack Crawford. However, the true brilliance of *The Silence of the Lambs* lies within the allure of its two serial killers. Jame Gumb, better known as "Buffalo Bill", is a nightmarish combination of six real-life murderers: Ed Gein (whose fascination with human skin was previously discussed in *Psycho*), Ted Bundy (who used ruses to capture his victims), the "Green River Killer" (who dumped his victims in rivers), Gary Heidnik (who trapped his victims in a pit in his basement), Edmund Emil Kemper III (who blamed his crimes on childhood abuse), and Jerry Brudos (whose murders included transvestic elements).

Aside from playing the part of Bundy in the killer-hunts-killer narrative, Dr Hannibal Lecter is based on three additional killers: the intellectual murderer Dr Alfredo Ballí Treviño, the elusive "Monster of Florence", and the cannibalistic "Rostov Ripper" Andrei Chikatilo. These last two influences are woven into Lecter's backstory, and their profound impact on the character's psychology and behaviour are made clear in Thomas Harris' subsequent novels *Hannibal* (1999) and *Hannibal Rising* (2006), both of which were later turned into eponymous movies in the Hannibal Lecter franchise.

—

The first of the murderers to have inspired the character of "Buffalo Bill" is arguably the most infamous serial killer in American history: Theodore Robert Bundy, who sexually assaulted and murdered at least 30 young women and girls from 1974 to 1978. Bundy was a highly organized and mobile offender, claiming victims in Washington, Oregon, Idaho, California, Utah, Colorado, and Florida. While his modus operandi evolved over three distinct stages, his use of elaborate ruses – starting with the March 1974 abduction and murder of Donna Gail Manson in Olympia – is generally considered the apex of his criminal sophistication.

Frequenting university and college campuses after dark, Bundy relied on props such as crutches and casts to feign temporary disability. Then, positioning himself within walking distance of his tan Volkswagen Beetle, he waited for an attractive young lady to emerge. Once he spotted a suitable victim, he began his routine, struggling to carry a stack of books to his car in an intentionally pathetic display. Inevitably, a female target would take pity and offer to assist him – a selfless proposition that Bundy accepted with feigned gratitude. The moment the victim reached his car, Bundy would bludgeon her with a tyre iron, bundle her unconscious form into the back of the Beetle, and drive out into the American wilderness. After he finished sexually assaulting and murdering his victim, he would decapitate them with a hacksaw, then drive back to Seattle, leaving their body in the pines. A necrophile, Bundy kept the severed heads in his home, periodically returning to the wilderness to further abuse the mutilated corpses.[1]

In August 1974 Bundy was accepted at the University of Utah Law School. He moved from Seattle to Salt Lake City, Utah, but continued to kill. After a string of murders that spanned the neighbouring states of Utah, Idaho, and Colorado, Bundy was finally arrested in Granger, Utah. But more were to die at Bundy's hands before he was stopped for good. Following two successful escapes from custody in Utah, he found himself on the FBI's Ten Most Wanted list. He was swiftly recaptured after the first escape, but after the second he stole a car and eventually made his way to Tallahassee, Florida, arriving on the morning of January 8, 1978. Whether unwilling or unable to suppress his homicidal urges, within a week of renting an apartment he rampaged through the Chi Omega sorority house at Florida State University, murdering Margaret Bowman and Lisa Levy and wounding two other sorority sisters. Bundy then headed east to Lake City where he raped and killed 12-year-old Kimberly Leach, leaving her body in a shed. His reign of terror finally came to an end at 1 a.m. on February 15, 1978, when policeman David Lee pulled over his stolen Volkswagen Bug in Pensacola, Florida. The two physically struggled, but Bundy was eventually cuffed, arrested, and transported to the local jail. Along the way, the still unidentified Bundy remarked, "I wish you had killed me."[2]

Bundy, a former law student, chose to represent himself at his June 1979 trial in Miami – the first nationally televised trial in American history. There, his psychopathic grandstanding and contempt for authority were on full display. Damned by forensic odontology and eye-witness testimony, he was convicted by a jury after less than seven hours of deliberation, and sentenced to die by electrocution for the murders of Lisa Levy and Margaret Bowman. Six months later he received a third death sentence, after a separate trial in Orlando convicted him of killing Kimberly Leach.

While awaiting his execution on Florida's death row, Bundy met with investigators from various police departments, offering droplets of information about his crimes, in the hopes that his death sentence might be commuted if he proved more useful to the criminal justice system alive than dead. When another particularly elusive and prolific serial murderer emerged in Washington State in 1982, Detective Dave Reichert and former Bundy sleuth Detective Robert Keppel seized the opportunity to visit and converse with Bundy on a regular basis. Though they privately doubted the prisoner could provide much useful insight into this new predator, Keppel hoped Bundy would inadvertently open up about his own murders during the process.

Ironically, some of Bundy's investigative suggestions would later prove to have been accurate. Not that he was able to gloat. On January 24, 1989, Theodore Robert Bundy met his end in Florida's electric chair, never having learnt the identity of the man the media had dubbed the "Green River Killer".

—

Whereas Ted Bundy was notable for his elaborate methods of procuring victims, the Green River Killer's moniker arose from his trademark body-disposal techniques. On July 15, 1982, two young boys in Kent, Washington looked into the Green River only to discover the corpse of 16-year-old sex worker Wendy Lee Coffield caught against the pilings of the Peck Bridge. She had been strangled to death. This grim revelation was followed on August 12 by the discovery of another missing sex worker from the Seattle suburb of SeaTac, Debra Lynn Bonner, 23. Bonner had died from strangulation, and her body was found snagged on branches in the Green River a quarter of a mile (0.4 km) south of Coffield's.

Though the Green River was beginning to give up its macabre secrets it wasn't until the fateful day of August 15, 1982 that the King County Sheriff's Office came to the grim realization that they had "another Bundy" on their hands. Rafting down the Green River in search of bottles, a local man spotted the bodies of Marcia Fay Chapman, 31, and Cynthia Jean Hinds, 17, floating just below the surface. The treasure hunter alerted the police immediately, and Detective Dave Reichert, Patrol Officer Sue Peters, and Major Dick Kraske soon arrived at the scene. Reichert and Peters began carefully treading down the muddy, overgrown riverbank to get a better look at the bodies. As they drew closer they noticed heavy stones on the victims' torsos which had prevented them from bobbing completely to the surface. Without warning, Reichert slipped, nearly falling into the river. To his horror, he now saw a third body – that of a teenage girl – lying by the river, a pair of blue shorts knotted around her neck. She would later be identified as 16-year-old Opal Charmaine Mills.

Following the terrible revelations of August 15, the elusive Green River Killer stopped dumping bodies in the water, choosing instead to conceal them in forested areas – sometimes leaving several in the same location – where he could revisit them for necrophilic sex. Despite the creation of a well-funded taskforce headed by Dave Reichert and Robert Keppel, the killer claimed dozens more victims over the next few years, until seeming to stop in the latter half of the decade.

With the arrival of the new millennium came significant improvements in DNA analysis, and the taskforce began testing and retesting the many biological samples they had collected from suspects over nearly 20 years. By October 2001 they had a match.

On November 30, 2001, Gary Leon Ridgway – a mild-mannered husband and father – was arrested at the Kenworth Truck Factory where he worked as an automobile painter, and charged with four counts of murder. Two years later, in exchange for being spared the death penalty, he pleaded guilty to murdering 48 women, mostly sex workers, in the SeaTac area. The body count rose to 49 on December 21, 2010, after hikers found the skull of Rebecca Marrero in Auburn, Washington, and Ridgway admitted to the slaying.

Gary Leon Ridgway is believed to be responsible for the deaths of 71 women from 1982–2001, and is currently the most prolific known "lust murderer" in the history of the United States.

—

Forty-three-year-old Gary Michael Heidnik was a walking paradox: a high school drop-out plagued by severe mental illness, who nevertheless managed to make half a million dollars playing the stock market. But for Heidnik, money was simply the means to a greater end.

Obsessed with building a "harem" of African-American sex slaves, Heidnik dug a pit in the basement of his Philadelphia home at 3520 North Marshall. Beginning with the abduction of Josefina Rivera on November 25, 1986, over the next two months, Heidnik added five more women to his subterranean pit. Keeping his captives on a starvation diet, he raped and tortured them on a routine basis, meting out severe punishments for insubordination. He encouraged the women to inform on each other, with some success, in exchange for preferential treatment. When Sandra

Lindsay unexpectedly perished after a violent "re-education" session, Heidnik dismembered her body with a power saw, sliced off her flesh, boiled her head in a pot, cooked the remains, and fed them to his dogs. In another fatal disciplinary exercise, Heidnik chained three of the prisoners in the pit and filled it with cold water. Next, after stripping the insulation from an extension cord to expose the wire, he pressed it to their chains, shocking them with the electrical current and fatally electrocuting 23-year-old Deborah Dudley. Heidnik transported Dudley's body to New Jersey where he concealed it in the Pine Barrens.

During her three months of captivity, Josefina Rivera cooperated with Heidnik, even aiding him in the abduction and torture of the other women. By doing so, she slowly gained his trust. On March 24, 1987, Rivera convinced Heidnik to let her pay a brief visit to her family. He agreed, telling her to return promptly, and waited for her in a nearby car park. Rivera calmly walked to a phone and dialled 911. Gary Michael Heidnik was arrested on the spot, his home raided, and surviving captives freed. Convicted on two counts of first-degree murder on July 1, 1988, he died by lethal injection in the State Correctional Institution at Rockview on July 6, 1999.

—

Having recently returned to the public imagination by way of the hit Netflix series, *Mindhunter*, Edmund Emil Kemper III remains one of America's most notorious serial killers. Standing 6 feet 9 inches (2 m) tall, "Big Ed" preyed on female hitchhikers over a period of 11 months in and around Santa Cruz, California. As the majority of his victims were students at Fresno State University or the University College of Santa Cruz, he was christened the "Co-Ed Killer". Unsurprisingly, given the circumstances of his crimes, Kemper is remembered as a lust killer: he mutilated his victims' corpses, engaged in post-mortem sex with their remains, and even dabbled in cannibalism. Yet, none of this would have transpired if he had remained incarcerated for a comparatively mundane double-homicide he had committed in 1964.

Ridiculed and derided by his alcoholic mother, Clarnell, a "sick angry woman",[3] 14-year-old Ed had gone to live with his paternal grandparents at their ranch in the mountains of North Fork, California. Unfortunately, he found his grandma Maude every bit as "emasculating"[4] as his allegedly man-hating mother. On August 27, 1964, the two became embroiled in a bitter argument at the kitchen table, and Ed stormed out in a huff. Seizing a hunting rifle his grandfather had given him, he returned to the kitchen and shot her in the back of the head, before firing two more bullets into her torso. Knowing that his grandfather would soon return home to find his wife dead on the kitchen floor, Ed intercepted him in the driveway and murdered him in similar fashion. Having given little thought to what would transpire after the killings, Ed telephoned the police and turned himself in. While in custody, he remarked, "I just wanted to see what it felt like to kill grandma."[5] Incorrectly diagnosed with paranoid schizophrenia, the 15-year-old was committed to the state psychiatric hospital at Atascadero, and released back into his mother's care on December 18, 1969.

Two-and-a-half years later, at the end of his co-ed murder spree, he beat his mother to death in her bed with a hammer, cut off her head – as he had with the young hitchhikers – and sexually penetrated it. When he attempted to put her tongue and larynx into the garbage disposal, the device rejected them, prompting Ed to note, "That seemed appropriate as much as she'd bitched and yelled and screamed at me over so many years."[6] Not long after, history repeated itself, and he telephoned the local authorities to tell them what he had done and to give himself up.

Edmund Emil Kemper III has been held at California Medical Facility at Vacaville for the past 45 years, where he continues to receive letters from adoring fans.[7]

—

With his ruddy face, double-chin, thinning hair, and complete lack of style, 23-year-old Jerry Brudos was hardly up to his girlfriend Ralphene Schwinler's standards. Yet, for all his outward faults, he seemed funny, sensitive, and dependable. More to the point, 17-year-old Ralphene was desperate to move out of her parents' house. Six weeks after she became pregnant with his child in 1962, they were husband and wife.

By 1968, the Brudoses had a son and a daughter, and after years of moving around Oregon, finally settled into a house in Salem, the state capital. Unfortunately, Jerry struggled to find work, and began puttering around the house becoming increasingly overweight. When Ralphene finally confronted her husband about his weight, the portly electrician sulkily left the room. Moments later he returned, now clad in a bra, girdle, stockings with garters, and high heels. He stood there, staring at her expressionlessly. Though Ralphene thought he looked completely ridiculous, there was something about his manner that made her fearful. In the end, she responded with an apprehensive laugh, and put it out of her mind. Jerry slouched out of the room with a disappointed look on his face.[8] Ralphene's reaction might have been somewhat different had she known what was going on in their garage.

Between January 1968 and April 1969, Jerry Brudos murdered four women in his home, raping them ante- and post-mortem, excising their breasts and feet, and keeping the latter in a chest freezer in the garage, next to the frozen peas. In some cases, he forced the women to model lingerie and stilettos while he snapped photographs, continuing to dress and pose their bodies after death. His fetish for women's clothing and shoes was also transvestic, and Brudos regularly pleasured himself while wearing high heel shoes.[9]

Fourteen years before Gary Ridgway made national headlines dumping bodies in the Green River, Brudos was doing a much more effective job sinking his victims in the nearby Williamette. Gifted with extraordinary physical strength, he not only carried his victims' bodies from his vehicle to the riverbank, but also the car engines, transmissions, and railroad irons he used to weigh them down. Eventually, his unsettling behaviour – lurking around Callahan Hall, a student residence building at the University of Oregon – brought him increased police attention, ultimately leading to his arrest and conviction. When the police raided his Salem home they found a trove of high heel shoes, stolen underwear, and incriminating photographs.

On June 28, 1969, Jerome Henry Brudos pleaded guilty to the first-degree murders of Jan Whitney, Karen Sprinker, and Linda Salee. He also confessed to the murder of Linda Slawson, but was not convicted, as unlike the other cases he had not photographed her body. He lived out the rest of his days behind bars at Oregon State Penitentiary, and spent the next 37 years stockpiling women's shoe catalogues in his cell. He died of liver cancer at the age of 67 on March 28, 2006.

—

Extremely intelligent, utterly devoid of empathy, and yet eerily charismatic, Dr Hannibal Lecter is the terrifying killer at the heart of the *Hannibal* books and films. Just like Buffalo Bill, the key aspects of the character – his backstory, personality, penchant for cannibalism, and affinity for Florence, Italy – were inspired by a number of real-life murderers.

During the early 1960s, long before Thomas Harris was the internationally-renowned author of the *Hannibal* book series, he was an English major at Baylor University in Texas, supporting himself by reporting on crime for local news. While the 23-year-old wrote for the respectable *Waco Times-Herald*, he also covered crime for *Argosy*: a pulp magazine always struggling to stay financially afloat. Founded in the 19th century, the publication relied heavily on the popularity of its true-crime section.

In 1963, Harris received an assignment from *Argosy* that would take him south of the US border. He was to interview the aptly named Dykes Askew Simmons, a Texan convicted of triple-murder while holidaying in Mexico and subsequently sentenced to die amidst great controversy.

When Harris arrived at Nuevo Leon State Prison in Monterrey to speak with Simmons, he learnt the Texan had been shot and gravely injured during an ill-fated escape attempt. If not for the efforts of one Dr Alfredo Ballí Treviño, Simmons wouldn't have been alive to give his side of the story. Intrigued, Harris sat down to converse with Dr Treviño, who appeared to be the prison doctor, and found himself in the presence of a highly composed and disarmingly intelligent gentleman. "[A] small, lithe man with dark-red hair",[10] Treviño rested his jaw elegantly on steepled hands as they spoke, probing Harris with incisive questions, almost as if he were psychologically examining the young reporter. Treviño even offered Harris advice on how to put Simmons at ease. Eventually, Treviño excused himself, saying he had patients to attend to – impoverished villagers brought in by the guards. Harris had enjoyed the good doctor's company so much that he invited him to lunch if Treviño ever found himself in Texas.

"Certainly, I will, when next I travel,"[11] he answered, sincerely.

It was only after Treviño's departure that Harris learnt he was not a prison doctor at all – he was actually an inmate who had been convicted of murder. The prison warden described Treviño as an "insane" surgeon who had used his medical knowledge to fit his victim's remains inside a tiny box.

According to the Mexican crime writer, Diego Enrique Osorno, Treviño was once known as "The Werewolf of Nuevo Leon". In 2013, many years after using the doctor as inspiration for Hannibal Lecter, Harris recruited Osorno to uncover as much detail about the doctor's crimes as possible. It transpired that as a young medical intern, Treviño had slashed his lover Jesús Castillo Rangel's throat with a scalpel in what had been called a "crime of passion". Then, using his significant surgical skills, he had dismembered Rangel's corpse, crammed the pieces into a small box, and buried it. The remains were later uncovered by Treviño's uncle, leading to the doctor's arrest.[12]

Dr Alfredo Ballí Treviño died in 2009, aged 81, likely never suspecting he had inspired one of the most infamous villains in cinematic history. Setting aside the intricate dismemberment along with his elevated social status and intellect, his crime was actually all too typical. By all accounts, the disgraced doctor spent the remaining years of his life trying to put his dark past behind him and treating the indigent at the poorest barrio in Monterrey.

—

Born on October 16, 1936, in Ukraine (then part of the USSR), Andrei Romanovich Chikatilo's childhood was deformed by the horrors of Communist economic policy. Thanks to Joseph Stalin's mandatory collectivization of agriculture, the Ukrainian people suffered terribly during the *Holodomor,* or Great Famine of 1932–33, which claimed the lives of between 3 and 12 million citizens. While the worst had passed by the time of Chikatilo's birth, food remained relatively scarce in Ukraine, and sometimes his family resorted to eating grass and leaves. Ukraine had once been known as "The Bread Basket of Europe", but Chikatilo claimed to have tasted bread for the first time when he was 12. From his earliest memories, he recalled his mother, Anna, telling him of how his four-year-old brother Stepan had been murdered and cannibalized by their starving neighbours.

Regularly beaten and shamed by Anna for repeated bedwetting, young Chikatilo's life became even worse when Hitler's armies rolled into Ukraine in the summer of 1941. His father, Roman, was conscripted into the Red Army and shipped off to fight the Germans, leaving five-year-old Andrei and his mother to fend for themselves. During this important formative stage of his development, Chikatilo saw countless people shot, incinerated, and blown to pieces by the invading forces. He often hid for hours or days at a time in darkened cellars or ditches to avoid being killed, once watching helplessly as his family's hut was burned to the ground. It has been speculated that he may have even witnessed his mother being raped by a German soldier, as she gave birth to a daughter, Tatyana, in 1943.

In September 1944, as the German armies retreated, Chikatilo began attending school. While he was a keen and intelligent student, he was bullied relentlessly due to his small stature, poor eyesight, and timidity. His situation did not improve after the war, when he learnt that his father had been wounded and captured by the Germans in 1943. Falling into enemy hands rather than fighting to the death was considered treachery in the Soviet Union, and cast a pall over his family. Worse, Ukraine was plunged into a second famine, which left Chikatilo so starved that his belly swelled up and he began passing out from hunger.

While many of his peers endured these same horrible conditions, upon reaching puberty, Andrei Chikatilo realized that he also suffered from a uniquely humiliating and endlessly frustrating condition – chronic impotence. Worse, he discovered to his horror that physically dominating smaller children was the only way he could climax sexually. Though he would have girlfriends and even marry, Chikatilo could never maintain an erection long enough for sexual intercourse. In the end, he satisfied his urges through hurting young women and boys. One day, while in his mid-40s, he murdered his first victim. From that point on, he killed relentlessly.

From 1978 to 1990, Chikatilo murdered more than 50 people,[13] often utilizing the Soviet railway system to prey upon young female sex workers, teenage girls, and pre-pubescent children of both sexes. During his frenzied stabbing, biting, and mutilation of his victims, he began to occasionally devour their flesh – a practice that would later be linked to his recollections of his brother's murder and cannibalization.

Chikatilo was eventually arrested on November 20, 1990, and

incorrectly deemed by the authorities to be the Soviet Union's first and only serial killer. Though he claimed more than 56 victims, in April 1992, Chikatilo was tried on 53 counts of murder in Rostov, and on October 14 was convicted of 52 killings by Judge Leonid Akubzhanov. On Valentine's Day, 1994, the "Rostov Ripper" was led from his cell to a sound-proofed room and executed by gunshot to the head.

—

In the *Silence of the Lambs*, Hannibal's love for the city of Florence is conveyed through the sketches of notable Florentine landmarks that adorn his otherwise barren cell. He claims to have drawn them from memory alone, and one of them – a view of the Duomo from Forte di Belvedere – is possibly a coded clue to Buffalo Bill's identity, as Bill is later tracked down in Belvedere, Ohio. The links between Hannibal and Florence are further expanded upon in the sequel book and film, *Hannibal*.

For more than 500 years, Florence has been associated with beauty and the pinnacle of human achievement. Under the ruling Medici Family, it became the "Cradle of the Renaissance", providing patronage to some of Europe's most brilliant artists and minds – Botticelli, Galileo, Leonardo da Vinci, Petrarch, Dante, and Niccolo Machiavelli, to name but a few. A city of stunning architecture, with the Palazzo Vecchio and the Duomo of Santa Maria del Fiore looming over the sun-baked streets, it is the urban embodiment of the Apollonian ethic: symmetry, order, and self-mastery.

In 1968, something wholly antithetical to the Florentine spirit appeared in the city – something violent and degenerate. It mocked Florence's high aspirations by exposing its hypocrisies. At the time, Italy held fast to its traditional Catholic values, including abstinence from sex until marriage. Socially, this manifested in a lack of spaces in the city for unmarried men and women to be together in privacy. Courting couples and philanderers responded to these prohibitions by driving into the hills on the outskirts of the city to kiss or have sex in their cars. There was even a local joke that a third of Florentines were conceived in a car. This practice was so prevalent that it attracted nearly as many voyeurs as lovers. Collectively, these peepers were given the name *Indiani*[14] for their skill at concealing themselves and creeping around in the dark. The *Indiani* sub-culture was shameless, dividing its members into "tribes" who laid claim to different areas of the surrounding hills as their own voyeuristic hot spots.

Though a married woman, 32-year-old Barbara Locci had developed a local reputation for promiscuity, earning her the nickname *Ape Regina*, or "queen bee".[15] On August 21, 1968, she was parked on a country road in the small town of Signa with one of her many lovers, 29-year-old Antonio Lo Bianco. Barbara's six-year-old son Natalino Mele lay sleeping in the back seat. At some stage, a gunman approached the car and shot the couple dead using a .22-calibre Beretta pistol. The child survived the attack and walked to the closest farmhouse. The *carabinieri* quickly concluded that Locci's older husband, Stefano Mele, had committed the murders in a jealous rage. He was convicted of the crime, all the time protesting his innocence and pointing the finger at Barbara's lovers.

Meanwhile, the killings continued. On September 15, 1974, unwed teenagers Pasquale Gentilcore and Stefania Pettini were being intimate in Pasquale's Fiat on a rural lane when they were rudely interrupted. The intruder shot Pasquale dead before dragging Stefania from the car and onto the road. After stabbing her 97 times, the killer thrust a grapevine stalk into her genitals, then fled.

The next double-homicide happened nearly seven years later, on June 6, 1981, near the commune of Scandicci. Though 30-year-old labourer Giovanni Foggi and Carmela de Nuccio, 21, were engaged to be married, they did not want to wait until their wedding night. The killer crept up to the driver's side door and fired a single bullet through the glass into Giovanni's temple, killing him outright. Then, after dragging the naked Carmela from the vehicle, the assailant stabbed her to death and used a notched knife to mutilate her genitals. A ballistics expert soon determined that the same gun used in the Foggi-de Nuccio murders had fired the bullets in the 1974 Gentilcore-Pettini case and the Lo Bianco-Locci slayings of 1968.

A few months later, on October 23, a near-identical atrocity occurred in a park near Calenzano. The victims were Stefano Baldi, 26, and Susanna Cambi, 24. Recognizing the handiwork of a serial killer, Florentine crime reporter Mario Spezi christened the perpetrator "The Monster of Florence".[16]

These 1981 slayings marked the beginning of a rash of similar sexually-motivated homicides that continued periodically until September 1985. With the exception of a 1982 double-murder in which the opportunity for post-mortem activities did not present itself, the genitals of the female victims were always mutilated. Towards the end of the series, the killer's signature evolved – specifically, the murderer amputated the breasts of the last two women. After the murders of French tourists Jean Michel Kraveichvili and Nadine Mauriot, the Monster mailed a portion of Nadine's breasts to the state prosecutor along with a note goading them to locate the whereabouts of the victims. Then the Monster seemed to vanish.

In the 1990s, Pietro Pacciani – a convicted sex criminal who had served 13 years in prison for the 1951 murderer of his girlfriend's lover – became a prime suspect, although the only physical evidence tying him to the crime was an unfired cartridge in his garden which was the same brand and calibre as the Monster's. Pacciani was convicted amidst much controversy in 1994, only to be subsequently acquitted and released in 1996. He died in 1998 before he could stand trial again. Instead, two men thought to be his accomplices – Mario Vanni and Giancarlo Lotti – were convicted and remain in prison as of the time of this writing. Few believe them to be guilty of committing the murders. Meanwhile, empty rumours of Satanic cult activity and links to San Francisco's Zodiac Killer have emerged to fill the void.

For all intents and purposes, The Monster of Florence case remains unsolved, and with it, the brutal murders of 16 men and women. As of the time of writing, it has been 35 years since the deaths of the last known victims.

Scream 1996

The Murder of Janett Christman and the Crimes of the Gainesville Ripper

***Scream* breathed new life into a genre that was suffocating under the weight of its own tropes. Rather than fighting against them, Wes Craven's ingenious slasher incorporated them into the plot. The idea of a killer targeting teenagers in the safety of their own homes was inspired by two separate real-life crimes: the "babysitter murder" of Janett Christman and the crimes of the serial killer known as the "Gainesville Ripper".**

The French film theorist Christian Metz famously argued that genres go through four developmental stages: classical, experimental, parody, and deconstruction. Beginning with *Psycho* and *The Texas Chain Saw Massacre* and ending with John Carpenter's *Halloween*, the "classic"-era of slasher films established the conventions of the genre. The boom of slasher films from 1979 to 1991 comprised the "experimental" period, where the certain deaths of sexually promiscuous characters and triumph of the virgin, the indestructible serial killer, and the masked antagonist became recurring tropes. However, by the end of 1991, audiences were growing bored of the formula. One of horror's most observant luminaries, Wes Craven, realized what was happening, and in 1996, released the acclaimed *Scream*: bridging the experimental period of the slasher and the inevitable next stage: the parody.

The plot was relatively simple: "Ghostface", a masked knifeman who harasses his victims with phone calls prior to attacking them, murders high-schoolers Casey Becker and her boyfriend, Steve Orth, before making a failed attempt on the life of their fellow student Sidney Prescott, the protagonist. With the small town of Woodsboro, California struggling to deal with these events, high school is indefinitely suspended, prompting the popular Stu Macher to throw a celebratory party. Predictably, it is here that additional victims are picked off one-by-one. The film ends when "Ghostface" is revealed to be a costume shared by two different slayers, Stu Macher and Sidney's boyfriend Billy Loomis. Gaining the upper-hand, Sidney manages to kill both men, bringing the story to a close. The charm of *Scream* was to include a cast of characters who, while being hunted to death, were not only aware of the clichés of the genre and situation they were experiencing, but actually high-lighted and vocalized these throughout the film.

One of the most terrifying aspects of *Scream* is that the victims are often attacked in the apparent safety of their homes. This element was inspired by two separate real-life incidents: the murder of babysitter Janett Christman in Missouri in the spring of 1950, and a series of brutal killings that occurred in the city of Gaines-ville, Florida, in August 1990 – the crimes of the so-called "Gainesville Ripper". Stylistically, another key inspiration for the movie was Edvard Munch's iconic painting, *The Scream*, which influenced the spine-chilling mask worn by the film's villain.

—

At 7:30 p.m. on March 18, 1950, Janett Christman arrived at the home of Ed and Anne Romack on the outskirts of Columbia, Missouri. She was there to babysit their son, Gregory, while they attended a card game. For Janett, babysitting for the Romacks was becoming a semi-regular affair. She also sometimes babysat for another local couple – the Muellers. It was a Saturday night, and while her fellow Grade 8 students at Jefferson Junior High were throwing a party, Janett decided to take the opportunity to earn some money to help pay off her newly-purchased burgundy suit. Though only 13 years old, she had matured faster than her peers, both emotionally and physically. Now, she was beginning to attract the attentions of older men; in fact, Robert Mueller had recently made some inappropriate comments about her to Ed Romack, even speculating on whether she was still a virgin.[1]

When Janett arrived at the Romacks' house, three-year-old Gregory was already fast asleep. Anne explained that the boy liked to listen to the radio while his mommy and daddy were out, while Ed showed Janett a shotgun in the hallway closet and showed her how to use it in case of an emergency. He instructed her to keep the front and back doors locked. In the unlikely event that someone paid a visit to their little bungalow on the hill, she was to flip on the porch light, and only answer the door to people she knew.[2] Ed and Anne Romack then drove out into the wind and sleet to meet their friends. It was now 7:50 p.m.

Despite the miserable weather, childminders were in high demand that Saturday evening. After Janett left for the Romacks', Robert Mueller phoned the Christman residence to ask if Janett was available to babysit. A family member politely informed him of her prior arrangement with the Romacks. Meanwhile, on the other side of town, Janett's best friend Carol Holt was also babysitting a sleeping child. Looking back 60 years later, she would recall the blustery evening as "eerie".[3]

For Officer Ray McCowan of the Boone County Sheriff's Department, the bad weather made for a pleasantly dull shift – few people were braving the storm. However, at 10:35 p.m., his phone suddenly rang. Picking up the receiver, Officer McCowan was greeted by a series of horrific screams, and a shrill plea to "come quick"[4] before the line went dead. McCowan was shaken. The voice had been female – there was little doubt about that – but the caller had provided no clues as to her whereabouts or identity. Worse, as there was nobody at the telephone company staffing the test board at this hour, tracing the call was impossible.

Thunder was rumbling in Boone County. Concerned that it may have awoken little Gregory, Anne Romack called home to speak with Janett and was greeted by a "busy" signal. Around midnight, Janett's friend, Carol, had an odd sense that something strange was happening and went to check on the child in her own care.[5]

When Ed and Anne Romack returned home at 1:35 a.m., they were shocked to discover their living room window smashed, the front porch light glaring, and both front and back doors unlocked. They entered the dwelling to find Janett Christman lying dead on a shag rug beside the living room piano, surrounded by blood. A length of cord cut from a nearby iron was cinched around her throat. Her partial state of undress seemed to indicate that she had been the victim of a sexual assault. Gregory was still sound asleep in his bed, though the radio had stopped broadcasting. The Romacks rushed to telephone the police.

Arriving on the scene, investigators from the Boone County Sheriff's Department found evidence of a violent struggle that had spilled out of the kitchen, through the hall, and into the living room. The front window had been shattered from the outside, with shards of glass littering the living room interior; however, the Venetian blinds, fixtures, and furniture were all undisturbed. Considering this forensic inconsistency along with the glowing front porch light and unlocked doors, the police formed the following conclusions: 1) The crime scene was staged, that is deliberately arranged to mislead the authorities. Specifically, the front window had been shattered to make it appear that it was the killer's point of entry. However, as the porch light was blazing, and Ed Romack had instructed Janett to switch it on if somebody came calling, the front door was unlocked, and the Venetian blinds remained perfectly aligned, the offender seemed to have gained entry to the home via the front door; 2) The victim likely knew the offender. Not only did she open the door to them, but the physical attack on her seemed to have begun in the kitchen, implying that she *may* have willingly let her killer enter the residence; 3) The offender seemed to be familiar with the layout of

Poltergeist (1982)

Poltergeist premiered on June 4, 1982.

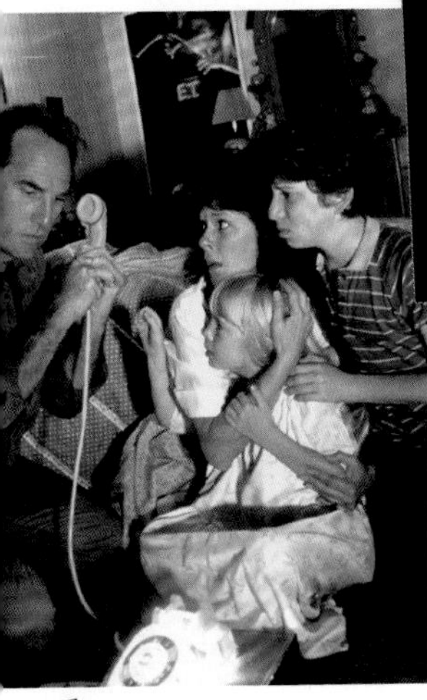

The Freeling family are assailed by unknown entities.

Clairvoyant Tangina Barrons, who was reputedly based on real-life medium Lorraine Warren.

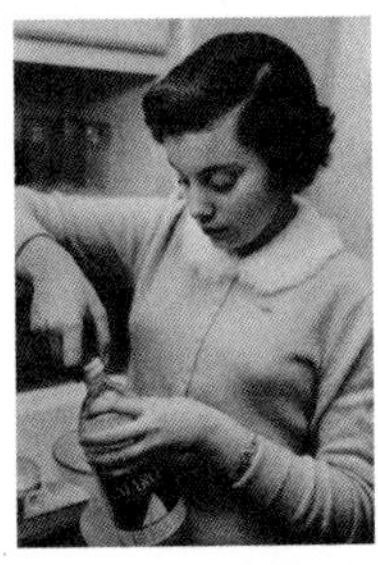

Lucille Herrmann examines a bottle that allegedly opened itself.

Parapsychologist Dr J. Gaither Pratt interviews Jimmy Herrmann.

The Herrmann family are seen in the basement of 1648 Redwood Path, next to a toppled piece of furniture.

Detective Joseph Tozzi examines just some of the mail sent to the scene of the "Seaford Poltergeist".

A Nightmare on Elm Street (1984)

Villain Freddy Krueger was inspired by a number of traumatising events from director Wes Craven's childhood.

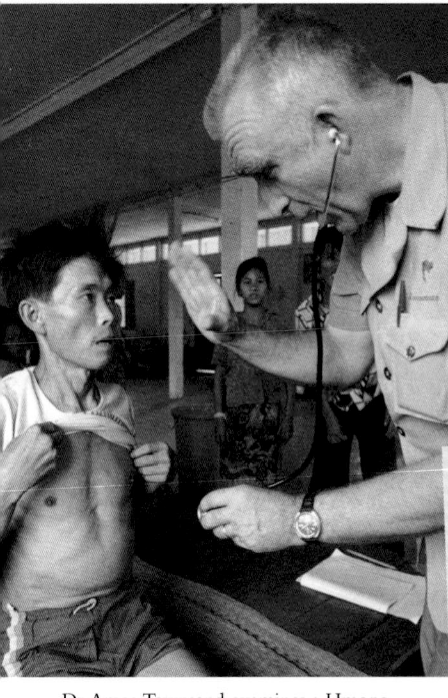

Dr Amos Townsend examines a Hmong refugee in Thailand. By 1978, more than 30,000 Hmong had been resettled in the United States.

The Hmong population in Laos was subjected to terrible treatment by the ruling communists.

The Serpent and the Rainbow (1988)

Actor Bill Pullman plays anthropologist Dennis Alan, who travels to Haiti at the behest of a drug company.

Clairvius Narcisse, whose story served as inspiration for the movie.

The theatrical release poster.

The Silence of the Lambs (1991)

"Buffalo Bill" (below and right), the skin-wearing killer who dumps the bodies of his victims into rivers.

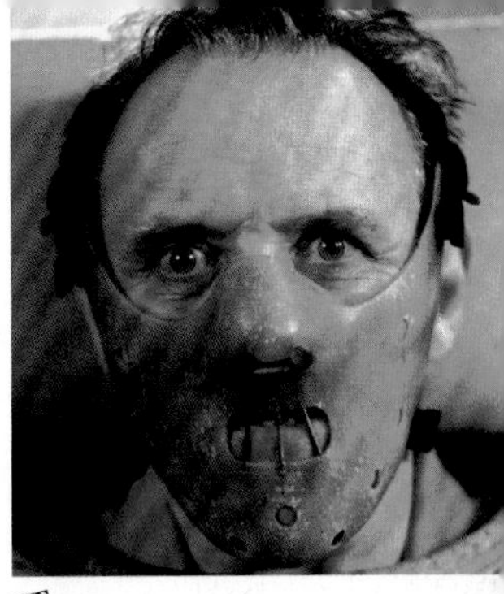

Anthony Hopkins as Dr Hannibal Lecter, a chillingly intellectual psychopath and cannibal.

Ted Bundy, perhaps the most infamous serial killer in US history.

WANTED BY THE FBI

INTERSTATE FLIGHT - MURDER

THEODORE ROBERT BUNDY

DESCRIPTION

CRIMINAL RECORD

CAUTION

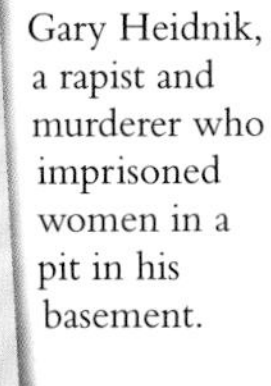

Gary Heidnik, a rapist and murderer who imprisoned women in a pit in his basement.

Ed Kemper, who at 6ft 9in tall, towers over his guards.

Heidnik's house, located at 3520 North Marshall Street, north Philadelphia.

Scream (1996)

"Ghostface", the masked killer who stalks the young people of Woodsboro.

Two victims of the so-called "Gainesville Ripper": Christina Powell (left) and Tracy Paules (right).

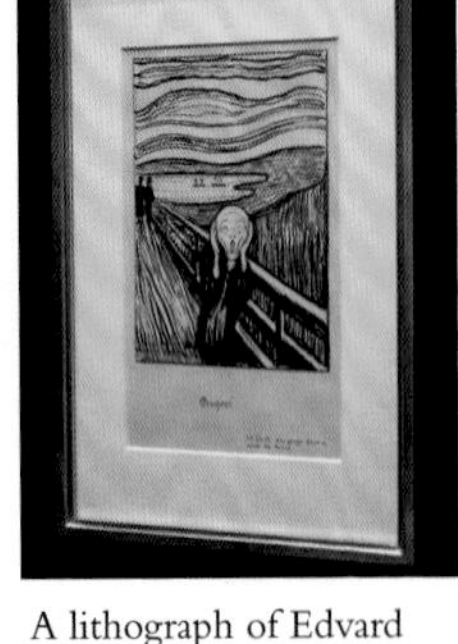

A lithograph of Edvard Munch's *The Scream*.

Two University of Florida students protect themselves with a shotgun while they study.

Danny Rolling, the "Gainesville Ripper". He was executed on October 25, 2006.

Rolling during his trial in April 1994.

The Mothman Prophecies (2002)

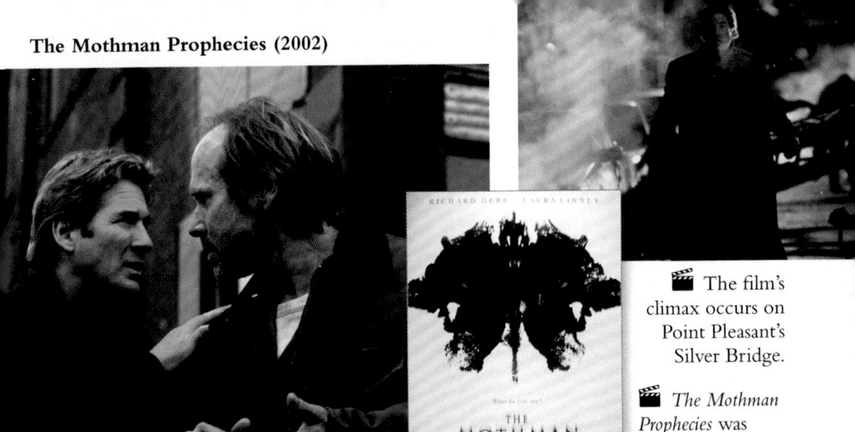

Richard Gere stars as journalist John Klein, who tries to get to the bottom of the strange events in Point Pleasant.

The film's climax occurs on Point Pleasant's Silver Bridge.

The Mothman Prophecies was widely marketed as "based on true events".

The remains of the Silver Bridge, which collapsed on December 15, 1967, killing 46 people.

Point Pleasant, West Virginia, scene of numerous alleged Mothman sightings.

Wolf Creek (2005)

Wolf Creek uses the vast, empty expanses of the Australian Outback to heighten tension.

Outdoorsman Mick Taylor, the terrifying antagonist of *Wolf Creek*.

The film's story follows three young backpackers: Ben, Kristy, and Liz.

The Kombi van belonging to Peter Falconio.

Ivan Milat, the "Backpacker Murderer" who killed at least seven young travellers between 1989 and 1993.

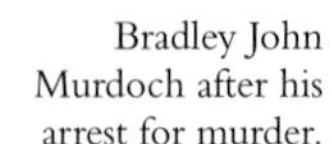

Bradley John Murdoch after his arrest for murder.

Peter Falconio and his girlfriend, Joanne Lees.

The Conjuring (2013) and Annabelle (2014)

In one of the movie's most memorable scenes, Carolyn Perron plays "hide and clap" in the cellar.

Vera Farmiga portrays medium Lorraine Warren in *The Conjuring* and its sequels.

The Perron family, as depicted in *The Conjuring*.

Lorraine and Ed Warren, whose cases inspired the movies of the "*Conjuring* Universe".

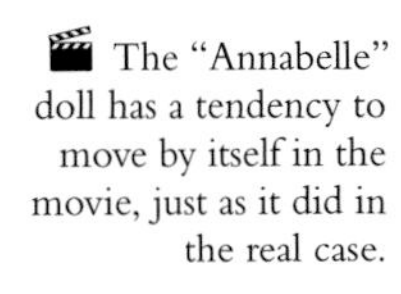

The "Annabelle" doll has a tendency to move by itself in the movie, just as it did in the real case.

The *Annabelle* movie release poster.

The real doll looks a lot less sinister than its depiction on screen.

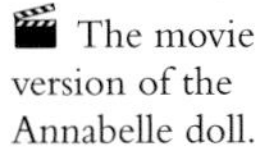

The movie version of the Annabelle doll.

The Conjuring 2 (2016)

Madison Wolfe portrays Janet Hodgson, the girl who was at the heart of the Enfield Poltergeist case.

In a scene that really happened, police officers who are called to the Hodgson residence witness the strange events first-hand.

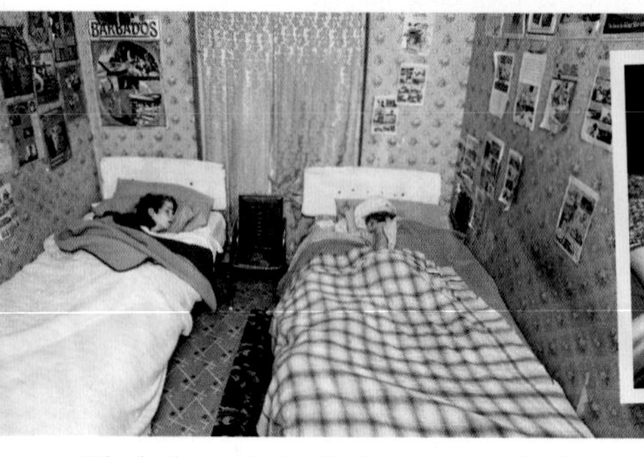

The bedroom in the Hodgson household that was supposedly the site of paranormal activity.

The Hodgson children (from left to right): Janet, Margaret, Billy, and John.

The Witch (2015) and The Lighthouse (2019)

In *The Witch*, an isolated frontier family is tormented by malevolent forces.

The "Witch House" in Salem, Massachusetts, which was standing at the time of the infamous witch trials.

Smalls reef, scene of the tragedy of 1801. This lighthouse replaced the original in 1857.

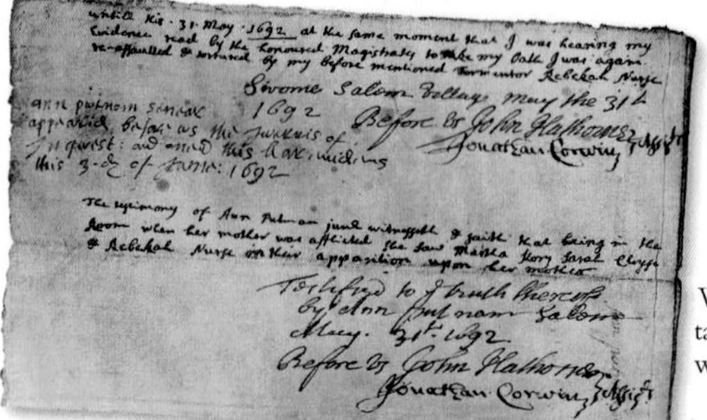

... 31 May 1692 at the same moment that I was hearing my
Evidence read by the honoured Magistrates to take my Oath I was again
re-assaulted & tortured by my before mentioned Tormentor Rebekah Nurse

Sworne Salem Village May the 31st
1692 Before us John Hathorne
Jonathan Corwin Assists

Ann putnam senior
appeared before us the Juriors of
Inquest: and owned this her evidence
this 3 day of June: 1692

The testimony of Ann Putnam junr witnesseth & saith that being in the
Room when her mother was afflicted she saw Martha Kory Sarah Cloyse
& Rebekah Nurse on their apparition upon her mother

Testified to the truth thereof
by Ann Putnam Salem
May. 31st 1692
Before us John Hathorne
Jonathan Corwin Assists

Witness testimony taken during the Salem witch trials of 1692-3.

the bungalow, and had found the murder weapon – the iron power cord – in a bedroom adjoining the living room.

A garden hoe used to shatter the front window lay in the flower bed. As Deputy Julius Wedemier put it, the murder had all the characteristics of "an inside job".[6] After collecting a series of bloody fingerprints, the investigators summoned hounds from Algoa Correctional Center, and managed to track the killer's trail through dense brush to the corner of West Boulevard North and West Ash Street, where the dogs lost the scent.

A medical examination of Janett Christman revealed that she had been raped and beaten. She had also suffered multiple tiny round punctures to the head from an unidentified metal instrument. Her death had occurred sometime between 10 p.m. and midnight: asphyxiation via ligature strangulation. Her face had been scratched, and there were traces of skin – almost certainly belonging to her attacker – under her fingernails.[7]

On Sunday, March 19, Carol Holt was readying herself for church, when she received a phone call that would change her life: her friend Janett had been brutally murdered. But Carol wasn't the only one to receive an unexpected call that morning. The Romacks were still struggling to deal with the horrific events that had just occurred under their roof when the telephone rang in the kitchen. Ed answered, only to hear the voice of his boyhood chum, Robert Mueller, offering to pop by to help "clean up the mess."[8] Ed thought this was strange, as word of the murder had yet to spread. It isn't known whether Ed Romack asked Mueller flat-out, or Mueller offered the information himself, but according to trial transcripts Mueller "told Romack that he did not have an alibi but [added] 'I don't have no scratches.'"[9] At this time, the results of the autopsy – including the skin found under the victim's nails – had not been made public.

Although the crime had occurred in Boone County, the investigation was complicated by interference from the Columbia Police, who repeatedly and unapologetically impinged upon the Boone County Sheriff's Department's jurisdiction. With his city of

31,000 souls plunged into a panic in the wake of the Christman murder, Chief E.M. Pond of Columbia PD sought to calm public fears. He immediately ordered the "3132" emergency number to be switched to "112", a crucial time-saver back in the age of rotary telephones; he assigned all of his officers to 12-hour shifts; he employed local businessmen to patrol the streets after dark; and he hired four new patrolmen. Among the new recruits was Paul Cheavens, whose first assignment was to spend a dozen 6 p.m. to 6 a.m. shifts at 1015 Stewart Road, in case Janett Christman's killer should return to the scene of the crime. Rather than culminating in an arrest, these invasive stakeouts only served to escalate pre-existing interdepartmental tensions.

While Chief Pond and his men paraded around Columbia nightly looking for shady characters and jotting down rumours, Sheriff Glen Powell of Boone County was busy gathering and eliminating suspects. As the list became narrower and narrower, it became abundantly clear that Robert Mueller was their "Number One Suspect".[10] On the surface, the 27-year-old World War II veteran seemed like an exemplary American citizen. During the war, Mueller had distinguished himself as a captain in the U.S. Air Force. When the conflict ended, he received an honourable discharge and returned to Columbia, where he married, started a family, and resumed his friendship with his old schoolmate Ed Romack.

However, Robert Mueller's friends knew him to be "hyper-sexual."[11] Aside from his comments about Janett Christman's precocious development, he frequently spoke to Ed Romack of "trying to get a virgin"[12] and suggested going to Hinkson Creek – a popular local spot for student picnics – to "get a nice young girl."[13] Two days before Janett's murder, he had run his hand over Anne Romack's dress while they were alone. Anne had often found Mueller's behaviour unsettling, and she had no hesitation in confiding her suspicions – that he was the only family friend who could have murdered Janett Christman – to local law enforcement.

In addition, the Muellers and Romacks often visited each other's homes. Robert Mueller was not only familiar with the bungalow at 1015 Stewart Road, but had repeatedly used the electric iron that was employed to strangle Janett Christman, and knew exactly where it was kept. He was also aware that little Gregory liked to sleep with the radio on when his parents were out, making him unlikely to stir during an altercation. Regarding the porch light and unlocked doors, Mueller not only knew Janett personally, but also that she would be babysitting at 1015 Stewart Road that night. According to Ed Romack, Mueller once even offered that he might have murdered Janett "and then forgotten it."[14] Perhaps most damning was Mueller's habit of carrying a metal mechanical pencil: its round end was consistent with the strange puncture wounds to Janett's head.

Convinced they had their man, on May 4, 1950, Sheriff Powell made his move. With the help of Ed Romack, they tricked Mueller into picking Ed up in his car, ostensibly to attend a card party. Mueller typically kept score, which meant he would inevitably bring the mechanical pencil. He picked up Romack shortly after 8 p.m. The sheriff and his two deputies arrested Mueller on the spot, and ordered him to drive several miles from the city to Deputy Julius Wedemier's farm. They questioned Mueller through the night but did not obtain a confession. The next morning, he was brought to Jefferson City, where he submitted to a polygraph test. With no significant deception detected, Mueller was taken back to Columbia and released. Nevertheless, there remained sufficient circumstantial evidence against him for Judge W.M. Dinwiddie to have a grand jury look into charging him with the murder of Janett Christman. Unfortunately, Sheriff Powell had failed to request an arrest warrant from the prosecuting attorney or notify him of the interrogation, allegedly because of the attorney's close relationship with Columbia Police Chief Pond. When the grand jury issued its report on June 17, instead of indicting Mueller, it ferociously criticized the Columbia Police and Boone County

Sheriff's Department for their "petty jealousies"[15] and total lack of cooperation in investigating the homicide.

Soon after, Robert P. Mueller re-enlisted in the air force and left Columbia. With his departure, a string of local sex crimes spanning back to 1946 abruptly stopped. Mueller eventually filed an unsuccessful lawsuit against Sheriff Glen Powell and his deputies for civil rights violations relating to the May 4 interrogation. In 2006, he died, a free man, in Tucson, Arizona, aged 83. The late Sheriff Powell's nephew, Wayne, informed a reporter for the *Columbia Daily Tribune* that his uncle remained convinced that Mueller was responsible for the Christman murder until his dying day. Powell was haunted by the suspicion that the suspect's family connections had helped him evade justice.

The still-unsolved murder of Janett Christman is now widely believed to have inspired the "Babysitter and the Man Upstairs" urban legend, which formed the basis for the trailblazing horror films *Black Christmas* (1974) and *When a Stranger Calls* (1979). Paying homage to these classics, the opening scene of *Scream* – in which a babysitter is attacked and murdered – is yet another fictionalized retelling of the chilling events that unfolded at 1015 Stewart Road on March 18, 1950.

—

While the Christman murder inspired *Scream*'s opening scene, the single greatest inspiration for the film's plot and antagonist was a series of murders that occurred in August 1990. To this day, the brutality of these crimes – dubbed the "Gainesville Ripper" murders – is perhaps unrivalled in American criminal history.

On Friday, August 24, 1990, a man wearing black clothing crept to the back of the Williamsburg Village Apartments in Gainesville, Florida, and opened his "hit kit". In the balmy darkness, his hands found a pair of leather gloves and a ski mask. He stretched them over his hands and face, then stared up at the lit windows of the green, four-storey complex. Later, he would claim to have been directed to apartment 113 by the voice of "Gemini", a demon bearing the same name as the serial killer in *The Exorcist III*. He had viewed the film in a cinema shortly after arriving in town, and identified with it profoundly. In truth, he had simply followed the young female tenants home from a nearby Walmart the previous evening, vowing to return under cover of darkness.[16]

Tip-toeing onto the deck, he gently turned the door knob. It was locked. He retrieved a screwdriver and penlight from his bag, began prying at the lock's frame, and finally gained entry. Swapping his break-and-enter tools for a Marine combat knife and duct tape, he ripped two six-inch (15-cm) strips from the roll, fastened them to his left arm, and entered the dwelling. He crept through the kitchen and into the living room, where he came across the sleeping form of a young woman on the couch. Bypassing her, he slowly ascended the stairs. Upon reaching the top, he spied a taller girl asleep on her bed. He traced the narrow beam of the penlight across her face. Quietly, he peeled a piece of duct tape from his arm, and leaned over her. Then, in a single motion, he placed the adhesive over her mouth and stabbed the blade into her right chest. The girl jolted awake and began to frantically kick at her assailant, but soon lay still.

Descending again to the lower level, he returned to the young woman snoozing on the sofa, and clamped his hand down over her mouth. He threatened her with the knife, telling her that if she screamed he would harm her. When he removed his hand from her mouth, she quietly asked him about her roommate, Sonja. Knowing the truth would jeopardize her cooperation, he lied that Sonja was upstairs with an accomplice. He pulled her off the couch, then bound her hands behind her back with duct tape and led her into the kitchen. There, he subjected her to a degrading sexual assault over the next half hour. Afterwards, he brought her back into the living room and ordered her to lie back down on her stomach. He stuck a second piece of duct tape over her mouth, and then stabbed her five times in the back.

After his second victim had stopped breathing, the man returned to the body of the girl upstairs. He removed the duct tape, stripped the body and, seizing her ankles, dragged her to the edge of the bed. He stabbed the knife into her left thigh, leaving a horrific wound, before leaving her in a degrading pose.

The killer then headed back to his second victim downstairs. He removed the duct tape from her mouth, and had post-mortem sex with her body. Next, he mutilated the victim, before using dish-washing soap to destroy any biological evidence. He left the bottle between her legs.[17] Grabbing an apple and banana from the kitchen, he beat a hasty retreat into the night, stopping only to discard the bloodied pieces of duct tape in a dumpster.[18]

The next night, Saturday, the killer rode his stolen bicycle to 3533 Southwest 24th Avenue, and ditched it behind a house trailer. He moved silently down the alley towards the chain-link fence that obstructed entry to his target's backyard. Patiently, he unhooked the links, creating just enough space to pass through. Once he was crouched outside the target's building, he retrieved the same implements from his kit – the recently bloodied combat knife, penlight, roll of duct tape, screwdriver, mask, and gloves. He removed his shirt and slipped the combat knife and duct tape into his waistband. Pulling on the mask and gloves, he crept towards the apartment's sliding glass door with the penlight and screwdriver in his hands. He scanned the interior to ensure nobody was home, and then stuck the screwdriver between the glass door and frame, prying it open. The killer entered the darkened apartment, tearing two six-inch (15-cm) pieces of duct tape from the roll and sticking them to his left arm. His penlight traced over a bookcase filling an alcove near the front entrance. Recognizing the perfect place to spring his trap, he easily lifted the heavy piece of furniture – he was more than 6 feet (1.8 m) tall and was very strong – relocated it to the bedroom, and closed the door. Then, he waited by the living room window for the occupant to return home.[19]

It was just after 10:15 p.m. when he spotted her strolling along the path towards her front door. The killer manoeuvred himself into the alcove and waited as she opened the door, entered, locked it behind her, and placed what looked like a racquet and balls on the table. Then he pounced, tackling her to the floor, and sending the racquetballs bouncing in all directions. Smothering her mouth with his left hand, he used the right to pull the knife out of his waistband, brandishing it before her eyes.

In the face of his threats, she agreed to comply. He removed a strip of tape from his left arm and placed it over her mouth, then used the roll of duct tape to restrain her hands behind her back. After groping her, he seized her arm, pulled her to her feet, and marched her to her bed. The attacker sexually assaulted her, then picked up the combat knife from the floor, turned her onto her stomach, and stabbed her once in her back, killing her. He then mutilated the body, ending by removing the victim's head. He left the head on the bookshelf and used a heavy object to prop it up. In one final act of degradation, he positioned the body so that it appeared to be sitting on the edge of the bed. He then cleaned himself up, gathered his things, and rode off into the night.

Having spent most of Sunday resting, the killer left his campsite in the hot, mosquito-ridden forest, climbed onto his bike, and headed towards Archer Road. He was searching for another victim, and thought the Gatorwood Apartments would be a good place to find one. Around 11 p.m. he arrived at the building, alighted, and began peeping through the windows. He found what he was looking for in the corner apartment – a young woman chatting on the phone with her friend. Obscured by a bush, he sat watching her.[20]

It was now 1:30 a.m. on Monday. He heard two young men pass by talking about a girl who had been decapitated, wondering whether it was the handiwork of a serial killer. Realizing his previous victims had now been discovered, he decided he would have to leave Gainesville soon. As with the previous attacks, he donned his balaclava and gloves. Leaping over the railing onto the back porch, he moved to the glass sliding doors and came face to face with a Siamese cat. The feline began wailing loudly, catching the attention of the young woman. Taking fright, the killer vaulted back onto the other side of the railing and lay flat on his belly. There he waited. At 3 a.m. he unzipped his bag and retrieved the same items he had used in the killings of his first three victims. Wedging his screwdriver between the seam and frame of the locked door, he began to jimmy it, and soon gained access to the apartment. He crept towards the woman's room, but stopped. Through an open doorway he saw the sleeping form of a large, athletic man: a potential problem.

The killer slipped soundlessly into the room, and closed the door. Raising the combat knife, he aimed right at the man's solar plexus and brought it right down. The young man instantly awakened and his fists flew up to strike his assailant, but the knife continued to rain down into his torso, striking his hands, arms, legs, and face. The victim shouted and then was still.[21]

The attacker was soaked in blood. He walked down the hallway to the kitchen and began to rinse off his hands, forearms, and blade in the sink. The girl's bedroom door squeaked open, catching his attention. She entered the hallway holding a curling iron and locked eyes with the blood-soaked stranger. Screaming, she dove back into the bedroom, quickly locking the door behind her. But the man had size and aggression on his side. With one heavy kick, he smashed the door open, threw the woman onto her bed, and then used the same tactics as always – a knife and some strong warnings – to ensure obedience.

He taped her hands behind her back, but not her mouth, then forced her to recite a degrading form of script as he sexually assaulted her. Finally, he drove the knife into her back three times.

Wiping the blade on the bed-sheets, he pulled the body into the hallway just outside the bathroom. He soaked a towel, covered it in liquid soap, and attempted to wash away any clues on the body. However, he was getting careless. He left a piece of duct tape on her bedroom curtain and his combat knife sitting on top of the television.[22]

On Saturday, August 25, 1990, the seemingly safe little college town of Gainesville was thrown into disarray with the discovery of two murdered University of Florida freshmen. The bodies of 18-year-old Sonja Larson and 17-year-old Christina Powell were found in Apt 113 of the Williamsburg Apartments. Police found the body of a third teenager – 18-year-old Christa Hoyt, a student at Santa Fe College – the very next day, murdered and mutilated with such brutality that it eclipsed even the horrific treatment of Christina Powell's body. The community experienced mass panic, and on August 27, two more victims, 23-year-old seniors Manuel Taboada and Tracy Paules, were found stabbed to death at the Gatorwood Apartments. The deaths of Taboada and Paules signalled not only that the so-called "Gainesville Ripper" had no intention of stopping, but that even the presence of a physically powerful male wasn't adequate defence against the killer. Students fled the town in droves – many never to return – replaced by members of the national news media, all struggling to keep pace with the crimes and anticipating more headline-grabbing homicides. But it soon became apparent that the killings had ceased.

On September 7, 1990, a fugitive named Danny Rolling was arrested in Ocala, Florida after robbing a Winn-Dixie supermarket at gunpoint and crashing his car in the ensuing high-speed chase. Rolling was already wanted for the attempted murder of his father in Shreveport, Louisiana, having shot him in the face during a quarrel, and the news of his apprehension soon reached the authorities there.

A disturbingly violent crime had occurred in Shreveport on November 4, 1989, when 55-year-old William Grissom, his 24-year-old daughter Julie, and eight-year-old grandson Sean were murdered in their family home. William and Sean had simply been in the wrong place at the wrong time and were quickly murdered, but the killer had taken his time with Julie, sexually assaulting her, then murdering her with a combat knife, before mutilating and posing her corpse. The killer had also used solvents to clean up evidence.[23]

While Danny Rolling had never been a serious suspect in the Grissom family murders, the fact that the Gainesville killings bore such a striking resemblance to them, and that Rolling was known to have been in Florida when they occurred, could not be overlooked. Shreveport police contacted the investigators in Gainesville to outline the connection and encouraged them to take a closer look at the man now in custody.

In early 1991, the taskforce investigating the Gainesville Ripper decided to reassess reports of an unidentified man who had fled town in August 1990. The man had escaped following a botched bank robbery, leaving behind a bunch of junk at his campsite in the woods. They re-examined items recovered at the time, and since put into storage. Among them were a screwdriver with multiple notches, indicating it had been used to pry things open, and cassette tapes of a whiny-voiced man identifying himself as Danny Rolling, making cryptic statements that might relate to the murders, and singing country songs about being an outlaw. Even more damning, news soon got out that Danny had been discussing the murders with his cellmate, revealing details only the Gainesville Ripper could know. A warrant was issued to obtain a DNA sample from him and this was then matched to the scenes of several of the Gainesville homicides.

Faced with this overwhelming evidence, Danny Rolling said "there are some things that you just can't run from"[24] and on February 13, 1994, pleaded guilty to all five of the Gainesville murders and their related charges. Despite his guilty plea, he was sentenced to death. Whether he was blaming his abusive father, his ex-wife, the American prison system, or the demon Gemini, Rolling never truly accepted culpability for one of the most horrendous series of murders in American history. In the days leading up to his execution, now claiming he wanted to walk with God and have a clear conscience, he finally penned a statement in which he also confessed to the Grissom triple-murder in Shreveport. On October 25, 2006, Daniel Harold Rolling was executed by lethal injection at Florida State Prison.

Screenwriter Kevin Williamson first formulated the idea for *Scream* in 1990, after watching news reports of the "Gainesville Ripper" murders and finding a mysteriously open window in the residence where he was staying. Rolling's home invasions and use of a knife, and his sowing of such terror in Gainesville that the university closed as students fled, all inspired elements of *Scream*. However, Williamson was forced to excise the Rolling-inspired mutilations from the script when his agent warned him it would be too violent to sell.

—

Undoubtedly, the most famous imagery from *Scream* features the iconic mask worn by its antagonist, "Ghostface". For that – and by extension, the title of the film – the filmmakers looked further into the past for inspiration.

In 1893, a 30-year-old Norwegian artist named Edvard Munch created one of the most iconic images of the 20th century: *The Scream*. In the foreground, a hairless humanoid figure stands on a long wooden bridge clad in a dark smock, hands clutching his endlessly screaming visage. Lingering far behind are the shadowy forms of other bridge-goers – indistinct, as if inhabiting a different reality – while a fiery turbulent sky churns over distant water.

There are in fact several versions of the artwork. The first version of the composition, created in 1893, was simple pastel on cardboard; it is far lighter than its more recognizable successor, created that same year, which was crafted from oil, pastel, and tempera. In 1895, Munch created a second pastel and cardboard version, along with approximately 45 black and white lithograph prints. A final rendition of the composition, using only tempera, was created in 1910.

Considered to be Norway's first Expressionist painter, Munch first conjured up the idea for *The Scream* in Kristiania, the former name for Oslo, during a most unusual stroll:

"One evening I was walking along a path, the city was on one side and the fjord below. I felt tired and ill. I stopped and looked out over the fjord – the sun was setting, and the clouds turning blood red. I sensed a scream passing through nature; it seemed to me that I heard the scream. I painted this picture, painted the clouds as actual blood. The colour shrieked. This became *The Scream*."[25]

The original title that Munch gave to the piece was *Der Schrei der Natur* (The Scream of Nature). In the years since, *The Scream* has come to be considered an exemplary depiction of the anguish of modern man – unsurprisingly, given Munch's own notoriously tortured psychology.

Born on December 12, 1863, into a family plagued by madness and premature death, Edvard was a sickly child who resented his father's extreme religiosity and was inspired by the tales of Edgar Allan Poe. Ever aware of his own mortality, he channelled his neuroses through art, referring to his style as "soul painting". In 1908, ridden with anxiety and addled by drink to the point of extreme paranoia and hallucination, Munch underwent eight months of electroconvulsive therapy in an attempt to quell his personal demons. The artist's later life was one of self-imposed solitude at his estate at Skøyen, in Oslo. He died on January 23, 1944, aged 80.

Many decades later, during a visit to a costume shop, film director Wes Craven and producer Marianne Maddalena came across an elongated, screaming mask, which they decided would be perfect for the antagonist of their latest horror film, originally titled "Scary Movie". The mask had been designed by an employee named Brigitte Sleiertin; she had based it on Edvard Munch's *The Scream*.[26]

The Mothman Prophecies 2002

THE MOTHMAN OF POINT PLEASANT, WEST VIRGINIA

***The Mothman Prophecies* is an eerie story of encounters with mysterious figures, unexplained phenomena, and tragic disasters. The film was based on a series of bizarre events that plagued the small town of Point Pleasant, West Virginia in the late 1960s.**

The early 2000s were not particularly well known for producing quality supernatural horror movies, but *The Mothman Prophecies* stands out as a creepy exception. In the film, a journalist named John Klein goes driving one night and suddenly finds himself in the rural town of Point Pleasant, West Virginia with no memory of how he got there. When his car breaks down he knocks on the door of the nearest house hoping to use their telephone, only to be confronted by a gun-toting owner who insists that this is the third night in a row Klein has knocked on his door at 2:30 a.m. Police officer Connie Mills arrives and drives Klein to a hotel, informing him that a lot of odd things have been happening in Point Pleasant lately. In particular, numerous locals have reported seeing a large, red-eyed, winged creature resembling an anthropomorphic moth. As Klein lingers around Point Pleasant to chronicle the situation, he learns that the residents are receiving messages telepathically or in their dreams warning them of impending disasters. He begins to receive regular calls at his hotel room from a being referring to itself as "Indrid Cold", who provides him with secret information that convinces Klein that Cold is not of this world. In one call, Cold reveals to Klein that there will be a horrible disaster on the Ohio River. Obsessed with learning more about the enigmatic Mothman, Klein contacts researcher John Leek who tries to warn him of the perils of going down the Mothman rabbit hole. On Christmas Eve, John Klein watches as a heavily trafficked bridge over the Ohio River suddenly collapses and dozens of vehicles plunge into the freezing water below. Though he manages to rescue Mills, he realizes that Indrid Cold's prophecy has indeed come to pass.

The Mothman Prophecies was based upon UFOlogist John Keel's eponymous 1975 book and its predecessor, *Operation Trojan Horse*. According to Keel, he was once a "hard-boiled sceptic" who had begun investigating UFOs (Unidentified Flying Objects) full-time in 1966. By 1967 his phone was regularly ringing off the hook with strange calls from "space people". He was followed by black Cadillacs that seemed to vanish into thin air, garish air vehicles, and often pulled in to random motels to find that he somehow already had a reservation and that there were indecipherable telephone messages waiting for him. Keel first travelled to Point Pleasant, West Virginia to investigate a string of bizarre reports that had surfaced in the area. The eerie stories that were relayed to him were even more chilling in light of the tragic events that followed.

—

It was November 1966 when John Keel got the call. Gray Barker, the author and UFOlogist, insisted that something strange was happening in Point Pleasant, West Virginia. Dozens of locals had reported seeing a large winged humanoid with mesmerizing red eyes. The creature had even taken flight, chasing terrified motorists down mountain roads in their cars. Keel was in Washington D.C. at the time, hassling the air force for information on UFOs – he and Gray had overlapping interests – but reluctantly decided to look into it after returning home to New York City. A bachelor obsessed with the paranormal, Keel had made his way in the world with his boundless curiosity and a pen. In his youth he had worked as a freelance journalist and scriptwriter, and in 1957 published *Jadoo*, a book about the unusual things he had experienced while travelling through Egypt and India. He had followed it up with a superhero spoof novel, *The Fickle Finger of Fate*, earlier in 1966. On December 7, the adventurous Keel drove 450 miles (720 km) southwest to Point Pleasant.

Located on the confluence of the Ohio and Kanawha Rivers, Point Pleasant is locally regarded as the site of the first battle of the American Revolutionary War, in which Colonel Andrew Lewis' men defeated a joint Shawnee-Mingo force led by Chief Cornstalk. The settlement had stagnated throughout much of the 19th century – some attributed this to the curse of Cornstalk's ghost. Arching over the murky waters was the Silver Bridge, which connected Point Pleasant to Gallipolis, Ohio. When it was first erected in 1928, the aluminium eyebar-chain suspension bridge was lauded as a triumph of modern engineering.

Armed with a notepad, a tape recorder, and an open mind, Keel set out to investigate the reported strange happenings. He began with Deputy Millard Halstead of Mason County who acknowledged, "there's something to it. The people who have seen this Bird were all mighty scared. They saw something. I don't know what. Some say it's just a crane."[1] When asked, Halstead denied there had been any reported UFO activity.

Keel had heard otherwise, and decided to visit the apartment of Park and Mabel McDaniel to interview them about an alleged sighting. Having met plenty of "oddballs" during his years of UFO investigation, Keel was surprised to find the McDaniels refreshingly normal. Not only did they welcome him into their home, but they telephoned a number of family members and friends who had also witnessed strange phenomena in the Point Pleasant area. They were soon joined by Park and Mabel's daughter Linda Scarberry, her husband Roger, the Scarberrys' friends Steve and Mary

Mallette, local journalist Mary Hyre, her niece Connie Carpenter, and Connie's fiancé Keith.

The McDaniels recounted how they had watched a round object hovering over Tiny's restaurant, across the street from their home. Numerous customers at Tiny's, among them a local police officer's wife, also saw the UFO, but didn't bother to report it. Mary Hyre – a journalist for the *Messenger*, based across the river in Athens, Ohio – told how she too had seen a UFO while driving along the west bank of the river that summer: "At first I thought it was a plane. Then I got a better look at it. It was perfectly round. I couldn't make out what it was but I didn't give it any thought at the time."[2]

The experiences of the Mallettes and Scarberrys were even stranger. Three weeks previously, on November 15, 1966, the two couples had gone out for a drive, hoping to bump into some friends. Eighteen-year-old Roger Scarberry was driving his '57 Buick around an abandoned explosives factory – Keel subsequently referred to this as the TNT Area – when his wife, Linda, spotted a pair of glowing red eyes in the darkness. She had screamed, prompting Roger to slam on the brakes. A grey humanoid "six and a half or seven feet tall"[3] with "big wings folded against its back"[4] and "eyes like automobile reflectors"[5] was shambling on powerful legs towards the ruins of the generation plant. Terrified, they had sped away down the exit road leading to Route 62, only to see the figure standing on the crest of a hill. Unfolding its wings, it flew directly towards them. Though Roger was pushing the Buick to 100 mph (160 kph) along winding back roads, they were unable to shake their winged pursuer. "It followed us to the city limits. Funny thing, we noticed a dead dog by the side of the road there. A big dog. But when we came back a few minutes later the dog was gone."[6] Mary Mallette recalled the figure's strange sound: "it squeaked like a big mouse",[7] while the Scarberrys emphasized that "it was those eyes that got us . . . they were hypnotic. For a minute we could only stare at it. I couldn't take my eyes off it."[8]

The Mallettes and Scarberrys had immediately raced to the Mason County Courthouse to alert Deputy Halstead. The lawman accompanied them back to the generation plant. There was no sign of the monster, but when Halstead attempted to radio the dispatcher in Point Pleasant, an ear-piercing screech emitted from the speaker, disrupting the communication. Sheriff George Johnson held a conference for the media the following morning, and reporters eagerly took statements from Roger, Linda, Mary, and Steve. Mary Hyre had wired the story to the Associated Press and suddenly all of Point Pleasant was talking about the "Mothman", as the creature had been rechristened by an imaginative copy editor.

More recently, Connie Carpenter, Hyre's 18-year-old niece, was driving home from church on Sunday, November 27, when she saw a massive grey humanoid with blazing eyes near a golf course. When she reduced speed to get a better look at the creature it unfurled its massive wingspan, quietly levitated, and hurtled right towards her. Connie's gaze had locked with its "fiercely glowing red eyes"[9] before the creature soared over her vehicle and out of sight. As Connie recounted the story, Keel observed that her eyes were red, watery, and swollen: a symptom he had noted in countless UFO witnesses, and which he attributed to conjunctivitis caused by ultraviolet radiation.[10]

According to John Keel, over one hundred adults would report seeing the winged behemoth from 1966–67. While most Ohio Valley residents dreaded running into the Mothman, 50-year-old Woodrow Derenberger supposedly managed to establish a personal relationship with the entity. John Keel documented Derenberger's accounts in some detail.

The tale began on November 2, 1966, almost two weeks before the encounter reported by the Mallettes and Scarberrys. Woody had been driving his panel truck home along Interstate 77 to his farmhouse in Mineral Wells, roughly 40 miles (64 km) northeast of Point Pleasant. It was 7 p.m. on a rainy night, and the sandy-haired appliance salesman was eager to see his wife and two children. He became aware of a vehicle behind him, and entertaining the possibility it could be a police cruiser, slowed down. To his astonishment, the charcoal-grey vehicle flew past, cut him off, and quickly reduced its speed. Woody's eyes struggled to comprehend what they were witnessing: "an old-fashioned kerosene lamp chimney, flaring at both ends, narrowing down to a small neck and then enlarging in a great bulge in the centre."[11] Suddenly the craft turned ninety degrees, blocking the road. Woody hit the brakes and came to an abrupt halt within ten feet (3 m) of the object. As he sat behind the wheel, heart racing, the craft's door opened and a grinning man stepped onto the highway. He stood about 5 feet 10 inches (1.78 m) tall, with black hair, tan skin, and a thin dark overcoat. His arms were crossed, hands buried in his armpits. Woody sensed the man wanted him to roll down his window, and complied. As the figure drew nearer, he spied what appeared to be pseudo-metallic green clothing beneath his coat.

Do not be afraid.

Somehow, Woodrow Derenberger knew the grinning man's thoughts.

We mean you no harm. I come from a country much less powerful than you. What's your name?

"Woody."

My name is Cold. I sleep, breathe, and bleed even as you do.[12]

According to Derenberger, the craft was now hovering 40–50 feet (12–15 m) above the highway. Cold – the grinning man – then gestured to the lights of distant Parkersburg, West Virginia. He wanted to know what it was. Woody told him it was a city. The grinning man replied that where he came from, they called these *gatherings.* After some further telepathic chit chat, Cold urged Woody to inform the police about their meeting and promised to see him again soon. The craft then returned to gather Cold and sped soundlessly into the night.

By the time he arrived home to his farmhouse in Mineral Wells, Woody Derenberger was visibly distressed. Observing her husband's state and learning of his strange experience, Woody's wife encouraged him to call the Parkersburg police. Astonishingly, they heard him out, processed his report, and enquired as to whether he would like to see a doctor. The next morning, he was questioned by local and state police. Within 24 hours, Woodrow Derenberger's encounter with the entity, Cold, was reported by newspapers, TV, and radio stations all over the Ohio River Valley. Numerous witnesses came forward to describe passing Woody and the grinning man during the encounter. Overnight, the Derenberger farmhouse in Mineral Wells became a favourite haunt for skywatchers. It also began receiving threatening phone calls instructing Woody to keep his mouth shut.[13]

On November 4, Cold resumed communication with Woody, telepathically blasting into his mind while he rode in the passenger seat of a workmate's car. Cold explained he lived on Lanulos, a planet similar to Earth in the Ganymede (or Genemedes) galaxy. Like Woody, he had a wife, Kimi, and two sons. The inhabitants of Lanulos lived for 125–175 years. Famine, poverty, violence, and despair were non-existent. Then, as soon as Cold had entered Woody's consciousness, he was gone, leaving nothing but a stabbing headache.

On another occasion, a black Volkswagen pulled up outside the Derenberger farmhouse, seemingly unnoticed by the skywatchers, and a man in a black suit alighted. Woody had since learnt the man's first name: "Indrid". Indrid Cold spoke with Woody for a few minutes, then handed him a vial of medicine for his stomach problems. Derenberger claimed that the medicine worked.[14]

At the insistence of a UFO research group named the National Investigations Committee on Aerial Phenomena (NICAP), Derenberger travelled to St. Joseph's Hospital in Parkersburg to be assessed by a psychiatrist and EEG technician. In summary, they "found Mr Derenberger to be normal."[15] Soon after, the Parkersburg psychiatrist claimed they had begun to hear a mysterious voice emanating from their television.[16]

Sometime later, Derenberger would assert that a Captain Bruce Parsons, claiming to be from the "NASA security police", arrived at Mineral Wells to invite Woody and his family for a week in Cape Kennedy. After Christmas, the Derenbergers supposedly travelled to the Florida space program station and were treated to a grand tour of the facilities. In the evenings, Woody was transported to a secret location on the Cape where he was questioned extensively about his interactions with Indrid Cold. One of his interrogators, a man named Charlie, actually claimed to be the head of NASA. As the week neared its end, they explained to Woody that they had interviewed other "contactees" who had given near-identical accounts of their communications with extraterrestrials. Then, pointing to a star on a map, they told him, "that's where they're from."[17]

When the Derenbergers returned to Mineral Wells, Woody came bearing photographs of Cape Kennedy and spacesuit material reminiscent of the metal-like clothing Cold had worn during their first meeting. Soon, Indrid Cold and several other Lanulos would meet Woody's wife and children. Unlike her husband, Mrs Derenberger found their presence to be chilling and felt that their intentions were malevolent. During an interview with John Keel, she reported they were so similar to humans that she suspected they might be blending slowly into the population. When the skywatchers finally dispersed from the Derenberger farm in March 1967, Indrid Cold supposedly landed his spacecraft in the field and invited Woody aboard. During this first trip, Woody claimed that Cold flew him to Brazil and back, though, eventually, he was taken to Lanulos.[18] Subsequently, Woody would wait by a highway for Cold's black Volkswagen to pick him up and drive him to the location of the spacecraft. Though the Lanulos took Woody on routine runs to the Ganymede galaxy, he conceptualized them as time travellers rather than spacemen, because despite travelling through space for what seemed like days at a time, upon returning to Earth he always found only a couple of hours had passed.[19]

Woody asserted that he was also introduced to Indrid Cold's

extraterrestrial entourage – Ardo, Clinnel, Hassan, Kemi, and Kletlaw – who granted him peculiar favours. For instance, immediately after two young skywatchers had spotted a cluster of red, white, and green illuminations from their parked car on Bogal Ridge, they were accosted by a telepathic man with a strange red light. He ordered the male out of the car, led him into the nearby forest, and robbed him of his watch, socks, and shoes. Familiar with Woody Derenberger's extraterrestrial run-ins, the next day, the couple drove to his Mineral Wells farmhouse and informed him of the incident. That night, Woody led them back to the exact same area of Bogle Ridge, to meet Indrid Cold, Karl Ardo, and Demo Hassan. The Lanulos informed them they had fallen prey to "humanoid" thieves and were fortunate not to have suffered a worse fate. Cold, Ardo, and Hassan vowed to find the culprits and return the items. The following day, the male found his freshly shined shoes, clean socks, and watch rolled up inside his morning newspaper.[20]

In light of the countless, independent Mothman and UFO sightings, when a rumour began to spread around the Ohio Valley that Woodrow Derenberger had been impregnated in an extraterrestrial experiment, rather than being met with derision, it was generally accepted. Within a year, the region had become so accustomed to utterly bizarre widespread phenomena that nothing seemed impossible anymore.

Taking stock of the totality of Woodrow Derenberger's accounts, Keel ultimately concluded that "either he was the world's most convincing liar, and had somehow trained his wife, children, and friends to back up his lies, or he had a very special set of experiences beyond the limits of UFOlogy."[21] In 1971, Woodrow Derenberger self-published *Visitors from Lanulos* through Vantage Press, detailing his experiences with Indrid Cold. At present, there are believed to be no more than half-a-dozen copies of the original printing in existence.

Before and during John Keel's investigations in Point Pleasant, he accrued a whole network of contactees who, like Woody

Derenberger, telephoned him on a regular basis, passing along messages from the entities. Around August or September of 1967, the contactees began talking about an "EM [Electro Magnetic] effect" – a massive power failure – that would happen in mid-December and affect a large portion of the United States.[22] Other predictions included the devaluation of the dollar and China's admission to the United Nations, along with cryptic warnings about how Senator Robert Kennedy should avoid hotels and that mankind must abandon its attempts to reach the Moon. They even prophesied that dozens of people would perish in a terrible tragedy on the Ohio River, alluding to a catastrophic factory explosion.

Indeed, by late 1967, the residents of the Ohio River Valley were eerily cognizant that something awful would befall their little community. On November 2, 1967, Mrs Virginia Thomas heard a loud squeaking coming from the TNT Area: "it was like a bad fan belt . . . but much louder. I stepped outside. It seemed to be coming from one of the igloos*. Then I saw a huge shadow spreading across the grass. It was just after noon so there shouldn't have been any shadow like that. Then this figure appeared. It walked erect like a man, but it was all grey, and it was much bigger than any man I ever saw. It moved very fast across the field and disappeared into the trees. It didn't seem to be walking exactly. It was almost gliding . . . faster than any man could run. It was the hunting season so I knew it wasn't a hunter. No hunter in his right mind would dress in grey. Around here they all wear red coats and red caps. And it wasn't a bear or anything like that. It really scared me."[23] Though she hadn't been physically harmed by the creature, Thomas was haunted by horrific nightmares in the aftermath. She dreamed of trucks carrying strange people across the Silver Bridge to the Point Pleasant side of the Ohio River. Once there, they descended upon the TNT Area, forcing her to evacuate with her children.

* Dome-shaped structures originally designed to store explosives

Mary Hyre – the local journalist Keel had met the previous November – had been having terrible dreams of her own. She envisioned Christmas presents floating in the Ohio River and desperate people thrashing and drowning in its waters.[24] She harboured a sense of foreboding doom: a feeling apparently shared by her community. When John Keel returned to Point Pleasant, he learnt that the rash of Mothman and UFO sightings had seemingly ceased overnight, replaced by a collective intuition that something just wasn't quite right.

By early December, Keel's contactees went into much greater detail regarding the dreaded "EM effect": they warned that when President Lyndon Baines Johnson switched on the lights at the annual Christmas tree ceremony on the White House lawn it would cause a nationwide power outage. The extraterrestrials had planned it that way. Believing himself well-versed in the complex machinations of Indrid Cold and his ilk, Keel believed the premonitions.

Around 5 p.m. on December 15, John Keel switched on the television in his Manhattan apartment and tuned in to the tree-lighting ceremony. Following a brief speech by President Johnson, the Texan statesman threw the switch and the Christmas tree lit up the White House lawn, wowing the crowd. The lights in Keel's apartment didn't even flicker, let alone go out. Just as he was about to curse the entities, a sombre voice suddenly announced from the television: "we interrupt this program for a special bulletin. A bridge laden with rush-hour traffic has just collapsed at Gallipolis, Ohio. Further details as soon as they are available."[25] Immediately, Keel realized the only bridge in Gallipolis, Ohio was the Silver Bridge stretching across the icy water to Point Pleasant. He suspected the entities had long known the exact nature of the December 15 disaster, but had misled him to prevent him from issuing warnings. After repeated attempts to reach his contacts in Point Pleasant, Keel finally got hold of Mary Hyre at 2 a.m. the next day.

"It's the most terrible thing I've ever seen," she cried. "You know those dreams I had . . . well, it was exactly like that. The packages floating in the water. The people crying for help. Those dreams came true."[26]

Keel eventually learnt that the stop light on the Gallipolis side of the bridge – notorious for staying on red for so long that locals routinely ignored it – had actually been stuck on green around 5 p.m., resulting in a major traffic jam on the Silver Bridge. At 5:04 p.m., the structure had collapsed with a metallic screech under the combined weight of the vehicles, falling into the waters of the Ohio River in a shower of sparks.

A subsequent analysis of the wreckage found that a defect in a single link of the Ohio-side subsidiary chain – one indiscernible to the naked eye in 1928 – had gradually worsened over time and caused the collapse. The Silver Bridge had originally been built for a trickle of small family cars and trucks bearing 20,000-lb (9-tonne) loads, rather than the constant stream of heavy sedans and 60,000-lb (27-tonne) truck hauls that were crossing the Ohio in the mid-1960s.

Whether they were watching the tragic news on TV or reading about it in their local newspapers, people all over America collectively grieved for the denizens of the Ohio River Valley and the men, women, and children who had perished in its freezing waters. In total, 38 bodies were retrieved from the river, though the sudden disappearance of people in both Ohio and West Virginia led authorities to conclude they had most likely gone down with the bridge, too. Ultimately, the estimated death toll was 46, with a number of UFO witnesses among them.

Soon after the Silver Bridge incident, many of the so-called contactees and witnesses that Keel had interviewed suffered mishaps, divorced, took their own lives, died of natural causes, or were institutionalized after suffering nervous breakdowns.[27] John Keel continued to research UFOs and other strange phenomena until his death in New York City on July 3, 2009, at the age of 79.

Wolf Creek 2005

The Crimes of Ivan Milat and the Murder of Peter Falconio

Wolf Creek captures every backpacker's worst nightmare – being stranded in a remote location with a psychopath. Director Greg McClean based his screenplay on two of Australia's most notorious and disturbing homicide cases: the "backpacker murders" perpetrated by Ivan Milat, and the murder of Peter Falconio and attempted abduction of Joanne Lees by Bradley Murdoch.

On its release, *Wolf Creek* was lauded for its poignantly realistic depictions of brutal violence and ability to elicit genuine empathy with the protagonists' desperate situation.

In the movie, three young backpackers – a man and two women – who are stranded in the Australian Outback accept the help of Mick Taylor, a seemingly good-natured local. Taylor subsequently drugs them unconscious before raping and torturing one of the female members of the group. When the two women escape, Mick hunts them down, murdering them and anyone who attempts to help them. Kept elsewhere and likely overlooked, the third abductee manages to free himself, collapses of dehydration in the bush, and is rescued by a passing Swedish couple. No trace of the murder victims' bodies or Mick Taylor are ever discovered.

Director Greg McClean revised his original screenplay for *Wolf Creek* in 1997, after learning of the crimes of Australian "Backpacker Murderer" Ivan Milat, and another case that bore some resemblance: the murder of Peter Falconio by Bradley John Murdoch. Combining

Milat and Murdoch's dark characteristics and backgrounds – Milat was a rugged outdoorsman with a small arsenal of firearms and fondness for off-road vehicles, while Murdoch was employed as a mechanic and truck driver – McLean crafted a terrifying fictional Frankenstein in Mick Taylor. Completed before Murdoch's trial, *Wolf Creek* was released in theatres all over Australia on November 3, 2005, except for cinemas in Northern Territory, where an injunction was placed on the film to prevent it from influencing Murdoch's ongoing trial. Forty days later, on December 13, 2005, Murdoch was convicted of the murder of Peter Falconio and the assault and attempted kidnapping of Joanne Lees.

—

On January 25, 1990, Englishman Paul Onions took the train from Sydney, Australia to the nearby suburb of Liverpool, planning to hitchhike to Melbourne down the Hume Highway. After reaching the suburb of Casula, he stopped to purchase a drink at a shop, where he was approached by a black-haired man in his early 40s with a handlebar moustache. Likely noticing Onions' cumbersome backpack, he asked the traveller if he needed a ride. The man stood nearly six-feet (1.8-m) tall with a muscular build – in some ways he reminded Onions of the Australian cricketer Merv Hughes[1] – but seemed friendly enough. Onions affirmed that he was trying to get to Melbourne, and the man offered to take him as far as Canberra: nearly a third of the journey. Onions enthusiastically agreed and together they headed to a white Toyota Land Cruiser 4WD in the car park. The moustachioed man introduced himself as "Bill". Onions hoisted his backpack into the rear of the vehicle, then hopped into the passenger seat, and together they sped off south. At first, Bill was genial, asking Paul about his travels and what he did for a living. Over the course of their conversation, Bill claimed he worked for the Roads and Traffic Authority in Liverpool, and regularly travelled around southeastern Australia.

About 45 minutes into their journey, the atmosphere in the Land Cruiser started to change. When Onions innocently expressed his surprise at Sydney's large Japanese population, Bill's demeanour darkened.

"We shouldn't have all them in the country," he scowled. "It's the same with you Brits, you shouldn't be in Northern Ireland either."[2]

Taken aback, Onions attempted to steer the discussion away from immigration, but Bill only grew angrier. For 15 minutes there was a tense silence in the Land Cruiser. Having become increasingly wary, Onions noticed the driver's eyes repeatedly flitting to the rear-view mirror. The vehicle started to slow. Bill pulled over to the side of the road, muttering something about wanting to grab some cassettes from under the front seat. Noting that there were already tapes within reach, Onions became increasingly nervous. Bill climbed out of the vehicle, and began rooting around under the driver's seat. Suddenly, he was holding a length of rope and pointing a black revolver in Onions' face.

"This is a robbery,"[3] he barked.

The passenger started frantically unfastening his seatbelt. Onions had previously served in the Royal Navy, and his military training now proved crucial. Bolting out of the car, he ran in a zig-zag pattern into the oncoming traffic.

"Stop or I'll shoot, stop or I'll shoot!" he heard Bill screaming.

Then the crack of a gunshot. Multiple cars swerved to avoid him, but not one of them stopped to help. Looking over his shoulder, he saw Bill chasing him.

"Get back in the car, get back in the car!"[4]

As they reached the grassy stretch of land splitting the highway, Bill seized him by the right sleeve, ripping his shirt. Realizing the danger he was in, Onions darted onto the eastern side of the highway, vowing to stop the next passing vehicle – whatever it took. When a van appeared, he stood directly in front of it, forcing the driver to slam on the brakes. Dashing to the passenger side sliding door, Onions wrenched it open, climbed inside, and hastily locked it. When he looked up, a puzzled female face was staring at him from the driver's seat.

"He's got a gun, he's got a gun!"[5] Onions pointed to the man on the grass.

The driver immediately made a U-turn and started heading in the opposite direction. Onions watched through the window as Bill hurried back to the Land Cruiser and continued towards Canberra.

Reflecting on his close call years later, Paul Onions would comment, "As soon as I seen [sic] the rope, I thought that's going to take a bit of time and he's going to do whatever he wants . . . I just thought, 'This is it, run or die,' so I undid my seatbelt and jumped straight out of the vehicle and ran."[6]

The woman drove him to Bowral Police Station where he filed an incident report and caught the next train back to Sydney. Paul Onions had lost his passport and backpack, but held on to his life. It wasn't until three years later, while watching the news back in the United Kingdom, that he realized how much worse things could have been.

In 1993, Soul Asylum – a band from Minneapolis – released a smash hit called "Runaway Train". The music video for the song sought to address the plight of missing children. Beginning with the title "There are over one million youths lost on the streets of America", the footage featured the names, photographs, and disappearance dates of 36 missing American children and teens. Alternate versions were made for the United Kingdom and Australia, displaying pictures and information related to missing youths in those countries. Among those featured on the Australian video were 19-year-olds Deborah Everist and James Gibson, who had vanished on December 30, 1989 while hitchhiking south from Sydney to a music festival in Albury. Within months of the video's release, the pair would resurface under some of the most gut-wrenching circumstances imaginable.

Roughly a year earlier, on September 19, 1992, two men were orienteering near the Longacre Fire Trail in Belanglo State Forest when they were struck by a foul stench emanating from beneath a rocky ledge. Peering under the rocks they spotted a bone and some clothes shoddily buried beneath sticks and leaves. The men immediately contacted the Bowral Police. Arriving on the scene, investigators uncovered the decomposing remains of an adult female – the garrotte beside her body left little doubt she had been the victim of foul play. A closer inspection revealed she had been stabbed a minimum of 14 times in the neck and torso.[7]

The following morning, a police search team discovered the body of a second woman just 30 yards (27 m) from the first victim, similarly concealed by deadfall. Red cloth had been wrapped twice around her head obscuring her face. An examination of her corpse revealed she had been shot 10 times in the head with a .22 calibre rifle – a finding supported by a cluster of spent Winchester cartridge casings found approximately four yards (3.6 m) away. Strangely, the bullets had entered the victim's head from many different angles, almost as if the killer had been using the corpse for target practice.[8] As in the case of the first victim, the police also observed multiple stabbing and slashing wounds to the upper body. Aside from their clothing and jewellery, whatever travelling equipment or additional personal effects the victims may have been carrying were conspicuously absent. However, the discovery of six cigarette butts near the second victim – five of the Longbeach brand – proved particularly valuable.

A forensic pathologist officially identified the first victim as 22-year-old Joanne Walters of Maesteg, Wales, and the woman wrapped in red cloth as her 21-year-old English travelling companion, Caroline Clarke. The young backpackers had last been seen leaving a hostel in Kings Cross, Sydney on April 18, 1992, bound for Adelaide. Clarke was known to have smoked Longbeach cigarettes. There was evidence that both women had been sexually assaulted.[9]

Well aware of the seven backpackers who had vanished in New South Wales in the past three years, the authorities assigned 40 police officers to scour the area. When no further evidence or human remains surfaced after seven days, the search was called off. Instead of providing additional manpower, New South Wales offered a $100,000 reward for information resulting in the arrest and conviction of the person(s) responsible for the slayings.

Over a year passed, and the police were still no closer to catching the murderer of Caroline Clarke and Joanne Walters. Troubled by the notion that more missing backpackers could be mouldering somewhere in the Belanglo Forest, local outdoorsman Bruce Pryor set out along the Morice Fire Trail to see what he could find. Eventually, he branched out onto the Clearly's Exit Fire Trail, following it until he reached an opening in the trees. There he spotted a bone large enough to belong to a human being. His speculation came to an abrupt end moments later when he happened upon a human skull with its lower jaw missing. Bundling it up in cloth, he raced off to the local orienteering club to telephone the police. They arrived half an hour later. Pryor passed the skull into their possession and showed them to the clearing.

Detective Steven Murphy's eyes scanned the area and rested upon a pair of sandshoes protruding from the brush. Beneath a gum tree was a set of skeletal remains clad in female clothing. The garments had been slashed, repeatedly and ferociously, leaving them in tatters, while scavenging animals had left the clearing strewn with disarticulated bone. The investigators found a small crucifix and bracelets entangled in the remains. At the base of another tree, a mere 20 yards (18 m) from the latest discovery, a canopy of foliage concealed yet another skeleton – only this one was male. Like the woman, he had been fully clothed when subjected to a frenzy of stabbing and slashing. Investigators came across a bullet-riddled tree trunk 440 yards (400 m) from the man's remains, from which they retrieved nine slugs. All but one, a .22 calibre, were unsuitable for forensic analysis.[10]

When news of the gruesome discovery surfaced, the media immediately began debating the identities of the remains. Had the fates of James Gibson and Deborah Everist – the missing teens who had featured in the music video for "Runaway Train" – finally been discovered? What about Gabor Neugebauer and Anja Habschied: a young German couple last seen hauling their backpacks from a Kings Cross hostel on December 26, 1991? Could the remains belong to somebody else altogether? This tactless media speculation came to an end days later when forensic pathology and odontology confirmed the victims were in fact Gibson and Everist.

With four victims recovered from the Belanglo Forest in 13 months, and potentially countless others concealed in the more than 9,000 acres of pine, Detective Clive Small created "Task Force Air"[11] – comprising 33 detectives, 11 intelligence analysts, and a myriad of forensic specialists – to apprehend the predator and restore order to the community. The initial failure to find the remains of Gibson and Everist, who had met their demise more than two years before Clarke and Walters, was not only embarrassing, but had also set the investigation back significantly. Thus, Task Force Air's first order of business would be to conduct a thorough search of Belanglo. Before doing so, they compared satellite images of the area from the late 1980s to the present, noting the changing patterns of vegetation. They formulated a strategy to search nearly 50 miles of paths and fire trails, also covering an area 160 yards to the left and right of each track for an additional 15 square miles. The 300-member search team was subdivided into groups of 40 people walking line abreast.

Their efforts bore fruit on November 1, 1993 when the skull and upper torso of a fifth victim were found protruding from a heap of deadfall 40 yards (37 m) off the Miner's Despair Fire Trail. Once again, the victim was fully-clothed and had suffered multiple stab wounds to her chest and back. Her spinal cord had been severed, perhaps intentionally to paralyze her. Harkening back to the discovery of Joanne Walters, a wire noose lay close to the body, though it seemed to have been used as a restraint rather than an instrument of murder. Searchers located the victim's jewellery, clothes, and backpack-contents nearby, along with a red T-shirt which had been sliced open from the front. As with the British and Australian couples, the backpack itself was nowhere to be found.

The victim was Simone Schmidl – another missing German backpacker – first identified informally by the distinctive headband round her forehead, then officially through forensic pathology and odontology. Simi, as she was known to her friends, had parted ways with her travelling companion Jeanette Mueller in Sydney on the morning of January 20, 1991. Despite Jeanette's warnings, Simi had assured her "all Australians were warm and friendly"[12] and that she always carried a knife for self-defence. The tall girl with the dreadlocks and headband was last seen by motorists standing on the side of the highway at Casula.

On November 3, a stray leather sandal in the Belanglo led the search team to two additional human skeletons concealed in a now all-too-familiar fashion. Twenty-one-year-old Gabor Neugebauer and his girlfriend Anja Habschied, 20, had finally been located – though Anja's head remained missing. Like Joanne Walters and Simone Schmidl, she had been stabbed and slashed to death through her pink top. A 5-yard (4.5-m) blue and yellow rope looped at either end, presumably to restrain the victim, was discarded in the immediate vicinity along with Anja's wrist watch and ankle bands. Gabor Neugebauer, on the other hand, had been used as target practice: a cloth gag was still clenched between the teeth of his bullet-riddled skull.[13] A thorough search of the area uncovered a sealed plastic bag with plane tickets bearing his name, and a money belt with the couple's International Student Cards, traveller's cheques, and cash. Twenty yards (18 m) from the money belt lay another makeshift loop-restraint consisting of a black plastic zip tie, black insulation tape, cord, and a leash. A cartridge holder built for 50 rounds was located approximately 200 yards (182 m) from Gabor's corpse, along with Anja's pink jeans, and two empty card-board packs of .22 calibre ammunition. The first was for Winchester

Brand, and the second for Eley Subsonic hollow-points. The medical examiner removed four .22 calibre bullets from Gabor's skull (though there were six points of entry in total) and a fifth from his upper chest. Furthermore, investigators had extracted six bullet fragments from tree trunks in proximity to his body.

The search continued for 12 more days before Detective Small was satisfied the Belanglo Forest had given up all of its secrets. But how long would it be before the killer returned to replenish its stock of horrors? From now on, the investigation would have to be proactive: the reward for information was increased to $500,000. Within 24 hours the taskforce had received over 5,000 calls.[14]

Three phone calls would prove instrumental in bringing the Belanglo Forest Killer to justice. The first came on November 9 from a Ms Joanne Berry of Canberra, who had been driving on the Hume Highway near Berrima in January 1990, when a young man forced his way into her van shouting, "Help me, he's got a gun."[15] Spotting an older man in pursuit, she had sped off. Along the way to Bowral Police Station, the escapee had told her his name was Paul Onions, and that he'd accepted a ride while hitchhiking, only to have the driver pull a gun on him.

Paul Onions called the taskforce from England just two days later. Reports of the horrific revelations from the Belanglo Forest had reached the UK, and were being widely reported in the media. Recalling his near-brush with death in New South Wales, Onions thought it crucial to relay his experience. He described his attacker as a male "in his early 40s . . . fit looking, about 5'10" tall [with] a Merv Hughes moustache . . . [and] black hair", driving a "white Toyota Land Cruiser 4WD with woolly seat covers."[16]

A third call implicated a local man named Ivan Milat, who owned a four-wheel drive vehicle and had a small arsenal of firearms which he was always using for target practice. Milat had already appeared on the investigators' radar, owing to his well-founded reputation for criminality, gun fetishism, and eccentricity.[17] The phone call helped to focus the taskforce's attention specifically on Ivan. When Detective Clive Small ordered an in-depth search into the 48-year-old's criminal record, he uncovered a history of theft and incarceration dating back to his teenage years. His crimes had worsened as he grew older, graduating to charges for armed robbery and rape. A 1991 photo of Ivan confirmed he had owned a silver-white Nissan 4WD until September 1992, and had changed vehicles around the same time as the discovery of the bodies of Caroline Clarke and Joanne Walters. The Nissan bore a striking resemblance to a Toyota Land Cruiser. Ivan was also known to use the alias "Bill" and worked for the Roads and Traffic Authority – both details consistent with Onions' story. He had been charged with picking up and raping two female hitchhikers at knifepoint in April 1971. The modus operandi and victimology foreshadowed those of the Belanglo Forest Killer. Moreover, he had not been at work during any of the dates of the murders.

On February 26, 1994, Ivan Milat was placed on round-the-clock surveillance to ensure he did not commit any further crimes or destroy evidence. In keeping with the hypothesis that the Belanglo Forest Killer took mementos from his victims to relive the slayings, Task Force Air was convinced that his home in Eagle Vale was a trove of "souvenirs" taken from the Belanglo Forest victims. The noose tightened even further when Paul Onions arrived in Sydney on May 2. After being shown photographs of 13 different men, one of whom was Ivan Milat, Onions easily identified him as "Bill", his attempted abductor.[18]

A decision was quickly made to arrest Ivan Milat for his 1990 attack on Paul Onions. This would allow the investigators to search his residence in Eagle Vale while detaining him in custody without bail. They strongly suspected that Ivan's house held the key to unlocking the murderer's identity – once he had been placed under arrest, they would initiate a series of surprise raids on a number of properties belonging to his family, while subjecting other Milats to questioning. Well aware that Ivan was armed and dangerous, the taskforce carefully assembled a team of four negotiators, 21 investigators, and 26 members of the SPG's Tactical Operations Unit to ensure his arrest went smoothly. Shortly after dawn on May 22, 1994, Ivan Milat was arrested at his residence. Among the many items recovered from the Eagle Vale house were: .22 calibre cartridges of the Winchester Winner and Eley brands; currency brought back from Indonesia by Gabor Neugebauer and Anja Habschied; rolls of black electrical tape and zip ties consistent with those recovered from the Neugebauer/Habschied crime scene; Deborah Everist and Simone Schmidl's sleeping bags; over a dozen pieces of camping equipment linked to Simone Schmidl; a photo of Ivan's girlfriend wearing articles of clothing that had belonged to Caroline Clarke; a map of the Belanglo State Forest; a .32 Browning pistol; remnants of a Ruger 10/22 rifle (one of the firearms that ballistics experts had determined was used on Clarke and Neugebauer); and a silencer built to fit a .22 calibre rifle.[19]

Ivan Robert Marko Milat was convicted of the murders of James Gibson, Deborah Everist, Simone Schmidl, Gabor Neugebauer, Anja Habschied, Caroline Clarke, and Joanne Walters on July 27, 1996. He spent the rest of his life in prison. On October 27, 2019, after a short battle with oesophageal cancer, he died on the Hospital Wing of Long Bay Correctional Centre, having never admitted to the Belanglo Forest murders or any of the dozen others of which he was suspected.

Unfortunately, a few years later it would become apparent that Milat was not the only killer who took advantage of the sparsely populated Australian Outback to abduct unsuspecting travellers. Just over seven years after Milat's arrest, another brutal crime would shake Australia.

—

In 1996, Peter Falconio and Joanne Lees met at Visage nightclub in Huddersfield, UK, and fell in love. Both had been raised in West Yorkshire and were in their early twenties. At the time, Joanne worked for a local branch of the Thomas Cook travel agency, while

Peter was earning his BSc in building and construction management at Brighton University. Hoping to move down south with her new boyfriend, Joanne was delighted when Thomas Cook agreed to transfer her to Hove. The two moved into a one-bedroom flat near the beach together and enjoyed a seemingly idyllic life, holidaying in Greece, Italy, and Jamaica, while Peter slowly chipped away at his degree. Though he planned to provide a life for them as a construction site manager, neither Peter nor Joanne were ready to settle down until they had seen more of the world. In 1998, they began plotting a year-long journey overseas to commence when Peter finished his studies. They spent many nights poring over Joanne's travel brochures.

Peter graduated in 2000, and by mid-November, the couple had landed in Kathmandu. They spent the next two months on an adventure through the snow-capped Himalayas, eventually flying to Singapore. From there, they travelled by bus through Malaysia into southern Thailand. The couple had been so enamoured with Nepal's monasteries and the resplendent temples of Thailand, that they longed to see the Buddhist remnants of the Khmer Empire in Cambodia. Young and fearless, they caught a flight to Phnom Penh: the Cambodian capital. It took less than two days for a pick-pocket to relieve them of their cash, plane tickets, and traveller's cheques.[20] Luckily, they managed to borrow enough money from a fellow tourist to return to Bangkok. Their time in southeast Asia had been transformative, but the couple realized they'd pushed their luck too far. It was time to head to Australia. As Peter told Joanne, "We might as well continue. We're over the worst that can happen."[21] After securing a working visa, on the morning of January 16, 2001, Peter Falconio and Joanne Lees boarded a plane. When they alighted, they were in beautiful cosmopolitan Sydney in the middle of the Australian summer.

They found a flat in North Bondi Beach, and both promptly found work. Joanne was smitten with the city and wanted to stay as long as possible. Peter thought the real allure of Australia lay within its vast and surreal tracts of wilderness. While Joanne explored, Peter set about looking for a vehicle for the next leg of their journey. He found it at Kings Cross Car Market – an orange Volkswagen Kombi pop-top van with a built-in fridge, gas cooker, CD player, and sink – and after managing to talk its former owners, two fellow British tourists, down from $3,000 to $1,200, he bought it on May 24. Peter spent the next month tinkering with it, knowing Joanne was reluctant to leave the Harbour City. But, eventually, it was time to see the rest of the country.

On the morning of June 25, 2001, they waved goodbye to their Sydney friends, and set off south through the Blue Mountains in the puttering orange wreck. Over the next two weeks, they passed through Canberra and into Melbourne, before veering west towards South Australia and the state capital of Adelaide. Next, they headed north along the Stuart Highway (aka the Track) – right along the centre line that splits Australia into east and west – and entered the Northern Territory. With a population of approximately 200,000 Territorians scattered across 520,000 square miles, it was essentially a sparsely inhabited wilderness of rock and scrub, fractured by the occasional canyon. Dangerous, perhaps, in its emptiness.

By Wednesday, July 11, Peter Falconio and Joanne Lees had reached Uluṟu-Kaṯa Tjuta National Park, home to the sacred monolith of Uluru. Like the thousands who had come before them, it left them awestruck, possessing a kind of spiritual resonance they had not felt since Thailand. They befriended a group of Canadian backpackers, and offered them a lift north in the Kombi. The group continued along the Track, stopping at King's Canyon, before heading to Alice Springs where they parted ways. Peter and Joanne spent the night sleeping in the Kombi on the edge of the town. They remained in Alice Springs through Thursday and into Friday, visiting the hiking trails and gorges, purchasing plane tickets, and catching up on their emails at the local library. This little town of 20,000 residents would be the closest thing to civilization until they reached Darwin, 800 miles (1,287 km) to the north. On the afternoon of July 14, they attended the annual Camel Cup in Blatherskite Park, where they watched the hump-backed creatures gallop clumsily around the dusty race track. They left Alice Springs in the Kombi soon after, continuing their odyssey along the Track. Around 6:20 p.m., Joanne pulled in to Ti Tree Roadhouse to refill the petrol tank. They lit a joint, passing it back and forth as they watched the sun set slowly on the dry scrubland. Sydney was exciting, but the last few days had been nothing short of magical.

Within half an hour they were back on the road. Night had fallen, and the petty thievery they had encountered back in Cambodia was about to be overshadowed by something far worse.

At 7:30 p.m., Peter was driving along an isolated section of the Track, when headlights appeared in the rear-view mirror. To their surprise, a white pick-up truck drew up beside them, almost running parallel. The interior light was on, and the driver – a man with a black baseball cap and moustache – was signalling for them to pull over. While Joanne was nervous about stopping in the Outback at night, Peter concluded it was obviously important. The vehicles parked on the side of the highway. Peter exited and approached the pick-up truck – a Toyota. Watching through the window of the Kombi, Joanne could see a dog in the passenger seat. Peter and the motorist were discussing sparks shooting out of their exhaust pipe.

Peter returned to the van and explained to Joanne that they were going to check the exhaust, and needed her to rev the engine. Joanne nodded and slid into the driver's seat. Grabbing his pack of cigarettes, Peter circled around to the back of the Kombi with the other motorist. As she pressed her foot on and off the accelerator, she heard a loud bang, and wondered if the van had backfired.[22] Suddenly, the man in the black baseball cap was standing outside the driver's side window, brandishing a silver revolver. He ordered her to turn off the engine. When her trembling hands struggled to complete this simple task, he climbed into the van beside her and did it himself. Pressing the muzzle to her temple, he instructed her to place her hands behind her back and keep her head down. The man secured her wrists together with cable ties, then forced her out of the passenger side door onto the ground. Straddling her, he attempted to bind her ankles with rope, but she flailed her legs, kicking out wildly at him. Angered, he punched her in the head, leaving her stunned. He picked her up by the scruff of her neck, and she cried out to Peter, but to no avail.

Dragging her over to his white Toyota, the man tried to tape her mouth shut. Somehow, she managed to resist his efforts, while continuing to scream for help. Her attacker instead pulled a sack over her head and pushed her into the passenger seat of the vehicle. Once she was inside, he removed the sack. Joanne's eyes settled on the black and white dog sitting on the driver's seat. She turned to her abductor, and got a good look at his face. Judging by his lined brow, greying moustache, and collar-length hair, he looked to be in his mid-40s, with droopy, deep-set eyes and sunken cheeks.[23] An ill-fitting checked shirt, dark tee, and thick trousers hung from his tall frame. Next, he grabbed her and shoved her under the canopy in the back of his truck. Joanne tried to speak with him, but he threatened to shoot her if she didn't shut up. She heard him move away from the vehicle towards the Kombi, followed by the sound of something heavy being dragged across the ground. Seeing her chance, Joanne wriggled her way onto the truck's tray, placed her legs over the side, and slipped onto the road. As soon as she felt her feet touch down, she sprinted towards the bush. The dry branches tore at her as she crashed blindly through the scrub. Once she was far enough away from the road, she crouched behind some tall bushes and went still. Out on the road she could hear her assailant's movements. A torch scanned the tangled scrubland looking for her, then eventually went out. After a few minutes, she heard a vehicle door open and slam shut, followed by an engine's roar. Headlights illuminated the highway momentarily, then shot off down the road.[24]

Wisely, Joanne remained in hiding. Sometime later, she heard the man return to the crime scene to remove the second vehicle. When he had disappeared once more into the night, she tried unsuccessfully to free her hands from the zip ties. Exhausted, she staggered up to the roadside and collapsed. Uncertain as to whether the man in the baseball cap would revisit the area yet again, she chose to remain lying in the grass, waiting for the first road train. Cars were too risky – she had no idea what vehicle her attacker might be driving. With the appearance of a road train, she stumbled out into the road and flagged it down. While the two men who occupied the vehicle, Vince Millar and Rodney Adams, used a tool to remove the zip ties, she recounted her experience to them and stressed the need to find her missing boyfriend. Millar and Adams did their best to search the area, but Peter Falconio had seemingly vanished. They decided to take her to the nearby town of Barrow Creek. Joanne Lees arrived at approximately 2 a.m.

At 4:20 a.m., policemen from Alice Springs arrived to gather forensic evidence from Joanne Lees' person and record statements. They waited until 7 a.m. to erect roadblocks and search the stretch of road where the attack had occurred, finding only a pool of Peter's blood, Joanne's footprints, and the Kombi concealed in the bush 90 yards (82 m) from the initial crime scene. After that, they more or less gave up on the crime for a few weeks, due to insufficient corroborating evidence. Yet Peter Falconio remained missing.

Though Joanne Lees garnered great sympathy for her terrifying ordeal, it wasn't long before a cottage industry of books and newspaper articles sprang up falsely accusing her of committing, or being complicit in, Peter Falconio's murder. The baseless accusations derived chiefly from discrepancies in Lees' recollections of the crime, her perceived inappropriate appearance and attire during television interviews, and the overblown revelation that she had cheated on Peter while the couple were staying in Sydney.[25]

Eventually, when the poverty of the Northern Territory police's investigation came under scrutiny, they were jolted into action and managed to retrieve an unknown male DNA sample from Joanne's t-shirt, the zip tie handcuffs, and the Kombi's gear stick. They publicly released CCTV footage from a Shell truck stop in Alice Springs revealing the face of a man who had paid at the register at 12:38 a.m. on July 15. They urged the man in the CCTV footage to come forward so he could be eliminated as a suspect, to no avail. A $250,000 reward was issued for information leading to the arrest and conviction of the attacker. Cross-referencing the names of 36 men who tipsters had identified as the man on the CCTV with registered owners of 1991–99 Toyota Land Cruiser 4WDs, the police identified one Bradley John Murdoch, 43.

Born in Western Australia on February 19, 1958, Murdoch had moved to the state capital of Perth with his family at the age of 13. A known thug and bully, he had dropped out of high school at 15, started a trucking company, and joined an outlaw motorcycle gang, the Coffin Cheaters. In 1980, the 21-year-old Murdoch struck and killed a cyclist while driving, was convicted of causing death by dangerous driving, and given a suspended sentence.[26] Murdoch had married that same year, though his trucking business went bankrupt in 1983. His physical abuse of his wife, Diane, led to the couple's separation in 1986. By this time, he was working as a truck driver and transporting drugs. During the 1990s, Murdoch had developed a White Supremacist viewpoint, even joining a chapter of the Ku Klux Klan. His left arm bore a tattoo of a lynched Aboriginal man with his legs on fire, while a tattoo on his right arm depicted a Klansman pointing at another indigenous Australian. On August 20, 1995, a drunk Murdoch had opened fire with a bolt action rifle on a crowd of Aboriginal Australians in Kimberley, and was subsequently incarcerated for 15 months. Released from prison, he had eventually settled in Broome, Western Australia.

On November 1, police in Broome brought Murdoch in for questioning, but in a baffling display of investigative incompetence, failed to ask him to provide a DNA sample. Fortunately, on May 17, 2002, the Falconio task force apprehended a drug-runner working with Murdoch who divulged details of the attack that had not been released to the public. DNA obtained from Murdoch's brother was found to be closely related to the samples taken from the t-shirt and Kombi, and a warrant was issued for Bradley Murdoch's arrest. But by that time, he had vanished.

After his police interview, Murdoch absconded to a farmhouse in South Australia owned by a former brothel keeper, which was also home to the owner's girlfriend, and her 12-year-old daughter. Hiding out there, Murdoch repeatedly claimed the police were trying to frame him for the murder of Peter Falconio. His constant use of amphetamines only fuelled his paranoid fire. Allegedly, on August 21, 2002, Murdoch kidnapped the woman and her daughter at gun-point, chaining them up with manacles affixed to the rear of his Landcruiser. It was later claimed he raped the 12-year-old girl.[27] While driving across the state, he supposedly rambled non-stop about the Falconio case and how he was being set up – all while wearing a t-shirt that he admitted belonged to the missing Englishman. After keeping the mother and daughter for a period of 25 hours, he let them go. Not long after, Bradley John Murdoch was arrested outside a supermarket in Port Augusta. When police searched his vehicle they found a knife, .308 rifle with telescopic sight, loaded .22 Beretta semi-automatic pistol, electric cattle prod, crossbow with 13 bolts, chains, shackles, 800 rounds of ammunition, and night vision goggles. He was charged with two counts of rape, false imprisonment, and one count of assault.[28]

Throughout the course of his South Australian trial, police learnt that Murdoch had returned to drug-running, transporting massive amounts of cannabis from Sedan, South Australia, up the Track to Alice Springs, and then back to Broome. This criminal enterprise netted him hundreds of thousands of dollars every year. Though Murdoch was ultimately found not guilty of the rape, imprisonment, and assault charges by a majority verdict, his DNA had been obtained during the process and matched to the samples in the Falconio case. Moreover, in November 2002, Joanne Lees was approached by members of the Northern Territory police and shown a series of photographs. She identified Bradley John

Murdoch as the man who had attacked her on the Track almost two years earlier.[29]

In April 2005, Murdoch was extradited to Northern Territory and charged with both the murder of Peter Falconio and the assault and attempted abduction of Joanne Lees. His trial commenced in Darwin on October 17, 2005. Murdoch pleaded not guilty to each of the charges. On December 13, he was convicted on all charges by unanimous verdict and sentenced to life imprisonment, with no possibility of parole for at least 28 years. In the years since, he has occupied cells at Darwin's maximum security Berrimah Prison and the Darwin Correctional Centre, continuing to maintain his innocence, and assailing the criminal justice system with repeated appeals and requests for special treatment.

In 2007, Joanne Lees' book *Joanne Lees: Murder in the Outback* was published, providing the general public with her first-hand account of what had transpired. Sadly, as of the time of this writing, Peter Falconio's body has never been recovered.

The Conjuring 2013
Annabelle 2014
The Conjuring 2 2016

THE HAUNTING OF THE PERRON FARM, THE CASE OF THE ANNABELLE DOLL, AND THE ENFIELD POLTERGEIST

***The Conjuring* is one of the most highly acclaimed and commercially successful horror films of recent years. So successful, in fact, that it has spawned an entire cinematic franchise – the so-called *Conjuring* Universe. In this series of interlinked films, all have one thing in common: they are based on the real-life cases of Ed and Lorraine Warren.**

Controversial yet fascinating figures, demonologist Ed Warren and his clairvoyant wife, Lorraine, became America's most famous ghosthunters through their well-publicized exploits in the 1970s, 80s, and 90s. Director James Wan took great creative liberties with their "casefiles" to create the most successful horror franchise of the 21st century: the *Conjuring* Universe. His first offering, *The Conjuring*, made a whopping $319.5 million. Its spin-off *Annabelle* was another success, making $257 million on less than a third of its predecessor's budget, while *The Conjuring 2* also put on a great showing, raking in a record $320 million. Every installment in the series has chilling moments, from the iconic hide-and-clap scene in *The Conjuring*, to the emergence of "The Crooked Man" in *The Conjuring 2*. With tasteful CGI, compelling settings, and solid pacing, the films of the *Conjuring* Universe have firmly established James Wan as one of the 21st century's foremost horror filmmakers.

The Conjuring (2013) tells the story of the Perron family, who move into a haunted colonial-era farmhouse in Rhode Island in the early 1970s, and find themselves the victims of paranormal attacks. When the Warrens arrive to help, they discover the property is haunted by the spirit of a child-killing witch, Bathsheba Sherman. Carolyn Perron is eventually possessed by Bathsheba, and attempts to sacrifice her own children, forcing Ed Warren to expel the spirit from her body through exorcism against the church's wishes. The film also introduces the haunted Annabelle doll.

The first spin-off movie, simply titled *Annabelle* (2014), provides an account of the doll's origins. The story begins when Dr John Form and his pregnant wife, Mia, are attacked by cultists in their Santa Monica apartment. Cult member Annabelle Higgins seizes Mia's antique porcelain doll and fatally slashes her own throat. Paranormal activity ensues. John and Mia throw the doll away and move with their newborn, Leah, to an apartment in Pasadena. But the doll inexplicably reappears, along with supernatural happenings which Leah interprets to be linked to Annabelle Higgins' spirit. Later, she and a neighbour, Evelyn, discover she is wrong, and that the cultists summoned a demon that attached itself to the doll. When the demon possesses a local priest and abducts Leah, a guilt-ridden Evelyn jumps out of the window with the doll. Leah is reunited with her parents and the demonic attacks on the Form family cease. The film concludes with a mother buying the doll from an antique shop as a present for her daughter, Debbie, setting the stage for the opening sequence of *The Conjuring.*

In *The Conjuring 2* (2016), Lorraine encounters a demonic nun while investigating the Lutz home in Amityville – scene of the infamous "Amityville Horror" – and again while in her own home. Before she can investigate, she and Ed are called away to Enfield, north London, England, where an unprecedented level of poltergeist activity is terrorizing the Hodgson family, particularly 12-year-old

Janet Hodgson. There they meet British paranormal investigators Maurice Grosse, who believes the haunting is genuine, and the sceptical Anita Gregory. Using Janet as a medium, they communicate with the ghost of Bill Wilkins, an old man who died in the home and refuses to leave. When Gregory produces evidence that Janet is perpetrating a hoax, the Warrens prepare to head back to America, but Lorraine has a sudden epiphany – the demonic nun was using Wilkins' spirit as a puppet to make Janet susceptible to possession. They return to find the other Hodgsons locked out of their house and Janet in full thrall of the demon. Lorraine drives out the evil spirit by uttering its name – "Valac" – restoring order to the home.

The first three films in the *Conjuring* Universe were inspired directly by the paranormal investigations conducted and documented by Ed and Lorraine Warren in Harrisville, Rhode Island; Connecticut; and Enfield, London.

—

In 1970, the travelling salesman Roger Perron and his wife Carolyn were living with their five daughters in a suburb of Providence, Rhode Island. The pair had married in 1957, and had generally led happy lives, but a spate of terrible luck found them that summer. The girls watched helplessly as a teenager in a speeding car ran over their beloved dog. Gangs sprang up in the neighbourhood and the family returned home from a vacation to find their house ransacked and their three cats slaughtered. After the eldest Perron daughter, 12-year-old Andrea, attacked the boy she thought was responsible, she found herself in court. Though the charges were dropped, the family's summer of misfortune continued when a neighbour suffered a heart attack and crashed his truck on the Perrons' lawn. To make matters worse, the man's wife accused Carolyn – a lapsed Catholic – of causing his death through witchcraft.[1]

The Perron family were certainly due for a fresh start, and Carolyn decided to make a down-payment on a farmhouse in rural

Harrisville, 15 miles (24 km) northwest of Providence, without consulting her husband. Though he was upset, Roger was an agreeable man, and when he saw the beautiful colonial structure, erected in 1736, he assured his wife that she had made the right decision.

An ice storm was raging when the Perrons arrived with their truck full of boxes in January 1971. Roger passed a box to Andrea and instructed her to bring it to Carolyn who was in the kitchen. Dutifully, Andrea carried the item in through the parlour door, and began the long trek towards the pantry. Entering the dining room, she saw a man in outdated clothing staring at Mr Kenyon, the previous resident from whom they had bought the house. A polite girl, Andrea bid the stranger good morning, but he did not respond. Shrugging, she continued on to the pantry.

"Mom, who's that other man with Mr Kenyon in the dining room?"[2] Andrea asked, handing Carolyn the box. "There is no other man in the dining room,"[3] her mother replied.

As if on cue, the other four girls, Nancy, 10, Christine, 9, Cindy, 7, and April, 5, entered and exclaimed, "That man in the dining room just disappeared!"[4] Before Mr Kenyon made his own exit, he bid the Perrons farewell and told Roger, "For the sake of your family, leave the lights on at night!"[5]

On one of the first nights in their new home, Andrea was lying awake when her sister Cindy entered the room and crawled onto her bed. Cindy asked if she could sleep in Andrea's bed, and Andrea pulled back the covers. "I hear voices in my room," Cindy told her. "They're all talking at once, but they're all saying the same thing."[6] When Andrea asked her what the voices were saying, Cindy replied "There are seven dead soldiers buried in the wall."[7]

Initially, the house – or whatever force was occupying it – seemed most attracted to Cindy. One day, the five girls were upstairs together and decided to play a game of hide and seek. They all headed off in different directions. Walking around the ground floor carrying a torch, Cindy was looking for a good hiding spot, when suddenly the cellar door creaked open. Seeing a perfect opportunity, Cindy turned on her torch and descended into the darkness. While shining the beam through the junk and cobwebs she noticed a wooden trunk, which was closed neither by a latch or hook. Excitedly, she rushed over, raised the lid, and climbed inside. Yet, to her surprise, the inside of the box was extraordinarily hot. Cindy tried to push the lid open to clamber out, but was met with strong resistance, almost as if there was a person on the other side holding it shut. Unable to leave, she began to panic, and started screaming at the top of her lungs and punching and kicking at the sides. As the air inside ran low, she found herself praying for her sisters to come save her. Just before she was about to pass out, the lid opened, and she saw her sisters standing over her, looking concerned. "The box wouldn't let me out,"[8] she gasped, her face drained of all colour.

Nine-year-old Christine was the second member of the Perron family to have an unsettling encounter involving the cellar. Tasked with washing the dishes, she was standing at the sink one evening, looking out of the window into the night. Without warning, she felt a cold draught encircling her ankles, and heard the creak of hinges from behind. Looking over her shoulder, she saw the cellar door had opened. But when she turned back to the window, she jumped back in fright – she thought she had seen a human face reflecting back off the glass, meaning somebody was standing right behind her. Spinning back around, she saw only the open cellar door and darkness beyond.

The final incident with the cellar came when Andrea Perron found herself alone in the house – a rare treat for the eldest daughter of a large family. She was sitting on her bed completing her homework, when she heard a baby crying. This was baffling: there was nobody else home at all, let alone an infant. Yet the wailing continued, seemingly luring Andrea out of her room and down the stairs in the direction of the cries. They seemed to have a pained quality, as if the baby was in agony. Suddenly, the cellar door swung open, and the temperature plummeted to the point where she could see her breath. The door then slammed shut and Andrea started screaming. About that time, Roger came home to find his terrified daughter in the hallway. She explained what had happened, and he decided to examine the door. Despite his daughter's claims that it had opened on its own, it could not be pulled open unless one first raised the latch, and the latch was in good condition.

Opening the door, Roger decided to explore the cellar. As he was making his way through the darkness, he felt a hand brush his back from right to left, and believed it was his wife's. However, when the sensation stopped, he turned around to find himself alone in the cellar. Though he had no idea what was going on, Roger Perron had no doubt that whatever had happened to him was out of the ordinary, and it was probably no coincidence that his daughter had been similarly unsettled. He went back upstairs, closed the door firmly, fetched a hammer and some nails, and sealed off the cellar.[9]

Andrea Perron was having a terrible dream. She was standing in the corner of her parents' bedroom, paralyzed by fear, as an old woman with sticks in place of hands hovered over her mother. Roger lay beside his wife, torn up as if mauled by a savage beast. Though Andrea did not move or make a sound, the woman eventually sensed her presence, and turned to face her. Andrea snapped out of the dream in a cold sweat. She took a moment to compose herself, before rising and making her way downstairs. When she reached the table, she saw her mother scratching on a piece of paper with a pencil. Leaning over to pick up Carolyn's cup of coffee, she caught sight of the image on the page and froze. It was a portrait of a woman with wood protruding from her sleeves – the same hag Andrea had seen hovering over her mother in her nightmare. Andrea told her mother about the dream and asked if the assault had actually happened. Carolyn replied that it had. At that moment, Roger Perron came down the stairs shirtless. Both Andrea and Carolyn noticed lacerations across his back, almost like claw marks, and brought them to his attention. They explained to Roger what had happened to them the night before, but despite being shaken by his own injuries, he thought their claims were far-fetched. Instead, he wracked his brains for a reasonable explanation to the past few hours' events. He drew a blank.

Several nights later, Carolyn awoke from her slumber once again. The bedroom stank of smoke. When she saw two tall men standing next to the doorway, she felt her body clam up in fear. Before she knew what was happening, a dark woman walked into the room carrying a large flaming torch. As she neared the bed, she began to bang the end of the torch on the floor in a primitive rhythm, chanting hypnotically. Carolyn got the sense that she was trying to summon something evil from another realm. Then, Carolyn felt something stab her leg. When she threw the covers off to take a look, the figures disappeared. In that instant, Roger also awakened. He asked her what had happened; looking down at Carolyn's leg they could both see a needle-thin puncture wound, oozing blood. There was no denying it anymore: whatever was happening to them in their dreams was harming them in their waking life.

From that day onwards, Carolyn Perron was not the same. Overnight, her appearance changed from that of a woman in her early 30s to someone decades older. It was as if some other entity was sapping her lifeforce. Realizing that whatever evil was plaguing their Harrisville home was linked to its history, Carolyn's obsession with the past began. Delving into the local historical archives, Carolyn learnt that her home had been the site of countless tragedies. A "Mrs John Arnold" had apparently hanged herself in the barn at the age of 93: just one of a number of suicides, drownings, and other fatalities which had occurred on the property over the centuries. But the sum total of all of these findings paled in comparison to the tale of Bathsheba Sherman. Born to the same Arnold family who had once occupied the property, Bathsheba had supposedly been both beautiful and extraordinarily cruel. Carolyn learnt that a number of children had once been left in Bathsheba Sherman's care, during which time an infant perished. It was claimed that a medical examination by the county coroner reported that a needle had been jammed into the top of the child's skull. Bathsheba was alleged to have sacrificed the child in exchange for eternal beauty and youth. Though never formally convicted of the murder, members of the local community had apparently made up their own minds regarding her guilt, and a pall had followed Bathsheba for the rest of her life. Noting the similarities between the supposed murder-by-needle and what had happened to her own leg, Carolyn became convinced that Bathsheba Sherman was the main entity haunting the Perron home.

But Carolyn Perron's fascination with the past went well beyond poring over historic documents. By now she was dressing in vintage clothing and adopted an anachronistic way of speaking. With Carolyn seemingly possessed or suffering from mental illness, Andrea stepped into her mother's shoes, presiding over the Perron girls. Then, one evening in 1973, Christine Perron answered the door to two strangers – a man and a woman – who told them they had heard about their problems and were here to help.

Ed and Lorraine Warren first asked if they could look around the family's farmhouse, assuring them it would not take long. As they went from room to room, Lorraine paused as if noting something ethereal. Suddenly, she started trembling and buckled over. "I sense a malignant presence in this house," she cried, "and her name is Bathsheba."[10] Lorraine turned to Carolyn and asked if that name meant anything to her. She nodded, and Ed gently moved the children into another room to speak with them.

Despite their previous assurances, the Warrens would end up conducting a year-and-a-half long investigation which came to a dramatic ending when Lorraine explained to Roger and Carolyn, "You've got the devil living in your house, and we'd like to perform a séance."

Though the long-suffering Carolyn welcomed help of any kind, Roger sensed that nothing good would come of the idea. Eventually he gave in, and agreed.

Not long after, the Warrens entered the home with a priest, medium, and camera operator to film the events. While all of the children were given strict instructions to stay on the upper floor, 15-year-old Andrea and some of the sisters crept downstairs, peering through the crack in the dining room door at the six adults seated around the table clasping each other's hands. Lorraine began by calling upon any spirits in the home to come forward and allow their grievances to be heard. Two minutes passed, and then the house started shaking. The Perrons watched in disbelief as the table slowly hovered off the floor. As it rose, Carolyn's eyelids lowered, and her form slumped, as if all the energy were draining from her body. Her face contorted, at first in a pained wince, but then transforming to take on the appearance of someone entirely different. As it did, her knees curled into her chest, her anatomy coiling into an impossible shape that in a normal situation would have broken her bones. The hideous form levitated in its chair, its mouth spewing words in a tongue that was both unfamiliar and indecipherable to those in attendance. Suddenly, she flew 20 feet (6 m) backwards into the adjoining parlour. Her skull hit the floor with a tremendous crack, and she collapsed limp on the floorboards.

Roger shouted that the Warrens had killed his wife, and ordered them to get out of the house immediately. As the Warrens fled the home, Andrea and Cindy rushed into the room. Both daughters and Roger held on to Carolyn, trying to shake her back to life, and begging her not to leave them. Against all odds it worked. Carolyn would later describe the experience from her perspective: "It took every ounce of my strength, my heart. It was the will of my children I'm sure that brought me back, but I was so gone . . ."[11]

The Perrons believed that whatever demon the Warrens had inadvertently invited into their home scared many of the other spirits inhabiting the house into silence. Months of peace went by, but then, gradually, the unusual events resumed. Finally, one night, Carolyn walked into the parlour, and heard voices emanating from the closed dining room. Turning towards them, she saw a large family around a completely different table as a woman cooked a meal for them in a fireplace that had long since been sealed. As she instructed the children to take their seats, one of the men in the room glanced into the parlour and straight into Carolyn's eyes. Peculiarly, he nudged another man beside him, and pointed in Carolyn's direction. In that moment, Carolyn Perron had an epiphany: the colonial farmhouse was actually a portal between time and space, and now she was being viewed as an apparition by two men in the past. Later, she would claim that this revelation helped her come to terms with what was happening. In June 1980, the Perron family finally sold their Harrisville home, and relocated to Georgia where their lives apparently improved, though Roger and Carolyn would eventually divorce.

Perhaps predictably, the footage of the séance was mysteriously destroyed during the ritual, barring any outsider scrutiny of the Perrons' and Warrens' claims. However, there were other, subtler means of disassembling their grand narrative, and these lay in the same historical documents Carolyn Perron claimed to have so meticulously pored over during her obsession with the house's past. Upon the release of *The Conjuring* in 2013, Norma Sutcliffe – the owner of the Perron farmhouse for 33 years – found her life turned upside down as paranormal tourists embarked on pilgrimages to the secluded and once-serene property at all hours of the day and night. Annoyed by these incursions, Sutcliffe, a lifelong sceptic, joined forces with journalist Kent Spottswood to investigate the Perron family's claims.

Their research revealed a complete lack of evidence that Bathsheba Sherman was ever suspected of killing a baby in a Satanic sacrifice. Furthermore, they learnt that Andrea Perron, author of three colossal volumes detailing her family's paranormal experiences, had lied about consulting with the local historian who had purportedly confirmed this information. Andrea tried to recast the Bathsheba Sherman myth as purely the Warrens' theory, instead offering the ghost of Mrs John Arnold – who had supposedly hanged herself at a barn on the property in the 1700s – as the malevolent spirit who had terrorized the family. This new idea foundered once more when it was revealed that Mrs Arnold had actually hanged herself in a house a mile away, in 1866.

This begged the question: if the Warrens were incorrect about Bathsheba Sherman, and the Perrons about Mrs John Arnold, how could any of the proposed narratives of what befell the Perrons be true? Moreover, this would make anyone claiming to be a psychic or medium who arrived at these conclusions inaccurate at best, but more likely a fraud. Such a deception would be made worse by the fact that the Warrens and Perrons may have accused a seemingly innocent woman, without any evidence to justify proposing her connection to sorcery or murder. Whatever the truth of the matter, for as long as she continues to be remembered, Bathsheba Sherman's name will be associated with evil, selfishness, and malice.

—

The story of the Annabelle doll also began in 1970, and concerns two young nurses, Donna Jennings and Angie Stapleton, who were living together as roommates in Connecticut. For Donna's birthday that year, her mother gifted her an adorable Raggedy Ann doll, telling her that it would lighten up her apartment. Surprised and delighted with the gift, Donna would make her bed each morning and place the toy on top, its arms resting at its sides and its legs pointing straight out.

The first sign of anything amiss came when Donna began arriving home to find the doll's arms were folded and its legs crossed.[12] After a week of this strange occurrence, Donna and Angie decided to perform an experiment: if they left the doll with its arms and legs already crossed, what would happen? To their astonishment, whenever they returned home after posing the doll this way, they found not only that its arms and legs were unfolded, but it was in dozens of strange, contorted positions. The toy now began appearing in other areas of the apartment, despite the fact that Donna always left it in her room, with the door closed. One evening they returned home to find it sitting on the living room sofa. On another, they opened the front door and were startled to see it kneeling on a chair, staring directly at them. Despite repeated attempts, it proved impossible to keep the doll naturally seated in this position – it just kept toppling over. When Angie's fiancé, Lou Carlo, learnt about the strange happenings, he immediately voiced his disapproval of the doll. It had a mind of its own – in his opinion it was a "damn voodoo doll"[13] – and it wasn't cute, it was just plain creepy.

Soon, Donna and Angie found little notes, handwritten in pencil, awaiting them when they got back from work. Scrawled on parchment in a childish hand, they contained curt and worrying phrases, such as "HELP US" or "HELP LOU".[14] These messages were even more bizarre in light of the fact that neither girl kept pencils or parchment in the apartment. Only at this point, oddly, did they suspect that a third party was entering the dwelling – either by using a key or jimmying the window – to play tricks on them. However, there were no pry marks on the potential points of entry, nor any other evidence that a third party had accessed the apartment.

Then, one night, they found the Raggedy Ann doll sitting on Donna's bed where she had left it. This was unusual, and on closer inspection there appeared to be three droplets of blood on its torso and another crimson smear on the back of its hand. Though this terrified them, they did not consider disposing of the red-headed doll. At Christmas, a tiny boot made from chocolate appeared on the stereo. Neither Donna, Angie, or anyone they knew had brought it into their apartment. By this point, the unexplained activity had been occurring for approximately six weeks.

Finally, the nurses, having long entertained the idea that the doll was possessed, contacted a spiritual medium. During a séance, the medium informed them that a 7-year-old girl named Annabelle

Higgins had died while playing on the field upon which the property was built, and that her ghost was haunting the apartment. Annabelle found she could relate to Donna and Angie, and had moved the toy around to get their attention. Now that she had their attention, the little dead girl admitted she just wanted to be loved, and asked the nurses' permission to physically inhabit the doll. Taking pity on the poor and seemingly harmless spirit, they granted her wish. In hindsight, this was a mistake.

Lou started to experience intense nightmares. One night, he claimed he awoke at home to find himself overwhelmed by a sense of dread. He looked around the room, but didn't see anything until he glanced down at his feet and saw the doll, Annabelle, floating towards him. Paralyzed, he looked on in terror as Annabelle hovered over his chest and clamped its arms on either side of his neck as if choking him. An electrical surge flooded from the doll through his body.[15]

On another occasion, he was alone with Angie at her apartment around 10 p.m., examining maps for an upcoming trip, when they heard a great clamour coming from Donna's bedroom. Racing into the room, Lou found Annabelle lying in a corner on the floor. As he went over to inspect it, he got the feeling something was looming behind him. However, when he turned around to look, there was nobody there. Suddenly, he felt a series of sharp pains on his chest and doubled over in agony. Angie ran into the room to see Lou's shirt was covered in blood. Returning to the living room, they unbuttoned his shirt, only to find what appeared to be bloody claw marks in his skin. They consisted of four horizontal and three vertical slashes – all felt burning hot.[16]

Though the incisions disappeared within two days, it was clear that whatever supernatural entity was inhabiting Angie and Donna's apartment was malevolent. As such, they decided to contact Father Hegan, a friendly priest at the local Episcopal church. Father Hegan listened sympathetically to their account and promised to contact Father Cooke, one of his superiors in the church.

Soon after, Ed and Lorraine Warren received a phone call from

Father Cooke at their Connecticut residence. Father Cooke provided them with a vague appraisal of the situation along with the nurses' names and telephone number. Ed telephoned them to verify the situation and obtain their address.

Within two hours he and Lorraine were standing outside the apartment complex. Donna Jennings answered the door and let them inside. As usual, Ed had brought his black attaché case, camera, and tape recorder. She led them into the kitchen where Angie and Lou were drinking coffee around the table, and everyone made their introductions. Ed began interviewing Donna and Angie, and soon learnt about Annabelle. When he enquired as to the doll's whereabouts, they directed him to the living room. Ed picked up the innocuous-looking little figure from the couch and inspected it, before returning to his questions. Once he had finished collecting the accounts of all three individuals, he was able to reach a conclusion.

"Although you never saw anything spiritwise [sic] in here," Ed started, "Lou said he felt a presence in the room before he got hurt . . ."[17] At this point Angie interrupted, telling Ed that the girls could not stand being in the apartment with the doll, and that they were going to move out and find a new one. Ed told them that this wouldn't help them. Donna asked him what he meant, to which Ed replied "in a nutshell folks you inadvertently brought a spirit into this apartment – and into your lives." He continued, saying "[you're] not going to be able to walk away from it that easily. We are going to be able to help you, beginning right now today. The first thing I'd like to do is to call Father Cooke and have him come over here."[18] After Father Cooke had agreed to come over and perform an exorcism, Ed returned to the table and decided to spell the situation out for Angie, Donna, and Lou.

"To begin with, *there is no Annabelle!* There never was. You were duped. However, we *are* dealing with a spirit here," he confirmed. "The teleportation of the doll while you were out of the apartment; the appearance of notes written on parchment; the manifestation of three symbolic drops of blood plus the gestures the doll made are all meaningful. They tell me there was *intent*, which means there was an intelligence behind the activity. But ghosts – human spirits – plain and simply can't bring on phenomena of this nature and intensity. They don't have the power. Instead, what's taking over here is something *in*human . . . *Demonic.* Ordinarily, people are never bothered by any inhuman demonic spirits, unless they do something to bring the force into their lives. And I regret to say, you girls did something to bring the demonic into your lives."[19]

Ed went on to outline how the nurses had erred in giving the Raggedy Ann doll too much of their attention. This was the demon's way of making them notice it. Rather than shutting its hijinks down from the onset, Donna and Angie had allowed their curiosity – and thus the demon – to get the better of them. Once they had brought in a medium and given the demonic spirit permission to enter the Raggedy Ann doll, their fate was sealed.

"To really interfere in your life, the demonic has somehow got to get your permission to do so," Ed explained, "and unfortunately through your own free will you gave it that permission. It was like handing a maniac a loaded gun."[20] Not only was there no Annabelle, but the doll itself was not possessed. The demon had created this illusion to trick the nurses into allowing it into their lives.

"You all stood in jeopardy of coming under possession by the spirit, this is what the thing was really after," Ed went on. "But Lou here didn't believe in the charade, so he was an ongoing threat to the entity. One way or another there was bound to be a showdown. And what happened? For starters it tried to strangle Lou to death. When that failed, it cut him with a symbolic claw mark."[21] Ed told them that he and Lorraine had witnessed this claw mark in other cases – it was an unmistakable signifier of the demonic.

At that moment, Father Cooke arrived. The Warrens briefed him on the nature of the demon and how it had infested the young people's lives: the first of three stages of demonic possession. When they offered to show him the entity, Father Cooke replied, "No, I don't think so. Why don't I just do what has to be done?"[22] He performed the lengthy episcopal exorcism blessing – one that infuses the dwelling with the power of God rather than seeking to drive out evil spirits – in each room of the apartment and on every individual present. Though Lorraine established that the house was now free of demons, Donna nevertheless requested that the Warrens take the Raggedy Ann doll away.

Apparently, Donna's request had been wise. On the way home the Warrens' car repeatedly stalled, until Ed threw holy water in a crucifix shape over the toy.[23] The Annabelle doll spent the next few days at the Warren home, apparently levitating off its chair and appearing in random rooms. On some occasions a black cat would somehow materialize beside it for a time. One evening, Lorraine returned from a meeting with a member of the Episcopalian church to hear the doll growling at her. On another occasion, Lorraine checked the couple's answer machine and found that two messages from Father Hegan were separated by the same hideous snarl.

Over the years, others seemed to encounter misfortune after interacting with Annabelle. During one visit to the Warrens, a Catholic priest jokingly chided the doll. Ed admonished him not to. Before he left, Lorraine asked the holy man to drive with caution. Soon after, they received a phone call from him, in which he asked Lorraine why she had told him to be careful. She replied that she knew his car would go out of control, and that he would have an accident. The man told her "[you] were right. The brake system failed. I was almost killed in a traffic accident. My car is a wreck."[24]

Once, Ed was speaking with a local detective about a murder that appeared to have occult elements, when Lorraine told Ed to come upstairs and take a long-distance call. Before excusing himself, he invited the detective to explore the items in his office but warned him not to touch anything. When Ed returned five minutes later, he found his guest as white as a sheet, muttering about how the doll was "real".[25] From that moment on, they convened at the detective's office for consultations. As for the doll, it remains in the Warrens' museum to this day, inside a case marked "Warning, positively do not open."

—

In 1977, the Hodgson family were living at 284 Green Street in Enfield, North London. The head of the household, 47-year-old Peggy, had divorced her husband a few years before, and was currently subsisting off a combination of welfare and her ex-husband's child-care payments. She had four children, two girls and two boys: Margaret, 13, Janet, 11, John, 10, and 7-year-old Billy.

On the night of August 30, the Hodgsons' lives changed forever. In the very first of what would become countless incidents, John and Janet Hodgson called their mother into their upstairs bedroom and told her that one of their beds was shaking. Peggy thought they were just messing about, and dismissed the incident. At 9:30 p.m. the following day, Peggy was preparing the eldest and youngest of her children, Margaret and Billy, for bed when she heard Janet and John talking in their room. Annoyed, as it was well after their bedtime, Peggy stormed into the darkened room and demanded to know what was happening. John and Janet explained that they had heard a sound on their floor, like a chair moving. Peggy whisked the chair out of their bedroom, turned the light back off, and was about to leave when she, too, heard the noise. Flicking the light on once more, she looked around the room, but nothing seemed amiss. Yet, the moment she turned the light off, the sounds returned – now it sounded like slippers shuffling across the floorboards.[26] Then, Peggy, Janet, and John all heard four distinct, loud knocks on the wall. As Peggy stood there trying to find a logical explanation for what was happening, they watched in amazement as a heavy chest of drawers slid about 18 inches (46 cm) out of the bedroom door, and into the hallway. The chest then manoeuvred itself into a position blocking the door. When Peggy tried to push it away it wouldn't move, and she claimed she felt an invisible force shoving from the other side. Eventually she forced it aside, grabbed the children's sheets and blankets, and ordered the family downstairs.[27]

After all four of the children were standing in the living room, Margaret noticed that their neighbours, the Nottinghams, still had their lights on and must be awake. The family decided they had little choice but to seek help.

Peggy went over and relayed the story to the quietly incredulous Vic and Maggie Nottingham, and asked if Vic would come over and have a look. He agreed, and entered 284 Green Street followed by his wife and 20-year-old son, Gary. They checked the entire interior of the house, including the attic, before doing the same to the garden. They had just re-entered the house when there were four hollow knocks on the wall. The Nottinghams also heard them. It sounded as if the rapping was coming from the other side of the wall, but when they rushed outside, they found the alley beside the house empty. When they re-entered the home, the knocking resumed, except now it was transferring from wall to wall, following Vic's movements through the house. It sounded as if somebody was behind the walls trying to get in. Everyone present could confirm the strange phenomena, but were at a loss about what to do next. They decided to call the police.

Police Constable Carolyn Heeps and her partner arrived at 284 Green Street, took statements from the Hodgsons and Nottinghams – seven people in total – and then were shown the chest of drawers by Peggy Hodgson. Vic Nottingham decided to turn off the light to test if the furniture moved again. Incredibly, it did, and this event was witnessed by PC Heeps and her partner. Four hollow knocks immediately followed. The police officers conducted a second search of the house, and found nothing. Yet, when they returned to the living room, John Hodgson drew Heeps' attention to an armchair that appeared to be wobbling back and forth. Then, a second chair slid three feet (1 m) across the room, in the direction of the kitchen, as eight people looked on in amazement.[28] Like Peggy and Vic, the police constables simply didn't know what to do – no crime had been committed. They recommended that the Hodgsons consult a scientist, and left shortly after midnight. Peggy set up a makeshift tent city in the living room, and the family spent the night trying to sleep downstairs.

If things had ended there, undoubtedly the Hodgson and Nottingham families would have soon put the events of August 31 out of their minds, and gone about their lives as usual. But the next morning, Billy's marbles and LEGO bricks began spontaneously soaring through the air, as if someone were throwing them. Peggy ran next door to fetch the Nottinghams, who came to their neighbours' aid once again, now accompanied by Maggie's father, Mr Richardson. Not only did they also observe the flying toys, but a couple of marbles actually passed close by Mr Richardson's head, narrowly missing him. Retrieving them from the floor, he found them to be scalding hot to the touch.[29]

These phenomena – the moving furniture and seemingly self-flinging objects – continued almost without pause until the evening of Sunday, September 4, by which point Peggy Hodgson found herself at her wits' end. As the police had proved sympathetic but unhelpful, she decided to call the *Daily Mirror* to report the strange happenings in her home. Reporter Doug Bence and photographer Graham Morris arrived at the scene soon after, to find the situation surprisingly calm. Though they stayed all evening, by Monday, September 5, the two men felt they were wasting their time. They bid the family farewell, and went outside to their vehicle. The moment they closed the door behind them, the LEGO blitz resumed. Mr Richardson raced out and summoned them back just before they drove away.

Running back inside with his Nikon camera snapping, Graham Morris was struck in the head by a large, sharp-edged LEGO brick, causing a bruise. A photograph taken at that moment would later reveal the only people in a position to have hurled the brick at him were his colleague Bence and Peggy Hodgson. Bence's hands were in his pockets, while Hodgson's arms remained folded.

By the time Senior Reporter George Fallows arrived to follow up, the Hodgson house was empty, as the traumatized family had relocated to Peggy's brother's house at 72 Green Street. Fallows quickly tracked them down and asked Peggy to recount her story.

"I accept what you say. I'm not an expert, but I have done a lot of reading on this sort of thing," Fallows said. "I think that what you have in your house is a poltergeist."[30]

Fallows provided a description of a "poltergeist" to Peggy Hodgson that was nearly identical to that given to the Herrmanns of Seaford back in 1958. He offered to escort her and the children back home and to stay with them for a few hours while they got some rest.

Half an hour after their return to 284 Green Street, the knocking resumed. Unable to find a source for it, Fallows assured Peggy he would contact an organization that had experience in investigating such matters. He went to the payphone at the end of the street and called the Society for Psychical Research (SPR) – a generally respectable group formed in Cambridge in 1882, boasting a number of esteemed historic members including Marie Curie, Arthur Koestler, Colin Wilson, and even Prime Minister Arthur Balfour.[31]

One hour later, a red Jaguar pulled up outside 284 Green Street, and a balding, bespectacled man with a handlebar moustache made his way to the front door. It was time for the Hodgson family to meet Maurice Grosse. A 58-year-old inventor and Dunkirk evacuee, Grosse had become committed to parapsychology research a year earlier, following the tragic death of his daughter. Introducing himself to the family, he quickly established three SPR protocols: he determined that the case was worth investigating, comforted the family by letting them know that poltergeist activity was more common than they believed and would likely soon be over, and encouraged Peggy Hodgson to keep a record of any seemingly supernatural events.

From Monday, September 5 to Wednesday, September 7, Maurice Grosse seemed to have been a godsend. John returned to boarding school and nothing extraordinary happened whatsoever. Then, at 1:15 a.m. on Thursday, Grosse, George Fallows, and two other men from the *Daily Mirror* were standing watch on the upstairs landing when they heard a crash coming from Janet's room. They opened the door and rushed inside to see her bedside chair lying upside down four feet (1.2 m) from where it had previously stood. Janet was wide awake and visibly terrified. An hour later, it happened again, and photographer David Thorpe was able to snap a picture of the item in its new position. This time, Janet remained in bed, apparently fast asleep.[32]

Over the next few days, Grosse personally witnessed flying marbles, chimes tinkling without cause, doors repeatedly opening and closing, and articles of clothing jumping about. A two-and-a-half-hour radio spot on LBC Radio's *Nightline* featuring Maurice Grosse, Peggy Hodgson, and Maggie Nottingham aired on Saturday, September 10. Shortly afterwards, Grosse received a call from a colleague at the SPR offering his help – Guy Lyon Playfair. The two would eventually spend more than a year at the Enfield home, documenting thousands of incidents and witnessing hundreds first-hand, leading Playfair to chronicle the case in his 1980 book *This House is Haunted*.

The level of poltergeist activity at 284 Green Street was so constant, extreme, and enduring that reciting it chronologically or expanding on each individual incident is impossible. Besides the shuffling sounds, moving furniture, and ongoing storm of marbles and LEGO bricks, there were events that seem to deny any logical explanation altogether. Items would "dematerialize" and pass through walls and ceilings. For instance, coins appeared seemingly out of thin air and fell on Grosse's head. Tables and kitchen appliances that grown men struggled to move would suddenly flip or shift great distances. It seemed a stretch to attribute these incidents to sleight of hand, let alone that of a child – after all, the upended and air-borne items in the Roland Doe and Herrmann cases were always light enough for a child to have conceivably flung them. Throughout the years, numerous family members, neighbours, and visitors also saw an array of apparitions, including a grey-haired old woman, an elderly gentleman in a blue coat, a little boy, and a man with long fingernails. One neighbour actually saw Grosse peering through a door at her, when at that exact time he was known to be elsewhere.[33]

While Grosse and Playfair managed to document hundreds of hours of phenomena on their audio tape recorders, almost everybody who entered the home with recording equipment of any kind experienced some manner of unexplained malfunction, from instantly draining batteries to inexplicably distorted material. Nor was the poltergeist activity confined to 284 Green Street. It followed the Hodgson family and their visitors to the Nottinghams' house, Peggy's brother's, and even Maurice Grosse's home.

Margaret and Janet were flung from their beds multiple times every night. Numerous people, both within and outside the family, saw both girls levitating off their mattresses, sometimes almost as high as the ceiling. Two of these witnesses were actually walking along Green Street and saw Janet's body rising and falling through the bedroom window. On one occasion, Janet's levitation was famously photographed by Graham Morris – an iconic image that continues to spark debate and controversy. At other times, spontaneous fires would break out. Grosse and Playfair would attempt to communicate with the entity or entities through "rapping", knocking once for "yes" and twice for "no". Though this would often initiate a conversation, the dialogue rapidly deteriorated into chaos.

First Janet, and then Margaret, began speaking to people in the same croaking, guttural male voice. While, at first, they would only do this when nobody was looking at them, eventually they no longer seemed to care. The voice would alternately claim to be Vic Nottingham's dead father, "Fred", and a five-year-old boy named Tommy. Maurice Grosse asked Margaret to describe the sensation she experienced when the voice spoke through her. "Just the vibration in my neck," Margaret replied, "as though it was right behind me."[34]

There were certainly plenty of reasons to suspect the girls of trickery. Professional ventriloquist Ray Alan had visited 284 Green Street and quickly established that the girls were practicing a basic version of his art. It also didn't take long for two other members of the SPR to get wind of the girls' tricks. Having clandestinely set up a video camera in the room next door, psychologist and parapsychologist Anita Gregory and John Beloff recorded footage of Janet sneakily bending spoons and attempting to do the same with an iron bar, along with rehearsing bouncing off her mattress in a manner that resembled levitation.[35] Amazingly, though Gregory, Beloff, and Playfair were all members of the SPR, and Playfair's book uses bent spoons as evidence of the haunting, it gives no account of his colleagues' discovery whatsoever.

Unlike the Herrmann family back in the 1950s, Peggy Hodgson had no problem letting Milbourne Christopher, now head of the Society of American Magicians, into her home to investigate. This may have been because she thought Christopher was a man named "Eric White" – Christopher and Playfair had conspired to concoct this pseudonym and keep his true identity from the family, lest it influence their behaviour.

That night, the strange voice began emanating from Janet the moment she climbed into bed. Maurice Grosse placed a large adhesive bandage over her mouth, which did nothing to stop it. Leaving Janet's door fully open, Playfair loudly stomped halfway down the stairs, then began sneaking back up again. When he reached a bend in the staircase, he heard an angry voice shout "Get out!"[36] from upstairs. Certain that something extraordinary was about to occur, Playfair crept back down, and encouraged Christopher to replace him on the staircase. Ultimately, nothing happened. Christopher would later tell Playfair: "When you went down, and I stayed there, I stayed until [Janet] softly – with no sound at all – was looking down the stairs . . . At that moment I produced a flare of light in the air . . . it's a magician's thing. And she immediately backed up, and that's why I thought nothing would happen from this point . . . I think she was coming to see if there was anyone in the stairwell, and, being sure, then it would have happened."[37]

In January 1978, Playfair caught the girls red-handed. Having left his tape recorder upstairs one morning, he went upstairs to fetch it, and found it missing. After searching for 30 seconds or so, he located it inside a nearby cupboard. When he played the audio back, he clearly heard Janet seize the recorder then stow it away. Playfair took the device downstairs, and showed it to Janet, whose expression clearly betrayed her guilt. Grosse later reprimanded the girl. Days later, Playfair was standing outside the open bedroom door, when he caught sight of Margaret's hand snaking behind her headboard. Her hand seized the edge of the door and shoved it violently. Playfair put his foot in the door, preventing it from slamming, and pushed it back open. Entering the room, he found Margaret lying in bed, seemingly asleep.[38]

Though both of these occurrences should have immediately raised red flags – why would two girls whose lives were being destroyed by a supposed haunting contribute additional mischief to the situation as if it was one big joke? – Playfair found ways to intellectualize these events and incorporate them into his pre-existing belief that the house was indeed haunted. Ironically, regarding Janet's antics, he later wrote: "The fact that I had spotted the trick at once, encouraged me to think I would have spotted earlier tricks, had there been any, and the fact that Janet had confessed without much prompting suggested that she was not a natural liar."[39] Similarly, the fact that Margaret had seemed to be asleep instead of looking surprised when he caught her in the door-shutting incident, led Playfair to believe she must have done it unconsciously. Considering this in light of the findings by Beloff, Gregory, Alan, and Christopher, Playfair's observation that "it was becoming apparent that paranormal events only took place in the presence of people who *believed* them to be possible"[40] seems strangely oblivious.

However, one event in particular stands out as being beyond any reasonable explanation, other than widespread conspiratorial deception. After hearing bizarre noises coming from Janet's room, Maggie Nottingham, who was visiting from next door, entered to find the heavily fatigued 12-year-old lying on her bed. "Oh, phew! I been [sic] through the wall . . ." Janet told Maggie. "I went into your room . . . it was all white."[41]

Though Maggie Nottingham typically believed Janet, she knew that the little girl had never been into her bedroom next door, and regardless, it was brightly wallpapered. Challenging Janet to try it again, Maggie left the room, went back to her house, and walked upstairs into the bedroom. While it was indeed empty, she noticed a copy of a book, *Fun and Games for Children*, lying on the floor by her bed. Maggie recognized it instantly, though the Nottinghams did not own a copy. It was the same book she had seen minutes before on the mantelpiece in Janet's room. How it could have got through the wall from one house to the other in such a short time was simply unfathomable. It is also difficult to believe that the girls could have thrown heavy furniture around with the necessary ease, and in the words of Maurice Grosse "these facts . . . were witnessed by at least thirty people; the Harpers, the Nottinghams and Burcombes [Peggy's brother's family] . . . plus several of their friends, neighbours, and relatives and a good many outside witnesses including the police, journalists, local tradesmen, social workers . . . What more evidence do you want?"[42]

Ultimately, most people who believe in the supernatural view the Enfield poltergeist case as proof that paranormal activity does exist, while sceptics brush it aside as the antics of two bored, energetic girls who successfully deceived a pair of troublingly credulous parapsychologists. Each side suffers from a confirmation bias, choosing to only highlight the facts that fit their pre-existing worldview, and ignoring those that contradict it. To this day, the events surrounding the Enfield poltergeist are not as clear cut as either side would claim – it is a truly remarkable tale.

Unsurprisingly, between 1977 and 1978, numerous psychics from as far away as Brazil visited the Hodgson household, providing many different accounts of what was occurring, along with utterly useless advice. Among the last of these visitors were a couple from Connecticut: a self-purported demonologist and his wife, a disarmingly pleasant medium.

By the time Ed and Lorraine Warren visited 284 Green Street in the summer of 1978, the deluge of poltergeist activity had reduced to a trickle. As Grosse and Playfair had done, Ed Warren claimed to have spoken with the entity through Janet. "Who are you?" he asked. "Fred-die,"[43] the voice answered through Janet. "You were Freddie, huh?" Ed replied, sceptically. "What's your real name?"[44] The entity responded with a horrid retching sound. When prompted, it claimed that it was five hundred years old, before seemingly transforming into a different character – a young boy named Tommy. "Tommy, how do you think we could get rid of all the problems that are happening in this house?" Ed asked, to which Tommy replied "Kill the ghosties!"[45]

Tommy went on to inform Ed that there were five spirits present: himself, Freddy, Billy, Charlie, and Dick. He then apparently switched back to being Freddy. The back and forth between Ed and Freddy continued for some time, with Ed asking what month the spirit thought it was, and Freddy claiming that he hated Americans and asking Ed to smash his tape recorder. Finally, Ed confronted the spirit with a crucifix, telling it that "[the] cross means your days are numbered here"[46] and that "the next time I come back here, Fred, you'd better be gone. Because the next time I come I'm bringing a very powerful exorcist with me, someone you won't want to mess with."[47]

But Ed and Lorraine Warren never returned to 284 Green Street. Instead, they went home and contracted an author to write a book claiming that Margaret and Janet had invited the entities into their home while playing with a Ouija board in 1976. According to the Warrens, the two girls had been tricked into inviting a demonic spirit into their family home, like the nurses in Connecticut who had been plagued by the Annabelle doll. According to Ed's own recollection, he had spent a week in Enfield. Guy Lyon Playfair disputes this, saying the couple only spent a single day at the Hodgson residence:

"They did turn up once, I think, at Enfield, and all I can remember is Ed Warren telling me that he could make a lot of money for me out of it. So, I thought, 'well that's all I need to know from you' and I got myself out of his way as soon as I could. I said [I] was not impressed . . . I don't think he went there more than once. And I did read somewhere a transcript of a lengthy interview which he's alleged to have with one of the girls – which they couldn't remember giving him – and it was describing all sorts of marvellous wonders which I don't think ever happened."[48]

The Witch 2015
The Lighthouse 2019

The Salem Witch Trials and the Smalls Lighthouse Tragedy

Horror director Robert Eggers has made a name for himself by drawing on the past for inspiration. His first two offerings, *The Witch* and *The Lighthouse,* are both unsettling, eerie tales of isolation and madness. Both are based on infamous historical events, namely the Salem Witch Trials of 1692–3, and the Smalls Lighthouse Tragedy of 1801.

In 2015, American filmmaker Robert Eggers wowed critics and audiences alike with his directorial debut, *The Witch* – a psychological horror set in 17th-century New England. The film grossed ten times its $4 million budget, earning comparisons with cinematic classics *The Exorcist*, *The Amityville Horror,* and *Poltergeist.* Overnight, 32-year-old Eggers was catapulted from obscurity to become one of the world's most promising movie directors.

The Witch centres on a small family of New England Puritans who are banished from their community. Forced to settle on an isolated farmstead surrounded by impenetrable forest, the family is thrown into turmoil when the youngest child, the unbaptized baby Samuel, is abducted. Faced with further unexplained misfortunes, the family soon come to believe they are being tormented by witchcraft, and accusations fly as the eldest daughter, Thomasin, comes under suspicion of being the witch. The film culminates in the family tearing itself apart, the apparent deaths of everyone except Thomasin, and an eerie encounter with a terrifying goat, the aptly named Black Phillip.

Rather than rushing to his next success, Eggers' second offering came more than four years later with another New England psychological horror, *The Lighthouse*. This 19th-century yarn garnered critical praise and an Academy Award nomination for Best Cinematography. Director of photography Jarin Blaschke shot the film in black and white, using a 1.19:1 aspect ratio to enhance the sense of claustrophobia – something not seen in cinemas since Fritz Lang's *M*.

In the movie, a young lighthouse keeper, Ephraim Winslow, is sent to work a four-week shift at a remote lighthouse on an island off the New England coast. Upon arrival, he meets an elderly, irritable keeper named Thomas Wake, who will be his only companion during the coming weeks. The two men soon take a dislike to each other, and when a storm traps them on the island, a succession of bizarre and seemingly supernatural events send Winslow into the depths of madness.

The infamous Salem Witch Trials and the Puritan culture that birthed them provided a basis for *The Witch*, while the character of Black Phillip and the association of goats with Satan stemmed from the art and literature of continental Europe. *The Lighthouse* draws heavily on the infamous "Smalls Lighthouse Tragedy" that occurred off the southwest coast of Wales in 1801. Though set in different centuries, both films turn to the history and belief systems of everyday people facing hardship and strange phenomena while in isolation. The dialogue the ill-fated Puritan family speak in *The Witch* is entirely in early-modern-English, while lighthouse keeper Thomas Wake's accent, vocabulary, and phrasing harken back to a West Country seafaring dialect. Both films also look at how folk superstitions – whether related to the nature and activities of so-called "witches", or the sea and its denizens – colour the protagonists' expectations and understanding of events. Eggers has also commented that the characters portrayed by Willem Dafoe and Robert Pattinson in *The Lighthouse* are modelled upon the Greek figures Proteus – the "old man of the sea" – and Prometheus, who stole fire from the gods. This potent concoction of numerous inspirations results in films that are highly original, surreal, and open to endless interpretation. With Eggers emerging as the most lauded horror filmmaker of the 2010s, it is very possible that the future of great horror movies is embedded in history.

—

Situated on the mouth of the Danvers River, about 14 miles (23 km) northeast of Boston, the town of Salem, Massachusetts was settled by Puritans in 1626. Originally known as Naumkeag, the settlement was built on fertile land, and a thriving fishing and farming community was soon established. In 1629, the settlement was renamed Salem, derived from the Hebrew word for peace – shalom. In actuality, the events of the infamous trials of 1692 mostly occurred in Salem Village, a separate settlement on the outskirts of the town.

In late December 1691, eight young women and girls in Salem Village were afflicted by mysterious "distempers" – convulsions, strange bodily contortions, screaming, speaking gibberish, and a propensity to throw objects around rooms. When local physicians found themselves at a loss to explain the girls' behaviour, in February 1692, Dr William Griggs raised the possibility of witchcraft. Thirty-nine-year-old Samuel Parris – a minister at Salem Village – initially scoffed at the suggestion. He was father to one of the afflicted girls, nine-year-old Betty, and uncle to a second, Abigail Williams, 11. After summoning a congregation of fellow ministers from nearby parishes, Parris was urged to wait patiently and see what time revealed.[1]

The seeds of a witch hunt had long been sown in Puritan culture. There was historic precedent in Europe, where efforts to eradicate paganism by churches and theocratic rulers had led to the slaughter of an estimated 50,000 people by burning or hanging from the 1490s to 1650s. Although it is tempting for a modern audience to find this hysteria ridiculous, it is easy to forget that the contemporary European population found the idea of witches genuinely terrifying. Among the many horrific acts attributed to them, witches were said to create an unguent from the intestines of unbaptized babies that would allow them to fly on broomsticks. Poisoning was also a common accusation: during the Elizabethan period in England, one woman accused of witchcraft was rumoured to have given poisoned apples to children.[2]

Witch hunts came to an end in the Old World with the dawn of the Enlightenment, when the scientific method and secular governance replaced the theocentric thinking of the past. However, as self-exiled religious devotees who had settled the New World largely owing to theological differences with established churches, the colonial Puritans inhabited a cultural bubble. Furthermore, they believed in a rigid interpretation of scripture, which plainly stated in Exodus 22:18 "Thou shalt not suffer a witch to live." This not only confirmed the existence of witches theologically, but offered instructions concerning what to do about them.

The Harvard-educated scholar and minister Cotton Mather had written in his influential *Memorable Providences, Relating to Witchcrafts and Possessions* about the ordeal of the Goodwin children of Boston, who in 1688, had suffered afflictions allegedly caused by witchcraft. The culprit had been "Goody" Ann Glover, an Irish Catholic captured during Oliver Cromwell's conquest of Ireland and sold into slavery in Barbados. Following the execution of her husband for failing to renounce Catholicism, Ann had fled with her children to Boston, where she worked as a servant in the house of John Goodwin. Ann's troubles began when Goodwin's 13-year-old child, Martha, accused Ann's daughter of stealing fabric, causing Ann to shout at Martha. Immediately after, Martha was "afflicted", along with the other Goodwin children. A physician tasked with finding a cause for their maladies suggested that the children were bewitched, and Ann Glover became an obvious and convenient suspect.

Arrested and tried for witchcraft, the Gaelic-speaking Glover was unable to recite the Lord's Prayer – fluctuating between her native Irish tongue and Latin – which corresponded with a belief that witches were unable to utter the holy words. Coupled with "spectral evidence" – the testimonies of "victims" claiming that a witch's spirit had visited them in a vision or dream – Glover was convicted of witchcraft. She was publicly hanged in Boston on November 16, 1689.[3] The Goodwin children continued to be afflicted, but Cotton Mather explained this away by stating that it should not "disappoint our expectations of their deliverance, but for the *detection* and *destruction* of more belonging to that hellish knot."[4] In other words, there were more witches living in the Massachusetts Bay Colony, and they needed to be ferreted out. Mather's cruel tenets established the interpretive framework for the afflictions of Betty Parris and Abigail Williams less than three years later.

When the Salem afflicted showed no signs of improvement, Samuel Parris' neighbour, Mary Sibley, successfully convinced one of Parris' slaves, Tituba, to bake a "witch cake" consisting of rye meal and Betty Parris' urine.[5] Mary fed the cake to her dog, convinced that if the girls had been bewitched, the enchantment would pass on to the pet, which would then lead them to the guilty party. When Parris found out about the creation of the folk-magic "witch cake", he furiously declared that a church member had "gone to the Devil for help against the Devil. By this means it seems, the Devil has been raised among us, and his rage is vehement and terrible."[6] Nevertheless, the minister was increasingly persuaded that his daughter and niece's afflictions were the result of bewitchment, and Parris pressured the girls to name their tormentor. As in the case of the Goodwin children, the girls singled out a woman who was below their social station, in their service, and of a different ethnicity – the dark-skinned Barbadian Indian, Tituba. This accorded with the Puritans' belief that those native to the continent they had settled were Devil worshippers: a likely result of their recent conflicts with the Wabanaki Indians, brought about chiefly by the expansion of the colony. The children soon named two other women, Sarah Good and Sarah Osborne. Tituba, Good, and Osborne were arrested on February 29, 1692, on the basis that the women's spectres had supposedly visited the girls.

When news of Tituba's alleged witchcraft reached Mercy Lewis, an 18-year-old servant in the household of Thomas Putnam, she suddenly became afflicted, too. Lewis' childhood aptly illustrates the constant state of dread that colonial societies must have existed in – she had survived a brutal massacre in 1676, where 11 men and 23 women and children had been killed by the Wabanaki tribe in Falmouth, Maine.[7]

Thomas Putnam was a good friend of Samuel Parris, and Putnam's own daughter, Ann, was also soon afflicted. By March, Salem women Mary Walcott, Mary Warren, Elizabeth Booth, and Elizabeth Hubbard, were also showing similar signs of "bewitchment".

This apparent escalation fuelled the Puritans' witch-hunting zeal, which rapidly resulted in a series of show trials that same year. Those accused of witchcraft were given the option of confessing and providing the names of other witches, or being hanged. Unsurprisingly, most took the former path, which meant the witch hunt grew exponentially, culminating in the execution of 20 people by hanging. One man, Giles Corey, who refused to participate in these grimly farcical proceedings, was pressed with stones to persuade him to cooperate. He died after two days of torture, having never faltered in his resolve.[8]

The collective madness finally wound down in January, 1693, when the Massachusetts Superior Court of Judicature took over. It brought 52 more of the accused to trial, but acquitted 49, while the three convicted were never executed. By May of that year, Governor William Phips ordered a general reprieve and more than 150 accused witches were released from jail.[9]

In an April 1976 issue of *Science*, psychologist Dr Linnda Caporael posited an explanation for the Salem witch panic, which, despite being controversial, remains a favourite talking point to this day – that the Puritans were suffering from hallucinations brought on by the psychotropic fungus, ergot (*Claviceps purpurea*). This fungus grows on rye and other cereals, and the ergot alkaloid isoergine approximates 10 per cent of the strength of the recreational drug LSD. Isoergine is also present in morning glory seeds. This could mean the initial symptoms of "affliction" were brought on by inadvertent poisoning, and the beliefs of the Puritans meant they viewed these symptoms as being caused by evil magic. However, the stop-and-start nature of the "fits" has been presented as evidence that the ergot hypothesis cannot be correct. Perhaps more chillingly, another explanation is a condition of social psychology known today as mass psychogenic disorder – a social contagion. It has been noted that Parris' niece and daughter, along with the many other afflicted girls in the village, seemingly displayed the exact same symptoms as the Goodwin children, as detailed in Cotton Mather's widely read *Memorial Providences.*

—

The Witch culminates in an encounter between the accused daughter, Thomasin, and the family's large and sinister goat, Black Phillip, shortly after Black Phillip has gored her father to death. Whether a demonic manifestation, or a hallucination brought on by ergot fungus, in a truly chilling climax, Black Phillip responds to the girl's pleas. Like the other imagery in the film, Eggers' inclusion of Black Phillip draws on a rich history, in this case the association between goats and Satan.

The popular association of the Devil with goats is actually relatively recent, though it does have some religious and historical context. A passage in the New Testament, Matthew 25:31–33, reads: "When the Son of Man shall come in His glory, and all the holy angels with Him, then shall He sit upon the throne of His glory: And before Him shall be gathered all nations: and He shall separate them one from another, as a shepherd divideth his sheep from the goats: And He shall set the sheep on His right hand, but the goats on the left." Here Christ is the metaphorical herder. His followers are conceptualized as a flock of sheep, owing to the animal's natural disposition to be easily led. Goats, on the other hand, are stubborn, disagreeable, and individualistic. In this passage they represent those who resist the path set before them by God. Aptly, Charlie, the goat who starred as Black Phillip in *The Witch*, was notoriously disobedient: "If we wanted him to be doing something violent, he wanted to go to sleep. If he was supposed to be standing still, he was running around like a madman."[10]

In England, goat farmers were looked down upon. Nevertheless, early British settlers brought goats to the New World because of their great capacity to clear land and their relatively small size, which made them easy to travel with. Historian Mary Beth Norton found "nothing about goats in the Salem record or, that I can recall, in any other American records of witchcraft prosecutions."[11] Regardless, the goat would have been a common farmyard animal in 17th-century New England.

In fact, the goat was more closely linked to witches in continental Europe than in Great Britain or its colonies. Scholars have proposed numerous theories for this. One particularly attractive explanation is that the "witches" of antiquity – in actuality, simply the remaining pagans – began to worship a new "horned man" deity, a fusion of the Celtic god Cernunnos and Faunus, the Roman version of the horned, cloven-hoofed Greek deity Pan. Antagonism between the expanding church and pagans led to the conflation of the Christian Satan with the pagan goat-god. The horned Devil featured prominently in medieval religious iconography, and the late-medieval period saw masterful woodcuts of satanic goats, perhaps the best examples of which are by the German artist Hans Baldung Grien, depicting nude witches riding the horned creatures.

It was only in the 18th and 19th centuries that the goat became prominently associated with Satan in the popular consciousness. In 1798, the Spanish Romantic artist Francisco Goya's captivating painting *The Witches' Sabbath* depicted a large anthropomorphic goat cavorting with a coven of witches in the moonlight. Goya later followed this with the similarly themed *The Witches' Sabbath (The Great He-Goat)*. This trend extended to literature, for around the same time, Jacob of the Brothers Grimm penned the folktale *The Lord's Animals and the Devil's*. In the tale, the ties between the Devil and goat were made explicit:

> "The Lord God had created all animals and had chosen out the wolf to be his dog . . . Then the Devil . . . created goats. Now when they went to pasture, they generally remained caught in the hedges by their tails, [and] the Devil had to go there and disentangle them . . . This enraged him at last, and he went and bit off the tail of every goat. Then he let them go to pasture . . . but it came to pass that the Lord God perceived how at one time they gnawed away at a fruitful tree . . . This distressed him, [and] he summoned his wolves, who soon tore in pieces the goats . . . When the Devil observed this, he went before the Lord and said, 'Thy creatures have destroyed mine.' The Lord answered, 'Why didst thou create things to do harm?' The Devil said, 'I was compelled to do it: inasmuch as my thoughts run on evil, what I create can have no other nature' . . . [and] in his rage [the Devil] put out the eyes of all the remaining goats, and put his own in instead. This is why all goats have Devil's eyes, and their tails bitten off, and why he likes to assume their shape."[12]

Perhaps the most iconic image of Satan-as-goat stems from Éliphas Lévi's 1856 rendering of the deity Baphomet in his book *Dogme et Rituel de la Haute Magie*. In 1910, this directly inspired the half-goat drawing of "The Devil" on the card in the Rider-Waite tarot deck.[13]

—

It was no secret in Pembrokeshire, Wales, that Thomas Howell and Thomas Griffith did not get along. Whether there was some particular grudge between them or they just rubbed each other the wrong way, the older and younger man had a reputation for constantly quarrelling and made no attempt to hide it. Howell and Griffith worked together as "wickies" (lighthouse keepers) at the Smalls Lighthouse: a 40-foot (12-m) wooden tower[14] anchored to a perilous reef, 20 miles (32 km) from the Welsh shore.[15] The lighthouse had been built by Mr Henry Whiteside, a Liverpudlian luthier, who had been stranded at the recently finished lighthouse for a month in 1777, owing to stormy weather conditions, and had nearly starved.[16] Whiteside's lighthouse consisted of a platform bearing the light and keeper accommodation, standing on nine tall oak piles that allowed the stormy seas to wash through the structure.

Typically for wickies, both Howell and Griffith had wives, families, and other occupations – Howell was a cooper residing in Kingheriot, and Griffith was a labourer from the village of Solva. In the winter of 1800–01, the two men were transported by boat to the Smalls Lighthouse to begin another months-long shift. A week or two into their latest stint, Griffith fell ill, and Howell was unable to help him. Hoisting a distress signal, the two men waited patiently for a vessel to arrive. Instead, they were greeted by a storm of catastrophic proportions. With no boats able to reach the isolated cluster of rock, Griffith languished in agony for weeks before finally expiring.

When Howell found that his colleague had died, he came to a terrifying conclusion: if he dumped the body in the sea, the mainlanders might think he had murdered Griffith and disposed of the evidence to cover it up. Unwilling to take that chance, Howell resolved to keep the cadaver in the lighthouse with him until a relief ship finally arrived. Fashioning a coffin to preserve the remains, he placed Griffith's body inside the box, closed the lid, and did his best not to think about it. Yet, the storm continued unabated. Weeks turned into months.

Back on the mainland, the Howell and Griffith families had little option but to stand on the cliff, night after night, gazing out at the distant lighthouse, and anxiously wondering when help would arrive. The customs houses of Bristol, Milford, and Liverpool all received numerous reports of the distress signal still flying at the Smalls Lighthouse, but nobody dared to risk approaching and shipwrecking themselves.

Eventually, Howell could bear the stench of Griffith's rotting body no longer. He moved the coffin onto the gallery outdoors, and fastened it to the railing, where it remained for three weeks, battered by rain.

The howling gale eventually broke open the coffin and caused Griffith's arm to spill out, but the reports of what happened next differ greatly. By most accounts, the constant winds caused the dead man's hand to bang against the lighthouse window, leading Howell to believe that Griffith's ghost was tapping on the glass.[17] Another holds that distant ships saw what they believed to be a man waving to them from the platform, and assumed everything at the lighthouse was well – apparently ignoring the distress signal.

Finally, after four months, the weather stabilized enough to allow a boat from Milford Haven, carrying two replacement wickies, to anchor at the Smalls Lighthouse. By the time they reached Thomas Howell, his hair had allegedly turned white, and he was half-starved, near-frozen, and teetering on the brink of madness. Throughout his ordeal, he had kept the lamp lit. Taken back ashore along with what remained of Griffith's corpse, Thomas Howell was apparently unrecognizable to even his closest friends.[18]

The Smalls Lighthouse Tragedy would forever change British protocol regarding the staffing of lighthouses. Henceforth, the crew would always consist of three men – at least until the mass automation of the 1980s eliminated the need for lighthouse keepers altogether.[19]

Picture Credits

The publisher would like to thank the following for their kind permission to reproduce their photographs:

(Key: a-above; b-below/bottom; c-centre; f-far; l-left; r-right; t-top)

Insert 1 Alamy Stock Photo: Historic Images (crb); SilverScreen (tl); The History Collection (c). **Getty Images:** ullstein bild Dtl. / Contributor (clb); John Springer Collection / CORBIS (tr); Bettmann / Contributor (cr); Imagno / Contributor (bc). **Insert 2 Alamy Stock Photo:** AF archive (tl, tc); Everett Collection Inc (tr); Everett Collection Historical (cl). **Getty Images:** Bettmann / Contributor (br); New York Daily News / Contributor (bc); Chicago Sun-Times / Chicago Daily News collection / Chicago History Museum (bl). **Insert 3 Alamy Stock Photo:** AF archive (tl); PictureLux / The Hollywood Archive (tr); Pictorial Press Ltd (cl). **Getty Images:** Bettmann / Contributor (cra, br); Frank Scherschel / The LIFE Picture Collection (bc). **Insert 4 Alamy Stock Photo:** Collection Christophel (tr); Everett Collection Inc (tl); Trinity Mirror / Mirrorpix (bc). **Getty Images:** Daily Mirror / Mirrorpix / Contributor (crb); BIPS / Stringer / Hulton Archive (ca); Staff / Mirrorpix / Contributor (clb); Keystone / Staff / Hulton Archive (br). **Insert 5 Alamy Stock Photo:** AF archive (tr, cl); Moviestore Collection Ltd (crb). **Getty Images:** Discovery / Handout (b); Silver Screen Collection / Contributor (tl). **Insert 6 Alamy Stock Photo:** Everett Collection, Inc. (tl); ScreenProd / Photononstop (tr); Everett Collection Inc (cra); PJF Military Collection (clb); James Nesterwitz (crb, br). **Insert 7 Alamy Stock Photo:** Archive PL (bl); United Archives GmbH (tr); Everett Collection Inc (cra). **Getty Images:** Ed Clark / The LIFE Picture Collection / Contributor (crb); LMPC / Contributor (tl). **Insert 8 Alamy Stock Photo:** Everett Collection, Inc. (tc). **Getty Images:** Hulton Archive / Stringer (cra); Stan Wolfson / Newsday LLC / Contributor (cl); Paul Hawthorne / Staff (crb). **Rex by Shutterstock:** Red

/ AP (br). **Insert 8 Alamy Stock Photo:** Everett Collection, Inc. (tc). **Getty Images:** Hulton Archive / Stringer (cra); Stan Wolfson / Newsday LLC / Contributor (cl); Paul Hawthorne / Staff (crb); Twentieth Century Fox Film Corporation / Michael Ochs Archives / Stringer (tl). **Rex by Shutterstock:** Red / AP (br). **Insert 9 Alamy Stock Photo:** AF archive (tl); TCD / Prod.DB (tc); Photo 12 (cra). **Getty Images:** Nina Leen / The LIFE Picture Collection / Contributor (cl, cb, crb, bl) **Insert 10 Alamy Stock Photo:** AF archive (tr); Photo 12 (clb); © Universal Pictures / Everett Collection, Inc. (crb). **Getty Images:** Alex Bowie / Contributor (tl); Serge viallet / Sygma / Contributor (cra); Jean-Claude FRANCOLON / Gamma-Rapho / Contributor (bc). **Insert 11 Alamy Stock Photo:** AF archive (tc); Pictorial Press Ltd (cla); Entertainment Pictures (tr); American Photo Archive (cr). **Getty Images:** Bettmann / Contributo (clb); Bettmann / Contributor (cl, cb); David Rentas / New York Post Archives / (c) NYP Holdings, Inc. / Contributor (br). **Insert 12 Alamy Stock Photo:** AF archive (tl, tr). **Getty Images:** Acey Harper / The LIFE Images Collection / Contributor (ca, ca/Tracy Paules, clb); Wiktor Szymanowicz / Barcroft Media / Contributor (cra). **Rex by Shutterstock:** Uncredited / AP (br); Chris O'Meara / AP (bl). **Insert 13 Alamy Stock Photo:** Entertainment Pictures (tr); TCD / Prod.DB (tl); Everett Collection, Inc. (ca); Jesse Thornton (br). **Getty Images:** Bettmann / Contributor (c). **Insert 14 Alamy Stock Photo:** AF archive (tr); Allstar Picture Library (tl); Photo 12 (ca). **Getty Images:** Tony Lewis / Stringer (br); Ian Waldie / POOL (crb). **Rex by Shutterstock:** (bc); Rick Rycroft / AP (cb); Austral Int (clb). **Insert 15 Alamy Stock Photo:** AF archive (bc); Allstar Picture Library (tl); Everett Collection Inc (tc, crb); TCD / Prod.DB (cra); Atlaspix (cb); AmityPhotos (bl). **Getty Images:** Russell McPhedran / Fairfax Media Archives / Contributor (cla). **Insert 16 Alamy Stock Photo:** Allstar Picture Library (clb); Collection Christophel (tc, tr); Trinity Mirror / Mirrorpix (cla, ca); Rebecca Beusmans (crb); North Wind Picture Archives (bl). **Dreamstime.com:** Cindy Goff (cb). **Cover images:** *Front:* **Getty Images:** Thegoodly / RooM

All other images © Dorling Kindersley
For further information see: www.dkimages.com

Endnotes

M: A City Searches for a Murderer 1931

1 "Prostitutes, Respectable Women, and Women from 'Outside': The Carl Grossmann Sexual Murder Case in Postwar Berlin" by Sace Elder in *Crime and Criminal Justice in Modern Germany.*
2–3 Ibid
4 *Die Welt*, 6 April 2008 – "Der Mädchenfänger von Berlin"
5 Ibid
6 "Prostitutes, Respectable Women, and Women from 'Outside': The Carl Grossmann Sexual Murder Case in Postwar Berlin" by Sace Elder in *Crime and Criminal Justice in Modern Germany.*
7 *Die Welt*, 6 April 2008 – "Der Mädchenfänger von Berlin"
8 *The Encyclopedia of Serial Killers* by Brian Lane & Wilson Gregg.
9 *Supernatural Serial Killers: What Makes Them Murder?* by Samantha Lyon & Dr Daphne Tan.
10 Ibid
11 *Crimes of Horror* by Angus Hall.
12 *The Sadist* by Karl Berg.
13–15 Ibid
16 *Vampire Forensics: Uncovering the Origins of an Enduring Legend* by Mark Jenkins.

Rope 1948

1 *The Gay Science* by Friedrich Nietzsche.
2 *For the Thrill of It* by Simon Baatz.
3 Ibid
4 *The Loeb-Leopold Case* by Alvin V. Sellers.

5 *For the Thrill of It* by Simon Baatz.
6 Letter from Nathan Leopold to Richard Loeb, written October 9, 1923 and available online at http://www.crimearchives.net/1924_leopold_loeb/html/letters.html
7 *For the Thrill of It* by Simon Baatz.
8–16 Ibid

Psycho 1960 and The Texas Chain Saw Massacre 1974

1 *Necrophilic and Necrophagic Serial Killers: Understanding Their Motivations Through Case Study Analysis* by Christina Molinari.
2 *Cannibal Serial Killers: Profiles of Depraved Flesh-Eating Murderers* by Christopher Berry-Dee.
3 Ibid
4 *Deviant: The Shocking True Story of Ed Gein, the Original 'Psycho'* by Harold Schechter.
5–13 Ibid

Frenzy 1972

1 *10 Rillington Place* by Ludovic Kennedy.
2 *Frenzy! Heath, Haigh, Christie: The First Great Tabloid Murderers* by Neil Root.
3–4 Ibid
5 *10 Rillington Place* by Ludovic Kennedy.
6 *Frenzy! Heath, Haigh, Christie: The First Great Tabloid Murderers* by Neil Root.
7 Ibid
8 *Handsome Brute: The True Story of a Ladykiller* by Sean O'Connor.
9 *Frenzy! Heath, Haigh, Christie: The First Great Tabloid Murderers* by Neil Root.
10–18 Ibid
19 *Sadistic Killers: Profiles of Pathological Predators* by Carole Anne Davis.

20–21 Ibid
22 *Found Naked and Dead* by Brian McConnell.
23–31 Ibid

The Exorcist 1973

1 *Possessed: The True Story of the Most Famous Exorcism of Modern Time* by Thomas Allen.
2–26 Ibid
27 *American Hauntings* by Robert E. Bartholomew and Joe Nickell.

Jaws 1975

1 *Twelve Days of Terror: A Definitive Investigation of the 1916 New Jersey Shark Attacks* by Richard G. Fernicola.
2–25 Ibid
26 *History*, 31 January 2019 – "USS Indianapolis: Survivor Accounts From the Worst Sea Disaster in U.S. Naval History"
27–33 Ibid
34 *In Harm's Way* by Doug Stanton.
35 https://www.history.navy.mil/research/library/online-reading-room/title-list-alphabetically/s/sinking-ussindianapolis/narrative-of-the-circumstances.html
36 Ibid
37 *Insight on the News*, 5 June 2000 – "For the Good of the Navy"
38 *East Hampton Star*, 2 July, 2014 – "Janet Mundus, 88"
39 *Lowell Sun*, 16 July, 2019 – "Turning in a hook report on Dad's shark hunting"
40 *New York Times*, 16 September 2008 – "Frank Mundus, 82, Dies; Inspired 'Jaws' "
41 http://www.fmundus.com/frank_mundus_frequently_asked_qu.htm
42 Ibid

The Town that Dreaded Sundown 1976

1 *The Texarkana Moonlight Murders* by Michael Newton.
2–11 Ibid

The Amityville Horror 1979

1 *The Amityville Horror* by Jay Anson.
2–19 Ibid
20 *Snopes*, 15 April 2005 – "Was 'Amityville Horror' Based on a True Story?"
21 *People*, 13 February 1978 – "The Amityville Horror Lives On – in a Snarl of Lawsuits and Suspicions"
22 *The Big Con: Great Hoaxes, Frauds, Grifts, and Swindles in American History* by Nate Hendley.
23 *People*, 13 February 1978 – "The Amityville Horror Lives On – in a Snarl of Lawsuits and Suspicions"
24 Ibid
25 *The Big Con: Great Hoaxes, Frauds, Grifts, and Swindles in American History* by Nate Hendley.
26 *Washington Post*, 16 September 1979 – "The Calamityville Horror"
27 *New York Times*, 25 June 1992 – "'Amityville' Prisoner Says Movie Money Tainted Defense"
28 *Washington Post*, 16 September 1979 – "The Calamityville Horror"
29 *New York Times*, 25 June 1992 – "'Amityville' Prisoner Says Movie Money Tainted Defense"
30 Ibid
31 *Skeptical Inquirer*, January/February 2003 – "Amityville: The Horror of It All"
32 Ibid

Poltergeist 1982

1 *American Hauntings* by Robert E. Bartholomew and Joe Nickell.
2–5 Ibid
6 *Life Magazine*, 17 March 1958 – "The House of Flying Objects"
7 *Life Magazine*, 7 April 1958 – Letters
8 *American Hauntings* by Robert E. Bartholomew and Joe Nickell.

A Nightmare on Elm Street 1984

1 *La Crosse Tribune*, 3 November 2015 – "Hmong vets to shed light on a secret war"
2 *The Black Book of Communism: Crimes, Terror, Repression* by Stéphane Courtois et al.
3 *The Times*, 30 July 2006 – "No Way Out"
4 Ibid
5 *Medical aspects of chemical and biological warfare* by F.R. Sidell.
6 *Tragic Mountains: The Hmong, the Americans, and the Secret Wars for Laos, 1942–1992* by Jane Hamilton-Merritt.
7 *Los Angeles Times*, 26 February 1981 – "'Nightmare Syndrome?' Deaths of Laos Refugees Puzzle Officials"
8–9 Ibid
10 *Los Angeles Times*, 14 July 1981 – "Mysterious Fatal Malady Striking Hmong Men"
11–12 Ibid
13 *Los Angeles Times*, 26 February 1981 – "'Nightmare Syndrome?' Deaths of Laos Refugees Puzzle Officials"
14–17 Ibid
18 *Los Angeles Times*, 10 July 1983 – "'Night Deaths of Asian Men Unexplained"
19 Ibid
20 *Journal of the American Heart Association*, 3 March 2018 – "Sudden Unexplained Nocturnal Death Syndrome: Hundred Years' Enigma"

21 *Wes Craven: The Man and His Nightmares* by John Wooley.
22 Ibid
23 *Dream Weaver* by Gary Wright.
24 *Wes Craven: The Man and His Nightmares* by John Wooley.
25–28 Ibid

The Serpent and the Rainbow 1988

1 *The Serpent and the Rainbow* by Wade Davis.
2–11 Ibid
12 *The Guardian*, 14 January 2010 – "Haiti: a long descent to hell"
13 *The Serpent and the Rainbow* by Wade Davis.
14–19 Ibid

The Silence of the Lambs 1991

1 *The Only Living Witness* by Stephen Michaud & Hugh Aynesworth.
2 Ibid
3 *KSBW8*, 11 October 2011 – "Santa Cruz Serial Killer Spotlighted In TV Documentary"
4 *Front Page Detective Magazine*, March 1974 – "Edmund Kemper Interview"
5 *Cosmopolitan*, 17 August 2019 – "The True Story of 'Mindhunter' Killer Edmund Kemper Is Almost Too Disturbing to Tell"
6 *SF Weekly*, 30 August 2016 –"Yesterday's Crimes: Big Ed Kemper the Coed Butcher"
7 *Cosmopolitan*, 17 August 2019 – "The True Story of 'Mindhunter' Killer Edmund Kemper Is Almost Too Disturbing to Tell"
8 *Lust Killer* by Ann Rule.
9 Ibid
10 *The Times*, 31 July 2013 – "Unmasked: doctor who was real life Hannibal Lecter"

11 Ibid
12 *The Sun*, 5 April 2016 – "My chilling meeting with the elegant killer doctor who inspired Lecter character"
13 *The Killer Department* by Viktor Bukarov.
14 *The Monster of Florence* by Douglas Preston and Mario Spezi.
15–16 Ibid

Scream 1996

1 *United States Court of Appeals Eighth Circuit. Mueller v. Powell et al.*
2 Ibid
3 *Killer Legends* (film) directed by Joshua Zeman.
4 *Columbia Daily Tribune*, 7 March 2010 – "Who killed Janett Christman"
5 *Killer Legends* (film) directed by Joshua Zeman.
6 *Columbia Daily Tribune*, 7 March 2010 – "Who killed Janett Christman"
7 *United States Court of Appeals Eighth Circuit. Mueller v. Powell et al.*
8–10 Ibid
11 *Columbia Daily Tribune*, 7 March 2010 – "Who killed Janett Christman"
12 *United States Court of Appeals Eighth Circuit. Mueller v. Powell et al.*
13 Ibid
14 *Columbia Daily Tribune*, 7 March 2010 – "Who killed Janett Christman"
15 Ibid
16 *The Making of a Serial Killer* by Sondra London & Danny Rolling.
17 *Beyond Murder* by John Philpin & John Donnelly.
18 *The Making of a Serial Killer* by Sondra London & Danny Rolling.
19–22 Ibid
23 *The Gainesville Ripper* by Mary Ryzuk.
24 *The Making of a Serial Killer* by Sondra London & Danny Rolling.
25 *Daily Art Magazine*, 12 December 2016 – "The Mysterious Road From Edvard Munch's The Scream"

26 *Fangoria*, January 2000 – "The Face of Scream"

The Mothman Prophecies 2002

1 *The Mothman Prophecies* by John Keel.
2–27 Ibid

Wolf Creek 2005

1 *Milat: Inside Australia's Biggest Manhunt, a Detective's Story* by Clive Small.
2–5 Ibid
6 *News Australia,* 2 November 2019 – "Death of Simi: The terrifying story of Simone Loretta Schmidl's murder"
7 *Milat: Inside Australia's Biggest Manhunt, a Detective's Story* by Clive Small.
8–11 Ibid
12 *News Australia,* 2 Nov 2019 – "Death of Simi: The terrifying story of Simone Loretta Schmidl's murder"
13 *Milat: Inside Australia's Biggest Manhunt, a Detective's Story* by Clive Small.
14–19 Ibid
20 *And Then the Darkness: The Disappearance of Peter Falconio and the Trials of Joanne Lees* by Sue Williams.
21 Ibid
22 *The Telegraph,* 19 October 2005 – "Backpacker tells of Outback attack and points out her boyfriend's alleged killer in court"
23 *Murdoch v The Queen*
24 Ibid
25 *And Then the Darkness: The Disappearance of Peter Falconio and the Trials of Joanne Lees* by Sue Williams.
26 *The Age*, 15 December 2005 – "Massive search for Falconio remains"

27 *The Guardian*, 13 December 2005 – "A gun-obsessed thug"

28 *The Independent*, 13 December 2005 – "Falconio killer 'a gun-obsessed thug'"

29 *Murdoch v The Queen*

The Conjuring 2013, Annabelle 2014, and The Conjuring 2 2016

1 *American Hauntings* by Robert E. Bartholomew and Joe Nickell.

2 https://www.youtube.com/watch?v=514di7CMcPY; Spot on *San Antonio Living.*

3–4 Ibid

5 *American Hauntings* by Robert E. Bartholomew and Joe Nickell.

6 https://www.youtube.com/watch?v=514di7CMcPY; Spot on *San Antonio Living.*

7 Ibid

8 *Paranormal Witness*; Season 4, Episode 10, *The Real Conjouring* [sic], directed by Sebastian Smith.

9–25 Ibid

26 *This House is Haunted: The Amazing Inside Story of the Enfield Poltergeist* by Guy Lyon Playfair.

27–34 Ibid

35 *Poltergeists: Examining Mysteries of the Paranormal* by Michael Clarkson.

36 *This House is Haunted: The Amazing Inside Story of the Enfield Poltergeist* by Guy Lyon Playfair.

37–47 Ibid

48 *Week in Weird*, 7 January 2016 – "Conjuring the Truth: Enfield Poltergeist Investigator Says Ed and Lorraine Warren Never Investigated Case"

The Witch 2015 and The Lighthouse 2019

1 *Account of the Life and Character of Rev. Samuel Parris of Salem Village* by Samuel Page Fowler.

2 *Slate*, 3 February 2016 – "All of *The Witch*'s Most WTF Moments, Explained: A Spoiler-Filled Interview With the Director"

3 *The History of the United States, Volume II* by George Bancroft.

4 *Memorable Providences, Relating to Witchcrafts and Possessions* by Cotton Mather.

5 *In the Devil's Snare: The Salem Witchcraft Crisis of 1692* by Mary Beth Norton.

6–8 Ibid

9 *Salem Witchcraft, With an Account of Salem Village and A History of Opinions on Witchcraft and Kindred Subjects, Volume II* by Charles W. Upham.

10 *Hollywood Reporter*, 2 March, 2016 – "Black Phillip: The Real Story Behind the Breakout Goat From 'The Witch'"

11 *Slate*, 26 February, 2016 – "Why Are Goats Associated With the Devil, Like Black Phillip in *The Witch*?"

12 *The Lord's Animals and the Devil's* by The Brothers Grimm.

13 *The Pictorial Key to the Tarot* by A.E. Waite.

14 *The Commissioners Appointed to Inquire into the Condition and Management of Lights, Buoys, and Beacons with Appendix and Index Vol. II*

15 https://www.nationaltrust.org.uk/solva-coast/features/heritage-hunting-along-the-solva-coast

16 *John Phillips and the Smalls Lighthouses Part II* by John S. Rees.

17 *BBC Wales*, 30 September, 2014 – "From the Skerries to the Smalls, the automation of Welsh lighthouses"

18 *John Phillips and the Smalls Lighthouses Part II* by John S. Rees.

19 *The Story of the British Isles in 100 Places* by Neil Oliver.